Protocol Matters

protocol matters

Cultivating Social Graces in Christian Homes and Schools

Sandra Boswell

Published by Canon Press
P.O. Box 8729, Moscow, ID 83843
800-488-2034 | www.canonpress.com

Sandra Boswell, *Protocol Matters: Cultivating Social Graces in Christian Homes and Schools*

Cover design by Paige Atwood.
Photography by Mark Lamoreaux.
Front Cover: (From left to right) Kallie Kohl, Jordan Hoffmann, Naomi Gray, Elisabeth Ryan, Mac Jones, Tyler Evans, Asela Nieuwsma, and Caleb Struble.
Back Cover: Mac Jones and Kallie Kohl

Printed in the United States of America.

Library of Congress Cataloging-in-Publication Data

Boswell, Sandra.
Protocol matters : cultivating social graces in Christian homes and schools / Sandra Boswell.
p. cm.
Includes bibliographical references.
ISBN-13: 978-1-59128-025-5 (alk. paper)
ISBN-10: 1-59128-025-7 (alk. paper)
1. Etiquette for children and teenagers. I. Title.
BJ1857.C5B635 2006
395.1'22--dc22

2006022099

08 09 10 11 12 13 9 8 7 6 5 4 3 2

I lovingly dedicate this book to the youngest ladies in my life, my granddaughters Ambeisa and Kamarebe; to the noble-hearted Boswell gentlemen, Bud, Brad, Tyler, Brock, and Kusiima; and to my parents, who insisted that their children politely put their "best foot forward." May the children in my life be inspired likewise.

Contents

Part I: The Meaning and Purpose of Protocol Training

Part II: Teaching Protocol to Children

Part III: Protocol Training Topics

Part IV: Four Contemporary Essays on Protocol

Acknowledgements

The Lord's frequent choice of weak and imperfect vessels to display His grace is always amazing and delightful to behold, for it reflects His strength. A sense of inadequacy rightly accompanied me while writing this book, and I greatly appreciate and admire the capable people who made this publication possible.

This was a long project, and many people, especially my family, provided steady support. I am also indebted to many people who originated or added to the content throughout the years and along the way. This book is theirs as much as mine.

I have been blessed by the teaching and influence of faithful Christians. Some I know well (my precious family and in-laws), and others less well (such as Joanne Wallace and like-minded authors who advance His beauty in manners), but their kindness and expertise helped educate and encourage me in His gracious ways over the years. I hope you will sense their fragrance, along with Christ's, on the pages of this book.

I owe much to dear Nancy Wilson for her shared vision on the importance of Christian kindness, order, and good manners. Without Nancy's invitation to teach protocol at Logos School, her friendship, her dedicated involvement when I was discouraged by my rusty writing abilities, and her very patient labors (without complaint) in wading through my first rough drafts, this book would still be in the drawer. Sharon Howell, a fellow protocol teacher and friend, supported me greatly during the process of publication and I toast to her across the miles. She too understands the importance of godly manners in our everyday lives, and her life reflects His beauty. I would also like to thank Katie Boswell, my niece, and Ellen Helsel, a talented friend, for their early suggestions.

Tom Garfield and Scott Oplinger, two of Logos School's many outstanding gentlemen, were a joy to work with as they unselfishly forwarded the idea of turning a small school booklet into a book available to a broader group of people who might benefit from its material. Like all true gentlemen, they are not at all "stuffed shirts," but instead are a pleasure to know. I am also grateful to Donna Grauke for her enthusiasm and our enjoyable time together in the Logos protocol program.

Lastly, I want to thank the gentlemen at Canon Press for all they have done, especially Douglas Jones for making this book possible. I appreciate his confidence in the project, his lack of pressure, his kind words, and his joyful willingness to encourage people like me. Thanks also to the multitalented Jared Miller for his focus, corrections, and final proofs.

The Lord's gracious beauty indeed draws us to Him and fills us with the joy of life. He teaches us how to live well, and His beauty shines through His faithful people not only by their kindly decorum, but by the timely helps they generously give to others. That He does such amazing things for His own good purposes, and to confound the world's strong, should reassure each of us—especially those just beginning to explore the path of protocol's kindness.

Introduction

If we are serious about the quest to discover, recover, and pass on the essential tools of learning to our children, we must look back to successful examples not only in academics but also in the cultural and social arts. A well-rounded education must also be a social education. Protocol—the social codes and skills of kind conduct and deference to others—is one art which everyone should learn in order to become a truly mature and well-educated person. Sadly, it is much neglected in our educational systems, and today, more than ever, it merits renewed attention.

Traditional protocol contains a plethora of "how-to" particulars that yield easy treasures, and indeed, protocol's little gems are worth recovery. Many teachers of protocol, however, fail to recognize that Christian principles inspire numerous rules for behavior in common social situations. For example, the apostle's instruction to regard others more highly than oneself plays out in many established manners. We should thus see protocol training as providing useful skills and prescribed procedures that help us to walk in a manner worthy of the gospel in our relationships and in social situations. When such knowledge is rediscovered, it transforms behaviors, characters, and cultures.

Of course, once we *find* something of value, the next step is *holding it fast* so it isn't lost or stolen. Good training should inspire the next generation to hold fast and apply the knowledge it has gained so it will not be forgotten or neglected. John Milton Gregory has said that this step is essential to any "successful education."

Your recognition of protocol's specifics and its advantages will increase as you read and consider the *P*s and *Q*s presented in this work. (Some of us are quite fond of the expression "mind your *P*s and *Q*s" because we heard it often as pint-sized children). The *P*s and *Q*s of course refer to the nuts and bolts of protocol, but those two letters also suggest some of the major themes I am trying to communicate. I advocate, without hesitation, *P*s of preservation and promotion of Christian standards. I have also included preparation and presentation ideas to help you teach young people duties in proper public behavior. You will find proven protocol techniques throughout the work. I trust you will note other important *P*s as you read these pages, and that you will find it a genuine pleasure to gather ideas for equipping your children to walk in a manner worthy of the gospel in their everyday lives and relationships.

This brings us to the *Q*s. The information you glean from these pages is designed to quickly answer questions you may have about teaching common courtesy, and to help you avoid mistakes so you may begin your quest for a quality program with confidence and practical wisdom. Resources and suggestions for younger children and ideas for high-school age students are included to inspire training ideas and reduce any qualms you might have about your preparedness.

This book, of course, contains much useful protocol information (especially in Part Three), and I hope it will help you gain an increased appreciation for this handy little tool known as protocol. However, this is not a comprehensive "etiquette book" per se. It is intended, first of all, to raise awareness of our culture's ignorance about protocol and to provide a solid grounding for teaching, studying, and practicing protocol from a Christian perspective—Parts One and Four provide much-needed discussion in this area. Second, this book is oriented toward those who need a crash course or refresher lessons in protocol so that they may begin training their children and young adults in protocol. Part Two focuses on implementing such training at home and in school, while Part Three provides an overview of the basic content that students (and teachers!) will need to know.

This book primarily discusses the why, what, and how of teaching protocol to children and adolescents. You'll discover it is a pleasurable and rewarding task for all involved. There are many faithful people quietly laboring in small classrooms and homes with a caring eye to the future and a loving heart for the next generation's welfare. (If you are still reading, I suspect you are one of those people, or wish to become one.) As with so many small duties, those who remain faithful will find a wellspring of satisfaction in their work because faithfulness in little things has its own valuable rewards. It is my hope, along with those who made this book possible, to see more children trained in the knowledge of practical protocol, so they in turn may embrace, apply, preserve, and enjoy the standards given to them.

You will discover it is always an enriching experience to work with other gracious souls who understand the importance of a Christian worldview in protocol training and who look forward to the next generation's welfare. For more than twenty-five years I have been given delightful opportunities to teach and be involved with protocol programs for various groups, in both public and private schools. This work contains ideas and materials from these associations. I also had the privilege to teach protocol to high-school students at Logos for several years. This classical Christian school has established one of the best programs in which I have taught. It is well organized, thoughtfully run, and lots of fun for everyone—you will find their innovative and trustworthy example to be worthy of your attention.

I owe many thanks to the dedicated people at Logos, and several other kind people including family and friends, for this book. Teachers, directors, parents, and others have greatly encouraged and helped me put pen to paper. They asked me to share my ideas, resources, and methods. We hold a similar vision to encourage other parents and teachers to use ideas and materials we have found helpful to children. If this work helps you and your children to better demonstrate small, kind duties with increased confidence and grace, then time spent on this project will have been worthwhile. If it assists you, as a Christian, to remain *ex fide fortis* as you teach the social arts to the next generation, then those of us involved in this publication will rejoice. Thank you for the honor of considering our ideas. It is a pleasure to share them with you. May God, through His Son, grant you willing learners, and fill your hearts with wisdom and joy as you labor with forward vision.

Part I

The Meaning and Purpose of Protocol Training

1

What Is Protocol Training?

WHAT COMES TO YOUR MIND when someone mentions the word *protocol*? Some people immediately sit up a little straighter; some think of stuffy, formal, official, state occasions; others imagine holding a teacup with a raised pinky finger. On far too many faces—especially young faces—the word just produces a blank stare. How extraordinary you are if you can help them fill in the blanks!

Of course, most people have some idea of what's what in the world of propriety and social codes, but perhaps you have wondered why we should emphasize protocol. Does it really matter? I hope this book will answer those questions as well. First, let's consider some closely related vocabulary words to recover a better understanding of protocol training and its importance in our lives. The various words and their origins can give us valuable insights into the realm of social conduct. This, along with a review of certain biblical principles, will help clarify what protocol is and what it is not. For Christians, the purpose of protocol—contrary to contemporary zeal for success, power, and status—is the development of relationships, self-discipline, and kind behavior toward others.

Protocol is a broad term for "preferred, correct codes of conduct" in general, but it can also specifically refer to the official procedural rules of conduct in state or diplomatic contexts. Thus some etiquette books have a chapter reserved for the "protocols" of official state occasions. The word also has broad application in many other areas, in its simple meaning of "correct, conventional procedures to be followed when doing something, so that it will be done consistently and with ease of cooperation" (e.g., safety protocols, data transmission protocols, international agreements or treaties, and so on). The word has a positive connotation of actions or ceremonies that should be performed, rather than what is forbidden. Other than these connotations, however, it is difficult to distinguish protocol from etiquette, though some define protocol as the "forms" of etiquette, and etiquette as more specific rules or practices.

Etiquette, as I have said, overlaps broadly with *protocol.* If, however, we want to distinguish them, we may think of "etiquette" as referring to the specific rules and practices in social (as opposed to diplomatic) protocol—learned "dos and don'ts" in a broad social context. For example, some particular rules could be about which is the correct fork to use, or what to wear to a White House dinner. *Etiquette* comes from an old French word for a "notice" or "label." Tradition has it that King Louis XIV and his head gardener were continually irritated when, during parties, the king's guests ignored verbal warnings to keep off the grass in his gardens. So the king issued an order "to keep within the etiquette"—the posted signs stuck in the ground to mark approved walkways. Thus, one could think of the word as having a negative connotation of protecting something by prescribing primarily what is *not* to be done, though it certainly also includes positive rules. Today's etiquette largely reflects common sense and, according to one dictionary, "social observances required by good breeding." Instead of the archaic word *breeding,* I prefer the term *training,* because it emphasizes clearly that etiquette is taught and learned.

Manners also comes from an old French word, but differs from etiquette in that it signifies a person's expressed and habitual social actions. In the singular, "manner" is the way in which anything is done. It a general sense, it means our habitual social behavior—and how that behavior matches up with the conventions of etiquette and protocol. Proper training encourages good manners everywhere and all of the time, emphasizing their ability to cover a multitude of personal imperfections. As one writer has said, "Good manners are not a sign of weakness; they are a symbol of strength."[1]

Polite, courteous, and related words suggest polished, courtly, and cultured refinement in social behavior. They also have connotations of grace and thoughtfulness toward others over and above mere conformity to the rules of etiquette. The etymology of *polite* includes the meaning of "polished," while *courteous* originally meant behavior worthy of a noble court. Farther back, the root is in "a cultivated garden" (Latin, *hortus*). The histories of

1. Nat Segaloff, *The Everything Etiquette Book* (Holbrook, MA: Adams Media, 1998), xvi.

both words remind us that laborious efforts and cultivation produce a desirable outcome; they imply a work in progress with a hope for the future. If we desire to have courteous and polite children, we must labor to produce such results.

Decorum is a charming, slightly old-fashioned word that should be used more than it is today. I first heard this word when my mother spoke about people she admired for their upright, moral behavior and poise. The word sounded very impressive and I wondered where a person could find such a grand thing as "decorum." My mother used it properly because it refers to someone of good moral character who respects and practices what is right, decent, and fitting. Decorum reflects honorable conduct, manners, words, and dress. It comes from a Latin word for "that which is becoming"—a concept much needed by parents who desire to aid their children's comeliness through good protocol training. Decorum is decency and goodness as opposed to rudeness, licentiousness, or levity. It adds connotations of ethics and morality as well as the idea of fitting behavior to the occasion—that words or actions may be right for certain contexts but wrong for others.

Social arts is contemporary-sounding but its roots are old. The Latin word *socius* means "companion" and obviously involves community interaction that takes us beyond close family relationships. ***Art*** comes from the Greek word *artunein,* "to arrange," suggesting "the making or doing things by human skill that have form and beauty." Art involves the mastery of certain skills to attain beauty. To master the many codes of protocol is an art that takes consistent practice, but it also has consistent rewards.

These definitions present a kaleidoscope of related meanings that define the world of cultivated social uprightness. They remind us that right training in protocol takes time, labor, and studied application. Parents and schools who devote time and effort in training produce more considerate, happier children, with God's blessing. For Christians, protocol training is a necessary labor with wonderful results in their children's self-discipline, habits, relationships, and behaviors. This stands contrary to the worldly goals of status, power, and success, which many people try to attain by using social codes as tools for selfish ambition.

By this time you may have noticed a very basic issue at stake in these definitions. The definitions of protocol and its related terms all include, in one way or another, the assumption of "correctness" or conformity to standards. But what is the source of these standards? Whose principles are best in protocol training? How and when do we, as Christians, practice "correctness" and to whose tune do we march? After all, in certain cultures, protocol dictates that women occupy rooms separated from the male family members, or that men will not touch a chair seat after a woman has vacated it, or that eye contact with a new acquaintance is rude. Religious principles and worldviews have influenced different social rules in different places and among different groups of people—this fact alone highlights the great importance of protocol. Even in our own culture, everyone displays various combinations of manners we recognize as good or bad, and we must ask ourselves whose protocol should influence *our* manners, and what standards are worth teaching our children.

Who determines protocol's codes? Judith Martin, the noted protocol writer of traditional "Miss Manners" fame, answered the question, a bit tongue-in-cheek, this way: "I do, that's who."[2] Although she is one of our most authoritative and entertaining etiquette writers, and her delightful humor satisfies most readers, this response begs the question on a serious level. The real issue behind this half-serious answer is one reason why the study of protocol has encountered its current difficulties in our society. A secular society suffers from lack of order based on God's truth—and this will be felt not only in laws, but in personal ethics and conventional social behavior.[3]

The question "Whose standards?" must be answered before parents understand what protocol is, and thus before they can know what to teach. Happily, the answer is neither hard nor obscure. We have inherited a rich system of protocol standards from our Christian ancestors. Christ's principles have steadily advanced though the centuries, deposing false standards, as His kingdom progresses in the hearts and minds of more and more people.

American protocol has deep roots in the Christian worldview, because earlier Christians followed biblical precepts and applied them to all areas of life.[4] Cornelius Van Til's observations are worth noting: "Man's conception of goodness and ethics cannot take precedence over God. And, for

2. *Miss Manners' Guide to Excruciatingly Correct Behavior* (New York: Atheneum, 1982), 12.

3. Francis Schaffer, in *The Christian Manifesto* (Westchester, IL: Crossway Books, 1982), discusses the fact that there must be some source of authority. Christians recognize God as this source, and that His laws apply to every area of life. When people attempt to remove Christ's standards, it disturbs the peaceful social order.

4. While there are many discussions of the Christian influence on American social and family order, a good example is Edmund Morgan's 1966 expanded revision of *The Puritan Family*. Morgan's book describes the mandates of respect, good manners, and

the Christian, this rests on a specific conception of the nature of God and Christ."[5] The invisible boundaries constructed from biblical principles and standards cannot be forgotten or surrendered in any realm, including the protocol of social actions, the manners, and the etiquette we employ.

For Christians, then, the answer to "What and whose protocol?" is easy from one perspective but challenging from another. It is easy because eternal truths prescribe standards that never change. These good standards rest on the nature of God and include principles of respect, deference, kindness, and consideration towards those around us. For example, we are told to "Honor all people" (I Pet. 2:17). Commands like these are enduring principles in Christ. True, how they play out in particular social codes will sometimes vary, but the basic concepts remain constant.

The challenge for today's Christian is that current tides of social norms are resistant to biblical standards, and it requires discernment and diligence to stand against the flow. Still, our duty is to acknowledge and maintain in our protocol training the "old paths" which we have inherited from a more Christian culture of the past. This does not mean that protocol can never change, but it does mean that the old paths are the best place to start.

Christian definitions of protocol must include inherited standards that demonstrate sincere respectful social actions towards others. Therefore, we maintain, promote, and practice rules that demonstrate honor, consideration, deference and humility.[6] Neglect of such standards in protocol diminishes Christ's influence in society and creates what we might call

---

honor towards others as part of early American practices in pursuit of a biblical social order. (See James Jordan's review of the book in *The Journal of Christian Reconstruction* 4, no. 2, 170.)

Another example of strong Christian heritage is the moral lessons and codes of conduct in the original McGuffey's *Eclectic Reader* series, published in 1836 and 1837. McGuffey was a Christian preacher and educator whose Christ-centered books sold by the millions and were intended to influence the young reader's manner of behavior. Its influence indeed permeated our culture as it taught thousands of American children reading and moral lessons. Children were trained in duties of Scripture-inspired behavior and etiquette as they learned to read. Practical codes of behavior were the norm, not the exception, throughout reading lessons: avoiding rashness, being kind to others, having gracious speech, and being punctual were common expectations for children. McGuffey believed in lesson books that promoted "practical application."

5. Dr. Rousas Rushdoony discussing Van Til's observations in *By What Standard?* (Tyler, TX: Thoburn Press, 1983), 82–83.

6. The following passage, from Charles Spurgeon's *Morning and Evening*, is a gem. Spurgeon comments on Philippians 1:27 ("Only let your conversation be as it becometh the gospel of Christ"): "The word 'conversation' does not merely mean our talk . . . but the whole course of our life and behavior in the world. What sort of conversation is this?

"boundary disputes." The boundaries of protocol can become blurred within one generation, causing a divide between those who uphold the forms of social respect and those who forget, ignore, or try to change them. Today there are those who seek to remove the ancient "stone markers" in attempts to redefine correctness and goodness in protocol. Those who hold fast to virtuous ways are commendable for their good work, and God will likely bless their efforts.

More and more people today realize this need to hold fast to biblically-defined ways, and to train their children in its codes of kind conduct. Increasing numbers of protocol training programs are springing up. Many homeschool parents now include etiquette instruction in their curriculum to prepare their children to live well with others. Practical lessons, such as how to write thank-you notes, how to address adults properly, and many other polite manners, add a distinguishing poise and admirable decorum to a young life. It is a delight to interact with these children and observe their calm exhibition of self-control and thoughtfulness.

I have tried to describe to some extent what protocol training is, but we also need to consider briefly what it is *not*. Protocol is not a panacea for all social ills. It is only as good as the standards behind it, and as the earnestness of those applying it. While compliance with protocol may dispose a person towards a more cordial posture, training is not a guarantee of a sterling character and upright heart. Protocol can be (and has been) arrogantly misused for selfish purposes. Some call this "gilded hypocrisy" or just being "hoity-toity," but protocol's underlying principles are not at fault—rather, it is the person who is misusing them. Therefore, the cultivation of the right attitudes behind respectful behavior is as desirable as learning the codes themselves. Rules applied without right attitudes produce rigid emptiness.

Another of protocol's limitations to keep in mind is that it cannot be followed inflexibly. There are times when it is best to be "impolite." Children need to understand that life is full of situations where conventional

---

In the first place, the gospel is very simple. . . . There should be about our manner, our speech, our dress, our whole behavior, that simplicity which is the very soul of beauty. . . . The gospel is a very fearless gospel. . . . But the gospel is also very gentle. . . . Let us seek to win others by the gentleness of our words and acts. The gospel is very loving. It is the message of the God of love to a lost and fallen race. Christ's last command to His disciples was 'Love one another.' O for more real hearty union and love to all the saints; for more tender compassion towards the souls of the worst and vilest of men! . . . For His sake, for our own sakes, and for the sake of others, we must strive day by day to let our conversation [behavior] be more in accordance with His gospel" (Evening devotion for May 24th). Rules of kindness, love, respect and deference to others governed our Christian forefather's manners. Their influence is still with us today.

politeness is not necessary or is even wrong. For example, it is better to turn away abruptly, and give one's reasons for doing so, than to participate in conversations of mean gossip or ridicule. This is superficially rude to the group, but truly considerate toward the person whose reputation they are damaging. A child should be taught not to speak to strangers or to respect a stranger's request to get into a car. This is not rudeness but prudence—do not confuse politeness with mindless compliance, or an appropriate rebuke with impoliteness.

Christian protocol is one of God's lovely means of grace. We all need much help in learning how to behave graciously towards one another, and protocol provides a simple means to that end—rules that demonstrate respect, kindness and brotherly love. So, what is protocol? It is a system of orderly codes that aid the development of social character and culture. It establishes behavioral habits by which we treat others with honor, deference, consideration and kindness. Its Christian content provides glimpses of Christ's example to strangers and brothers alike. The everyday details of protocol may seem mundane or of small importance, but their impact in a community and society is great. Protocol matters!

2

The Purpose of Protocol

Some think that success and self-confidence are the key reasons for protocol training. Confidence and success are certainly frequent benefits, but the nobler Christian intent is to teach and equip children so that they will behave in a manner worthy of their gospel calling.

Protocol training promotes the valuable character-building habits of self-control, humility, and thoughtfulness. Good training is practical, providing our children with a working knowledge of how the Christian worldview applies to social actions, relationships, and culture. Calm manners equip us to better handle minor conflicts, and to downgrade potentially major conflicts, in everyday life, making things run more smoothly and pleasantly—hence the term "social pleasantries." Further, protocol training aids in the orderly fulfillment of social duties no matter what our age (even children have responsibilities). We all have a duty to show honor, kindness, respect, deference, and courtesy towards others. Protocol teaches us how to anticipate the needs of others and make them feel respected, comfortable, and cared for—precisely how we ourselves would wish to be treated.

Protocol training involves much more than the "keeping off the grass" of King Louis's etiquette. It is a primary step in learning to be faithful in real, daily actions. Almost every Christian is familiar with the commands "Honor all people" (I Pet. 2:17) and "Let nothing be done through selfish ambition or conceit, but in lowliness of mind let each esteem others better than himself" (Phil. 2:3). Of course, learning to put these commands into consistent practice can be challenging, but protocol training is an effective tool in making such considerate behavior a part of Christian life.

For many of us, it is a great relief and comfort to have existing, inherited customs to follow. Numerous courtesies in our country are based on Christian principles which, over time, have developed as reliable rules for polite behavior in both common, everyday situations and special occasions. We don't have to chart new paths; we don't have to reinvent the wheel each time we go out to dinner or a reception. We can hold fast to what is good and proven. We do well to practice prescribed order, for in this way we can concentrate on giving respect rather than on trying to figure out (often at a moment's notice) *how* we should do it. This category of faithfulness has been aptly called "love in the trifles."

The practice of protocol is good for our own souls and, more broadly, it is a means to preserve those aspects of the Christian worldview embodied in many of our nation's traditional social actions. Since customs are symbolic reflections of societal values, we should seek to preserve and maintain those values which best symbolize deference, honor and respect, and soundly reject those which do not. As we train children to faithfully perform their duties, we pass this heritage on to the next generation.

Who wouldn't agree that children must be trained in good behavior? They are certainly not born with it. Even those privileged few born with a "silver spoon in their mouth" need instruction on how to use that spoon properly. Advocates of protocol training, and any parent with a child past the infant stage, agree that courteous manners and good character do not happen on their own. Parents have a great influence over the kind of character developed in their children.[1] "Train up a child in the way he should go, and when he is old he will not depart from it" comes with promise for our earthbound youth. It speaks of preparation and preservation; it also implies protection. In the context of protocol, youth are prepared for social interaction, protected from wrong ways, and thus preserve and pass on the right ways to their children. Once a child experiences right ways, he discovers the satisfaction and beauty of Christ-like behavior. Who, then, would want dismal substitutes?[2]

1. "We are all creatures of imitation: precept may teach us, but it is example that draws us. There is that in us all, that we are always disposed to catch the ways of those with whom we live; and the more we like them, the stronger does the disposition grow. Without being aware of it, they influence our taste and opinions. . ." (J. C. Ryle, *Thoughts for Young Men* [Moscow, ID: Charles Nolan, 2002], 43). If this is true of friends, how much more important the influence of example by parents?

2. Among God's amazing acts of goodness are His revealed principles of truth, love, beauty and kindness. These are often provided through common grace, even to the unregenerate heart. This is not a history paper on the origin of manners nor is there a claim

Parents who missed out on etiquette education in their youth often understand the importance of early protocol training. A middle-aged mother of two teenagers once shyly asked me, "Can I join your classes? I always feel like such a klutz in social situations. I am so nervous and uncomfortable when meeting new people that I can't even remember my friend's name. I end up embarrassing myself and my friends. I don't know when and how to introduce people, or what to say." A father with similar inadequate feelings asked if he could sit in on a school protocol session: "I'm uncomfortable in social situations. I need to know what to do in some of these situations that you are talking about because I was never taught very good manners." Another typical parent said, "I need to learn table manners. I don't even know what fork to use. It's embarrassing! I can't enjoy myself when we are invited out—in fact, I often don't want to go out."

These admirable parents refused to be bound by their lack of training and took steps to correct it. They recognized that this disadvantage carries into adulthood, and also that etiquette is not a luxury meant only for the rich or famous, but a helpful set of rules available to everyone. Indeed, we have all heard or read true stories about people who lost job opportunities because their table manners were offensive or they had sloppy grooming habits. Parents who didn't learn such *modus operandi* in their youth are often protocol training's strongest supporters.

Another reason we teach protocol to young people is simply that childhood is the best time to do so. The sooner parents and teachers begin training, the better. Inquisitive youthful minds, without wisdom or experience, are like magnets attracted to information. Young people are keen and impressionable observers; they look everywhere and anywhere to discover how to live and how to understand their place in the order of things. Protocol gives them practical and detailed knowledge about how to act. When training begins in childhood, good manners are more likely to become an automatic, spontaneous part of one's character. Early practical training has the impressive ability to help mold quality character traits.

C. S. Lewis once noted, in a discussion about choosing reading matter, that life doesn't have optional voids: "If you don't read good books, you will read bad ones. If you don't go on thinking rationally, you will think

---

that all manners are godly. It is, however, without dispute that all good and right behavior is beautiful and that it originates with God. The Bible is indeed complete and trustworthy guide, not only in the good news but also in its wisdom and instruction on how people should live. Therein we find distinct principles for kind and gracious living, the kind of life that is full of satisfaction and joy.

irrationally. If you reject aesthetic satisfactions, you will fall into sensual satisfactions."[3] He could have easily added that if you don't practice of good manners, you will have bad ones. Voids will always be filled and so will young minds. You ought not to coast through life—coasting is always downhill.

So we teach protocol precisely because it is good training, and good training shapes good attitudes, which in turn develop habits that fortify good character. Protocol instruction gives clear specifics on how to "put on" considerate social behavior, thus eliminating many wrong inclinations. Some call this process "accentuating the positive," but it is more than that. True, many protocol rules discourage conceited behavior and self-centeredness (which are not good traits at any age), but the right training replaces those tendencies with the positive traits of deference and pleasant manners. This may seem like a small matter, but the cultivation of a pleasant ways offers a valuable defense against pride and arrogance. Small courtesies, when practiced regularly, have the ability to foster a sense of gratefulness and humility in a child's pliable character. Spoiled, unruly, demanding children are unhappy children. They are also unpleasant company—we know it and they know it. By establishing thought-out boundaries, protocol training prepares young people for mutually pleasant and beneficial social interactions.

We can now begin to see the far-reaching effects the right type of protocol training produces: it prepares, it equips, it preserves, and it protects. Its goal is a kinder, more orderly society, which has important implications for future generations and culture in general. Failure to teach our children how to live and act responsibly has serious consequences because a child is then forced to learn behaviors dictated from other sources—and not necessarily good or appropriate ones. The damage eventually manifests itself in individuals, homes, and the culture.

In a recent *CBS News* poll, sixty-one percent of American parents interviewed thought that they were doing a poor job in parenting. Fathers and mothers are worried about their lack of discipline and their children's lack of self-control. The parents interviewed said that they were concerned over emerging trends in America which hurt the family unit, and cited negative influences from video games and entertainment, economic trends that take both parents out of the home, families not eating together, and children being left unsupervised as all being harmful to children's character devel-

3. C. S. Lewis, *The Weight of Glory* (Grand Rapids: Eerdmans, 1949), 46.

opment. The void left in the absence of positive training is being filled by outside forces.

When we teach children simple, respectful social actions, such as standing when an adult first enters the room or speaks to them, they learn about honor in a tangible way. On a more subtle level, the child's attention is drawn away from himself towards his responsibility to another person—in this case, to his elder. Inclinations towards self-centered disinterest or shyness give way to proper duties of acknowledgement and respectful action. In the same way, when a gentleman rises from his seat as a lady or older man initially approaches, he gives honor by this small courtesy.

We must not separate the idea of good character from virtuous conduct. It is not enough to be invisibly "good" deep down in one's soul. All the best intentions and feelings are worth little to the recipient if they are never expressed. The ways we treat other people matter, not only in the acts themselves, but in the effects they have on our own personal development. Honor, respect, deference, and kindness[4] are worthy of cultivation, and this cultivation requires self-control—a foundational virtue. We teach protocol because it provides opportunities to develop and practice self-control. Peter's second epistle opens with the following exhortation and addresses the subject of virtuous character perfectly:

> Grace and peace be multiplied to you in the knowledge of God and of Jesus our Lord, as His divine power has given to us all things that pertain to life and godliness, through the knowledge of Him who called us by glory and virtue, by which have been given to us exceedingly great and precious promises, that through these you may be partakers of the divine nature, having escaped the corruption that is in the world through lust. But also for this very reason, giving all diligence, add to your faith virtue, to virtue knowledge, to knowledge self-control, to self-control perseverance, to perseverance godliness, to godliness brotherly kindness, and to brotherly kindness love. For if these things are yours and abound, you will be neither barren nor unfruitful in the knowledge of our Lord Jesus Christ. (2 Pet. 1:1–8)

Peter's instruction applies to our discussion here and beyond. Christ's promises and power are for everyone who follow Him, both adults and children.

4. The common word *kindness* has a rich and active significance. The Hebrew word *chavad,* meaning "kind," denotes both "to bow" (from the neck) in courtesy to an equal, and "to be kind"; the closely connected word *cheved* means "beauty, favor, good deed, kindly or merciful." May we, too, associate our word *kindness* with beauty and active courtesy.

Good protocol training strives to promote these qualities by the manners it advocates.

A dramatic reminder about the cultural, communal benefits of kinder manners comes to us from the pages of history. Christianity survived the ruins of the Roman Empire's fall, and it prevailed against the barbarians during the third and fourth centuries. It is well known that northern barbarians ravaged and destroyed the land. It is less well known that while barbarians won violent, forceful victories, they were eventually subdued and conquered as they witnessed a higher culture in daily operation. Christianity, even when imperfectly employed, stood in victorious contrast to the brutal, anarchistic savagery of the invaders. Such was the power of kind manners and respectful decorum.[5]

Fortunately, across our nation, there now is a growing desire among many private schools and homeschools to again cultivate gracious manners according to Christ's laws. An increasing number of parents recognize the value of protocol to train children in demonstrating brotherly love through Christian social skills and graces.

If we desire faithful children and a kinder culture, it is important to instill attitudes of honor, respect, kindness and love in them. They must also be trained in virtues of humility and self-control. Herein lies a compelling validation for protocol training: protocol is worth teaching because of its quality influence on relationships and character, and the important habits of self-control that it establishes in our children. Thus, we have better equipped them to walk in a manner worthy of the gospel. I don't dismiss the benefits of success and self-confidence, or the satisfaction gained from living with others considerately, but we must not underestimate protocol's impact on development of a faithful, humble character, and in a larger sense, upon an entire culture. A rich heritage awaits the seeker of such manners.

5. "We have learnt that barbarism is not a picturesque myth or half-forgotten memory of a long-passed stage of history, but an ugly underlying reality which may erupt with shattering force whenever the moral authority of a civilization loses its control. . . . [I]t was only by Christianity and the elements of a higher culture transmitted to them by the Church that Western Europe acquired unity and form" (Christopher Dawson, *Religion and the Rise of Western Culture* [New York: Image Books/Doubleday, 1991], 23, 27).

Part II

Teaching Protocol to Children

3

Teaching Protocol in the Home

A child should always say what's true
And behave mannerly at the table:
At least as far as he is able.
—Robert Louis Stevenson, "The Whole Duty of Children"

ESTABLISHING protocol and teaching manners in the home promotes self-control in children and increases their consideration toward others, as well as preparing them for more advanced protocol training later in life. It forces children to think beyond themselves as they anticipate the needs of others. Good manners create a wonderful atmosphere of order and respect. When parents begin right instruction early, and diligently practice it throughout childhood, they foster the virtues of humility, kindness, and competence in the little lives entrusted to their care.

At times this seems to be a daunting task for "us ordinary folks," but we must remember that it is not optional. A parent's duty requires them to develop the skills of responsible social behavior in their children's character. Fortunately, many helps exist, and most children love learning and practicing etiquette's rules. They appreciate the security of set boundaries. In a sense, protocol will always be applied in the home—it is only a matter of whose and what protocol is followed. You simply must firmly establish that the children's duty is to apply mannerly actions as far as they are able. Recognize that in order to do this, they need something from you: *precept*, *praise*, and *example*.

It is absolutely essential to recognize that the old parental standby "Do what I say, not what I do" just doesn't work, especially in the realm of etiquette. Small children are imitators. If Dad fails to say "Please" and "Thank you" or sticks a toothpick in his mouth at the table, so will Junior. On the other hand, parents who set an example by their good manners are richly rewarded with an amazingly well-ordered and peaceful household in a few short years. Children, even as toddlers, respond to visual and verbal instruction as well as praise for obedience and right actions. There is only one letter difference between *goodly* and *godly*, and Christian parents with goodly manners demonstrate godly, principled behavior, which inspires their little ones to do the same. Good etiquette training is not difficult, but it does require thought, time, and effort on the parents' part. Children need more than guidelines; they must see their parents consistently practice what they preach.

Children need constant reminders, gentle corrections, and frequent praise. Mom and Dad have the advantage of on-the-spot, 24/7 training. When Tommy is somewhat less than his cheerful little self, a parent can kindly say, "Tommy, how do we say 'Good morning' cheerfully?" When Susie forgets to say "Pardon me" as she bumps into Tommy, Mom or Dad is there with an instant reminder. In large families, an older sibling (not too close in age) may offer gentle reminders. My youngest son, now a man, was inspired by his older brothers' examples and takes his manly duties seriously (and to this day, he lovingly scolds me if I forget to allow him to open my door for me).

Imitation doesn't have to be confined to examples from real life. Children also enjoy examples from literature, so story time provides another opportunity to learn about manners from the many children's books which treat the subject either directly or subtly.

Respectful Speech

Children require specific instruction in proper communication skills so their little mouths begin to utter right words. Learning when to speak appropriate words gives them a head start in life. This section offers some practical tips for teaching basic verbal manners.

Voice and Address

Children should speak clearly but not loudly, avoiding slurred words. For example, instead of "Yeah" they should say "Yes." The best standards require children to answer adults with an appropriate "Yes, ma'am," or "No, sir," although proper titles may also be used: "Yes, mom," "No, Mr. Teacher," "Good afternoon, Mr. Neighbor."

It is polite for children to look others squarely in the eye when they or someone else is speaking. Even toddlers should be able to say "Hello" and make eye contact when others speak to them.

Acknowledgment and Greeting

Respectful acknowledgment of other people with a cheerful tone of voice, saying "Good morning," or "Hello" the first time they meet throughout the day is polite. "Hey" or "Hey there" is inappropriate. Mothers and fathers provide good examples by greeting each household member, upon seeing them for the first time in the day, with a pleasant "Good morning."

Requests

Children should make respectful requests with a "Please, may I" when asking for favors, and a "Thank you" when receiving any favor, compliment or consideration. Even children just learning to talk are well able to learn these expressions, and it is delightful to hear them try their best at saying them.

Apology

Words that belong in every child's vocabulary are "Pardon me," when having caused a distraction, inconvenience, or interruption, and "I'm sorry, please forgive me," in the case of having hurt or wronged someone.

When learning to handle embarrassments, children are relieved to know that a softly-spoken "I'm sorry" or "Excuse me" covers most situations. Remind them that embarrassments happen to everyone. A mistake does not signal the end of the world and shouldn't be given much attention after an apologetic word is spoken. Reassure your child that everything is fine, once he says "excuse me." Also, it is impolite for other children to draw attention to the fault or embarrassment. It is rude to point fingers or laugh at someone who slips and falls, spills food, stutters, burps, or worse. For a yawn, cough, or sneeze, one turns one's head away from others, covers nose and mouth, and follows it with a quiet "Excuse me."

Words for Difficult Situations

Children of all ages must learn to express appropriate words. Many sensitive situations warrant thoughtful, compassionate words. Teaching children to reflect a moment and think about what they say and how it impacts the other person in various hard situations, from minor to serious, is a worthwhile part of etiquette training. If a sister has accidentally torn her new dress, an encouraging comment such as "I'll bet it can be mended and look fine" can bring relief and comfort.

When a child hears of bad news from a friend, such as a divorce or death, it helps them to know that it is all right to say, "I'm sorry. This must be very hard for you;" or a simple and sincere "Oh, I'm so sorry." When children are faced with the death of someone they often want to say something kind, but don't know what to say. Kind, ready words are a soothing comfort to those in distress and a relief for those who are trying to provide the comfort.

Phone Protocol at Home

Phone manners are a necessary skill. Faithfulness in this small detail prepares children for responsibilities at home and in the workplace later in life. Many children, generally, are ready by age six or seven to handle phone calls properly, and they certainly should be ready by age eight or nine. Talking on the phone is always more difficult than in person (especially for children), and parents should establish their phone rules and teach children what to say before they need to use them in a real situation. (Phone protocol is discussed further in chapter 6.)

Advance instruction prepares children to respond to calls that are urgent, give bad news, or are otherwise important. One protocol writer notes the specific example of a child answering the phone and being asked to relay a message of a death in Mr. Caller's family. This is highly unusual, but possible, and would catch any unprepared child off guard. In any case, established rules help children to thoughtfully consider the other person and their need so they may respond appropriately. This includes, "I am very sorry to hear that. Yes, I will tell my parents immediately."

Interruptions

It is rude to interrupt others who are talking. Small children need good examples and frequent but gentle reminders about not interrupting others who are in mid-sentence. Parents need to set a good example by paying attention to children when they have something to say, and by not being too long-winded when talking to them, considering the short attention spans and patience of little ones.

Other Conversational Don'ts for Children to Remember

- Don't brag.
- Don't whisper or tell secrets in front of other people.

- Don't speak loudly or yell.
- Don't whine or complain.
- Don't participate in malicious gossip.
- Don't curse or use coarse language.

Thank-You Letters

Good home training includes showing children how to formulate and write letters. Teach children proper letter formatting, with salutations and recipients' names on top, endings and personal signature at the bottom. Thank-you notes are prompt, handwritten expressions of appreciation for gifts, special favors, dinners, and hospitality. Their purpose is to express appreciation and to acknowledge how much the gift or courtesy means to the recipient. Notes need not be lengthy but should be sincere, well-written expressions of appreciation and praise that mention the gift and aspects of the child's appreciation of it, along with a compliment.

With the exception of wedding gifts, most notes should be written within a few days—some say the next day—but no longer than two weeks after the fact. It is best when they are mailed as soon as possible.

Young children need guidance about writing thank-you notes, but should use their own words and thoughts. Parents can help them think about what they like about a gift and to express sincere appreciation. Every gift has positive aspects, even when it is not well liked.

Overnight Hospitality

A thank-you note is obligatory for overnight visits, unless the visit is in the home of relatives or very close friends, who may be thanked verbally upon leaving and with a follow up call after one's arrival at home. A thank-you note left on the bed is always a welcome surprise.

Dear Mr. and Mrs. Hospitality and Susie,

Thank you for inviting me to stay overnight. Breakfast was delicious. Your family's blueberry pancakes are the best! Susie and I enjoyed swimming in the pool, and it was fun to roast marshmallows. Thank you for including me in your family time. It was really nice to be with you.

Sincerely,

Holly Guest

Dining Hospitality

A considerate dinner guest always thanks the hosts upon leaving, and has the option of following up with a phone call in the next day or two if the hosts are very close friends or relatives. Thank-you notes are required when a person is the guest of honor at a dinner party. A note is the best way to express appreciation, unless the host is a relative, in which case a follow-up phone call is satisfactory. Sending a note of thanks is always appropriate. Sisters and brothers may combine a thank-you note. Some of the nicest notes I have received have been from families when each individual signed the note.

Dear Mr. and Mrs. Host,
Thank you for dinner Sunday afternoon. What a treat! Your turkey casserole was delicious. We enjoyed the clever ice cream cake you made for dessert. We had never tasted an ice cream cake before and really liked it. Your hospitality warmed our hearts.
With fond thanks,
Ambeisa and Kama Guest

Gifts

Handwritten notes, in addition to personal verbal thanks, are also obligatory whenever congratulatory personal messages and gifts are received. Get-well, graduation, and wedding gifts must all be acknowledged with handwritten thank-you notes, which should specifically name the gift and why you appreciated it. Thank-you notes for Christmas and birthday gifts from relatives are always appreciated, even when verbal thanks have been given in person. Such gifts from friends or acquaintances should always be acknowledged.

Dear Grandmother and Grandfather,
Thank you for the bicycle you gave me for my birthday. It's just what I wanted. I like it! I have been riding every day since you gave it to me. Next time you come I want to show you how well I am riding. Thank you for always being so loving and generous to me and for giving me this wonderful gift. I hope you are well. I'm looking forward to seeing you both soon.
Love, Kusiima

A Special Favor

Appropriate occasions for thank-you notes don't stop with hospitality and gifts. Any special act of kindness or thoughtfulness merits recognition. Often such recognitions are even more appreciated because they are unexpected.

Dear Mr. Thoughtful,
Thank you for coming to see me when I broke my leg. I miss playing with my friends so the time you spent helping me learn chess was fun. It's a good game. Thank you for taking time to show me new moves and strategy. I know you are very busy so the time you spent with me meant a lot. I hope to see you again when I am up and about. May the Lord bless you for your kindness to me.
Fondly,
Holly Grateful

Children's Parties

Invitations to birthdays (or any special party) require an acknowledgement. When a child learns that an acknowledgment is polite, he is happy to call or tell a friend, "Yes, I can come to your party" or "I'm sorry I can't come, but thank you for inviting me." The child may ask about expected dress if the invitation is not specific.

Well-taught children also learn it is polite to greet the host(s) and the guest of honor on arrival and on departure, thanking them for the invitation. When presents are involved, the invited child gives the gift to the honored person and does not reveal what is in the package. The birthday child greets guests on their arrival, and as Miss Manners says, should "offer greetings rather than grabbing."

When determining a guest list, the host child should include close friends, children whose parties he has attended, and those whose feelings would be hurt by not being invited. Children learn diplomacy and social skills from these rules. As to the number of invited guests, some suggest as many children as the birthday child's age. Very young children do better with a special family birthday dinner rather being subjected prematurely to social responsibilities involved with a large number of child guests. Budget is another factor in the number of guests and types of activities.

The birthday child always thanks each person for his gift as it is opened and says something good about it, even when it is not a favorite item.

Thank-you notes for each gift should be written within a few days of receiving them.

Teach children that parties are times to practice good sportsmanship, avoid crowding or running, wait patiently for their turn when being served, and say "thank you" to the person who gives them food or prizes. Well-mannered children also learn to have fun together without screaming or yelling, especially indoors.

On the subject of parties, a protocol party for young ladies at home is delightful event that young girls enjoy. A tea party with teddy bears or dolls is a wonderful way to help little ladies learn about manners. Little boys need different and more active ways of enjoying their protocol lessons. My sons, who were typical, busy boys, responded well to training for real-life situations rather than sitting still for tea parties.

Other Manners to Live By

Manners with Adults

- Stand up whenever an adult enters a room, approaches you, or greets you for the first time.
- Stand up to say goodbye to adults when they leave.
- Always offer your chair to older people when other chairs are occupied.
- Always allow an adult to speak first.
- Always allow adults to enter a door or room before you.
- Always knock on doors and wait for permission to open them before entering a room or home.

Manners in Daily Activity

- *Playing fair.* When playing, children must play fair, take turns, follow rules, be good losers, and congratulate the winners. They should be willing to share. If children don't want to share something in their toy box with guests, they should remove it beforehand and put it out of sight until later.
- *Coming when called.* It is polite to come immediately when called, whether it's getting out of bed, coming to the dining table, or in from play. It is rude and disobedient to ignore such summons. This teaches children to value other people's time.
- *Being a willing helper.* A willing offer to help with packages or small

chores, whenever possible, is polite and sharpens a child's awareness in the needs of others.

Other Dos and Don'ts

Do:

- Be on time.
- Smile.
- Walk inside homes, churches, or other buildings.
- Respect other people's property. This includes returning borrowed items quickly.
- Show respect by being polite to those in authority.
- Practice proper grooming (see chapter 8).
- Dress appropriately for the occasion (see chapter 8).
- Pick up toys and clothes after done using them.

Don't:

- Take things without permission.
- Laugh at others.
- Stare at others.
- Shove, pinch, spit, bite, or pull on someone.
- Run or roughhouse inside buildings and churches.
- Climb on furniture.
- Be shy or bashful.
- Comb hair or pick teeth in public.
- Be messy.
- Yell, scream, or talk loudly. Speak face to face, not across a room.

Table Manners at Home

Some of the best time that parents can spend with their children is at dinner together. Food needn't be fancy. It is the togetherness and happy fellowship that matters most to little ones. Our four-year-old grandson often requests a special family breakfast at our big table when he spends time with us, because he enjoys the congenial table talk when everyone gathers at the table to start the day. His sisters request dinners at the big table complete with crystal and unhurried conversation.

We all realize that there are days when it's difficult to coordinate schedules for everyone to sit down and eat together, but such days should not create a routine routinelessness. Mealtimes provide important opportunities in family life. They are perfect opportunities for enjoyable fellowship, hands-on training, and praise and encouragement to nourish little souls along with their bodies. Don't let your family be robbed of quality time at the table—make family meals the norm in your household. McDonald's shouldn't be the only place in town serving "happy meals." Parents who are serious about protocol training establish regular family dinners at home—they provide a perfect training environment whether one is learning to eat spaghetti or oysters on the half-shell.

Training should begin as soon as the child is able to sit with the family at the home dining table, but training must be suitable for the age. Small children are capable of learning to sit up straight, stay seated, eat neatly with child-size utensils, and practice civil behavior. Wise parents set attainable goals, though children are usually capable of much more than we give them credit for. Children can successfully master basic aspects of etiquette bit by bit as they are able.

It is important always to maintain a happy atmosphere—even when there are accidents or mistakes. When one of our grandchildren accidentally spills a drink, their father smiles and says, "What's the best thing about a mess? The children all say, with joyful relief, "It can always be cleaned up."

It is best to begin with a few rules at a time, and choose rules that apply to the child's situation. Young children need to master neatness and competency with basic utensils before learning finer points of dining etiquette. In other words, we don't teach a two-year-old how to use a finger bowl when he has yet to master holding a spoon.

After the child has mastered a particular rule, introduce another. Of course, parents should offer gentle reminders about learned manners as they move onto new ones. Soon a system of protocol will emerge in the child's daily practice as old rules become second-nature behavior. Even very young children can ably learn to apply the following basic rules at the table:

- Wash hands and face immediately before dinner and proceed promptly to the table when told to do so.
- Wait until all adults, but particularly their mother or the hostess, are seated before taking their chairs.
- Sit up straight in a chair, even with a booster seat.
- Wait until mother (or the hostess) picks up her napkin before taking theirs.
- Wait until mother picks up her fork or otherwise gives the signal to begin eating.
- Learn to use fork and spoon properly instead of fingers.
- Patiently wait without complaints until food is prepared and served.

- Take reasonably-sized portions and pass food counterclockwise (to the right).
- Never throw or spit food.
- Always take one bite at a time, not slurp, and chew with mouth closed.
- Return drinking glasses back to their proper position to avoid spills.
- Speak with an empty mouth.
- Speak with a quiet, cheerful tone of voice.
- Wait in turn to speak so that only one person is speaking at a time.
- Never interrupt or monopolize conversations.
- Say "Please" when asking for anything.
- Say "Thank you" for things given to them or done for them.
- Always thank mother or the hostess for dinner.
- Always remain at the table when a guest in another home until the hostess excuses guests or children. At home, always ask parents "May I be excused from the table?" when finished.
- Offer to help clear the table or carry a dish to the sink when old enough to do so.

Young children can practice many basic manners while still in a high chair. Our sixteen-month-old granddaughter was trained never to yell and never to spit or throw food. Banging on her high-chair tray was also a no-no. She says the sweetest "Please" and "Thank you" and receives frequent reminders to sit up straight and chew with her little mouth closed. She loves family praises, especially her father's, when she remembers her good manners.

Other miscellaneous table topics for children are discussed below.

Dinner Is Announced

It is polite to proceed immediately to the table when dinner is announced; conversely, it is rude for family members (or guests) to require second announcements. Wise mothers give a pre-dinner announcement a few minutes before dinner is served so that children may wash hands and arrive at the table neat and clean.

Seating Protocol for Home or Private Dinner Parties

Some gentlemen still practice the courtesy of steadying a lady's chair as she sits down for a daily family meal, while others do not. We should train our children to remember that protocols in homes vary.

Seating is assigned by the hostess at private, informal dinners. If family members have their usual places, then when guests are present for a special dinner, the family members should courteously await the hostess's (usually the mother's) instructions before being seated, in case of changes.

During a special sit-down dinner party in a home, the tone is more elevated than for routine daily meals. Therefore it is customary, and polite, for a gentleman to automatically assist the lady on his right side with her chair before taking his seat. (This is why a hostess assigns a seating pattern that situates a man next to each woman around the table.) Gentlemen should remain standing until the hostess and all ladies are seated in place. Ladies, young and old, accept this courtesy with a smile and sincere verbal thanks. The mechanics of seating is discussed in chapter 7. After ladies are in place, younger men remain standing for just a few seconds before sitting down, in order to allow elder gentlemen to take their seats next.

Respect for seating protocol is one sign of a true gentleman. This gentleman makes the dinner, no matter how humble, and the day, no matter how ordinary, a bit more special.

Seating Order for Everyday Dinners

By nature, daily family dinner protocol is informal—still respectful, but less strict than when company comes for dinner. Some families, unaware of seating protocol, all sit down at the same time, missing the opportunity to establish a sense of respectful order.

Properly speaking, mother is always seated first. Men remain standing by their usual chair until mom is seated. In addition, many protocol authorities advise training children to respectfully stand at everyday dinner tables until adults are seated. A few experts prefer the sense of order and dignity conveyed by gentlemen, young and old, standing until mother, and then daughters, are seated, whether or not chair assistance is given at home. Father sits down next, followed by the young men.

In either case, the essential point is that children do not take their chairs before mother is seated. Of course, protocol is difficult to maintain if mother has to run back and forth to the kitchen. Therefore she needs to be organized enough to have all the food ready if she wants to maintain daily protocol training (and an uninterrupted dinner).

On a side note, good training also includes teaching children job responsibility. Helping mother with dinner is a good place to start. Children may (and should) set dishes on the table when they are safely able, so that mother doesn't need to run back and forth to the kitchen. My young granddaughters have been cheerfully setting and clearing the table since they were big enough to carry plates.

Prayer

Grace—asking for God's blessing and thanking Him for His provisions—is usually said before the meal begins, though sometimes a meal ends with a prayer. Many families say grace while standing, before sitting in their chairs; others sit and then pray. Whether standing or sitting, a bowed head is the general symbol of respect. Train children not to take their seat until the host or hostess indicates to do so. Nor should they take a napkin until after grace is said and the hostess has taken her napkin.

Serving Protocol

Informal family meals have a common protocol. Very few of us have household servants, so we eat family style and serve ourselves. Food is passed to the right (counterclockwise) by the hostess before filling her own plate. This allows one to take the dish with the left hand and serve with the right (sorry, left-handers). The hostess is only served first when she is the only lady at the table or is alone with her husband and children. Otherwise, she is served last, but everyone still waits until the hostess picks up her fork before taking a fork or first bite.

Sometimes a host or hostess puts the food on plates (or soup in the bowls) herself and directs the presentation of dishes to guests, beginning with the eldest lady (such as a grandmother). Other ladies at the table are served next, then the gentlemen, beginning with the eldest one at the table (excluding the host).

When the host carves meat to be served at the table, he passes the platter counterclockwise for others to take their portion, and fills his plate last. While it is polite to wait until all are served before beginning to eat, it is also polite for the hosts to advise everyone to eat while the food is warm, after several people have been served. Train children to take the host at his word.

Other Protocol for Informal Meals

During informal meals, when hosts offer second servings the guests may either take seconds or decline it politely. Second helpings are considered a compliment to the "chef." During formal or semiformal dinners, however, second portions are not offered.

In a home, one or two able guests may offer assistance to the hostess at an informal dinner. A helping hand in serving or clearing plates as the hostess serves dessert is considerate, though be sensitive to the hostess's preference of whether or not she wants help. Common sense dictates which guests are most conveniently situated to perform help. Everyone should not get up to help while a meal is in progress—it would leave the table empty. If the home has a wait staff, help is not offered. The more formal the dinner, the less proper it is for a guest to offer assistance.

If you dislike or are allergic to some food served, you may discreetly move the food in question to the edge of the plate, but say nothing. A guest will not be asked about this at a formal or semiformal dinner. During an informal meal, however, if a concerned hostess asks about remaining food, you can simply say, "It's a nice meal. I'm fine, thank you." The point is to avoid making a big distraction over personal dislikes or lengthy discussions over allergies.

Protocol for Dining Out

Brunches, Buffets, Receptions, Cafeterias, and Potlucks

Young people are highly capable of considerate behavior at casual affairs. They may allow elders to proceed before them or yield a chair to a senior when necessary. I have observed thoughtful teenagers first fill a plate for an elderly grandparent before returning to the line for their own food—a very impressive indication of good training and fine character.

Children—especially younger ones—need continual guidance in remembering their manners. Protocol teaches that civil conduct applies to every age group and situation. Some well-trained youngsters still find it tempting to forget manners at picnics, potlucks and buffets when they see other children unsupervised or behaving badly. How should they behave? Protocol is full of common sense rules. Yelling, crowding, pushing, and running to be first in line is obviously inconsiderate behavior. The proper way for children to approach food lines is with their parents. Misbehavior is less tempting when parents are nearby.

Brunches and buffets, with limited wait service, are informal, mostly self-service meals, while cafeteria and potluck meals are even more casual. Young people are more able to enjoy large, casual dinner events of this kind when they obey the following simple rules. Realize, however, that variations occur in circumstances, group size, and the practices of each host. Tips for brunches, buffets, receptions, cafeteria meals, and potlucks:

- Always begin with and fill a clean plate. Don't carry a dirty, used one back to the food line for refills.
- Don't overload a plate or make excessive return trips to the food table.

- Use both hands to carry the plate when possible to avoid spilling.
- Use the appropriate plates for salad, dinner, and dessert courses.
- Never eat or taste food while in line.
- Do not cut into a group already in line.
- A buffet line usually moves in a clockwise direction unless foods are mirrored on each side of the table. Begin at the end of the table, not the middle, with the salads. Don't skip ahead or slow down the line.
- Always replace the serving utensil on the service plate provided. Utensils left in the serving dish may become hot or fall into the food.
- In homes, the host should instruct guests about seating and food line procedures. If the hosts direct guests to dish up and be seated, then guests do so. In this case, it is best to wait until after several others are seated at the table before beginning to eat. Gentlemen at the hostess's table should remain standing until the hostess is seated, and all those seated at the host's table wait for hostess to pick up her fork unless hosts urge those guests to begin eating immediately.
- Remember that home buffet dinner parties differ from casual restaurant brunches or cafeterias. Informal evening dinners are by nature more formal affairs than daytime meals.
- When a buffet dinner has a higher degree of formality, second servings from the food table are not the norm.
- When dessert is buffet style and self-service, wait until everyone at your table has finished their main course before going to the dessert table. Etiquette says, "Don't get more than one course ahead of the others at your table." And don't take more than you can eat.
- Seating may be limited at receptions. Children should honor older adults by permitting them the first use of available chairs.
- If you must stand while eating, as sometimes happens at a reception, find a safe spot away from "traffic" flow or food lines. Keep your food plate portions manageable and avoid difficult foods that might slip off the plate or require cutting.
- Dispose of dirty paper plates in the trash. Discreetly clean up your spilled food, if any.
- Children can help clean up after picnics and potlucks, fold chairs, help carry items to the car. Even toddlers enjoy a small job. Children grow in character when they learn to cheerfully lend a hand—and stay with the job until it is completed.

Restaurants

Dining out with children need not be a stressful or embarrassing experience. Rather, children should regard it as a privilege that comes with the responsibility to practice proper conduct. When children have practiced proper table manners at home, dining out is easier. Many of the table manners basics mentioned earlier apply to restaurant dining; at a restaurant, however, special attention should be given to avoid causing interruptions and distractions, which are rude. Children will do better (and parents will have less stress) if they know beforehand what is expected of them, so they should be given instruction on restaurant etiquette *before* going out to dinner. If their behavior does break down and they create a noisy distraction for other diners, they should be removed until they can behave.

Here are some general rules for dining out that should be a part of every child's training:

- Be neat and clean when you leave the house.
- Dress appropriately for the occasion.
- Stay close to parents; do not rush ahead or lag behind.
- Allow mother to go first behind the maître d'hôtel to the table and be seated first.
- Speak quietly. Noisy behavior or loud voices are impolite distractions.
- Walk, don't run, in the restaurant.
- Make menu choices without delay, changes, or complaints.
- Eat at the same pace with others at the table.
- Remain seated at the table with parents until it is time to leave.
- Young men should assist the ladies to their right with their chairs.
- Thank those who bought the dinner, even if it is your parents.

Conclusion

Can we really expect young children to behave well at the table or in a restaurant? Of course! For their sakes, we can't afford *not* to expect good behavior. Many families are successful in early training, and yours can be also. Just take it a step at a time and focus on what is needed most. Of course, with toddlers at a table parents cannot realistically expect perfect manners, but early and daily training pays off with a more enjoyable dinnertime for everyone, especially in restaurants. Circumstances once dictated, against our preference, that we take our eighteen-month-old son with us to a very nice restaurant for a special dinner occasion. He wore his little suit and tie with a bib, and sat in a highchair at our table. His limited previous training paid off, even at this early age. (His naptime just before dinner helped too.) We had a pleasant dinner and his admirable little manners were noticed by everyone around us. Even though he still could not manage a fork perfectly, his quiet decorum was wonderful for such a young age.

We have been guests in many homes where the children's good manners are a genuine contribution to the fellowship, and have seen many examples that illustrate how ably young children respond to diligent parent's good training. Quite recently, my sister and her husband were invited as first-time dinner guests into the home of new church friends. As they stepped out of their car, they were immediately greeted by five smiling children, from ages four to fourteen years. Each child spoke a warm welcome, introduced him- or herself, and then happily led the new guests into the home. Evidence of admirable training didn't stop here. All children eagerly assumed their proper positions without delay as older ones helped the youngest ones to the dinner table. A small beaded bracelet was by my sister's plate—a gift made by one of the children. During dinner, polite manners were the norm. When the youngest child began monopolizing conversation, as four year olds are prone to do, his father gently asked, "Do we need to leave the table to talk about manners?" The child immediately (and cheerfully) bridled his talk, allowing others at the table to speak. When the meal was finished, each child said, "Thank you for dinner, Mother—may I please be excused?" The children's protocol training resulted in a most delightful experience for everyone.

These well-trained children did not learn their good table manners and considerate behavior overnight. Their training, like all good training, required time and consistent effort on the parent's part. Comprehensive training is progressive—as reflected in the father's diligent reminder to his little "work in progress." This type of steady instruction provides your children with valuable capabilities and good attitudes.

Wise parents set good standards and then set good examples. They offer on-the-spot guidance, reminders, and corrections. Wise parents lavish consistent praise along with their reminders and corrections for their growing children. Children don't resent reminders and corrections when they are spoken gently and balanced with praise. Children readily welcome instruction in how to greet people, how to speak in different situations, how to handle compliments and embarrassments, the art and timing of deference, how to show respect for elders, how to dress appropriately, and myriads of small practical helps that etiquette provides.

In fact, praises should outnumber corrections. Sincere praise reaffirms correct behavior: "Timmy, how nice that you remembered to open the door for Grandmother and carry her package. Did you notice her smile? She told me later you were a fine boy, and I think so, too." Even a simple "Good job" or "Well done" reminds a child they are on the right track in life.

Etiquette provides nurturing guidelines for children as they practice respect and kindness on the phone, in public, and in the home. Should parents fail to impart specifics on a minor point or two, all is not lost. The overall effect produces humble, kind character, social competency, and self-control that make living with one another quite pleasurable. Wise parents prepare their children for the future, and this must be done in a slow, steady, incremental fashion. The small things we do every day will influence the future most. As Julia A. Carney put it in her children's poem "Little Things,"

Little drops of water, little grains of sand,
Make the mighty ocean and the beauteous land.

And the little moments, humble though they be,
Make the mighty ages of eternity.

So our little errors lead the soul away,
From the path of virtue into sin to stray.

Little deeds of kindness, little words of love,
Make our earth an Eden, like the heaven above.

4

Establishing a School Program

"WHO ARE these outstanding young people?" is a question that onlookers frequently ask when our students are on a field trip or protocol event. The benefits of a school protocol program extend beyond classroom walls and school culture, reaching far into the students' future lives. Beyond home protocol education, school programs have the advantages of large group classes. Protocol in this context builds a strong sense of community and social responsibility among students, apart from the excitement and heightened school spirit that generally accompanies it. Students eagerly anticipate a special event and the opportunity to immediately practice in public what they have learned in the classroom. Best of all, a protocol program provides students with tools to conduct themselves in a considerate manner as they serve one another day to day in the academic environment, all of which gives them a head start towards competency in broader community life and future social situations.

Whether you desire to establish a program in your school or have already begun a program, the information in this chapter is designed to speed you on your way with some time-saving suggestions and ideas. A good program, while flexible to its own school's needs, will operate according to certain tried and true basics.

Anatomy of a Successful Program

The ideas and suggested teaching material shared in this chapter are designed to help you avoid common problems in developing a successful program. Like a roadmap, it highlights proven routes and helps you to avoid wrong turns and bumps in the road. I hope it will hasten your program on its journey. In this first section, we review a few key characteristics you should have in place right away. Successful school protocol programs do the following:

Determine the program's scope early on. Will it include general manners for grade-school children, previous to and separate from the secondary program? Will it include only a high school program or both junior high and high school programs? Will the curriculum include just the basics, or will it be more thorough? What are the students' needs?

In a K–12 school, start early and continue consistently. Are there consistent etiquette codes in place to ease students' transition through the grades and into the secondary program? Do classroom and school rules help the smaller children exhibit self-control and demonstrate respectful behavior toward authority? What happens on the playground—does good sportsmanship prevail? What is hallway behavior like? What current classroom protocol exists? Most teachers establish classroom rules and can easily incorporate more general etiquette into those rules.

The answers to these questions affect overall program development. Though we should remember young children have slight interest in formal occasions, theirs is a good age to lay the right foundations and promote polite daily habits. (For more specific information, there are suggestions for children at the Grammar and Dialectic stages later in this chapter.) Later on, especially in the Rhetoric phase,[1] young people tend to be much more receptive to extensive protocol instruction, and this is an opportune time for special classes culminating in a formal event.

Determine which grades and how many students will be included in the program. Students are easily accommodated at most events when each class size does not exceed fifty students. Of course larger numbers are possible,

[1] For readers unfamiliar with the classical model of education, it works on the assumption that there are three basic yet overlapping stages in child development. The "Grammar" stage covers elementary school, with instruction tailored to young children's ability to memorize and imitate. The "Dialectic" (or "Logic") stage includes late elementary and seventh to ninth grades, with instruction tailored to the students' growing analytical skills and their desire to question and debate ideas. The "Rhetoric" stage corresponds roughly to grades ten through twelve, with lessons tailored to the students' desire to express themselves eloquently by organizing and polishing their thinking, style, and appearance. For more detail on classical Christian education, see Douglas Wilson's *Recovering the Lost Tools of Learning* (Wheaton, IL: Crossway Books, 1991) and Dorothy Sayers' essay "The Lost Tools of Learning," which is reprinted in Wilson's book.

but logistical challenges greatly increase. Smaller schools often successfully combine all secondary levels while larger schools can establish a two-part program—*beginning* or *junior protocol* for freshman and sophomore grades, and *advanced* or *senior protocol* for juniors and seniors. You will need to make adjustments according to your group's size and gender mix.

Remain flexible to meet the specific needs of each group. Needs vary from school to school. Every school and community situation is unique, so flexibility and creativity are important for a good program. Programs customized for group size, ages, and available resources are most successful. Your gala evening options will vary from year to year. Arrange classes and an interesting gala event so that students can practice what they learn. Mix new, fresh ideas with past, proven program techniques to keep students interested and ensure that the program succeeds.

Start early, allowing ample time for program planning and finding the right director and teacher(s). Lack of time usually means lack of planning, and lack of planning tends to lead to disaster. Imagine coming to a restaurant with forty well-dressed students, only to find that there is no seating because the reservation was not double-checked. Or, the last plays or concerts of the academic year are sold out two months in advance. A smart program director avoids these blunders—reliable people with good planning skills are a must-have for a good program. In most situations, two staff members are needed: the *program director* oversees and coordinates logistical details and keeps the program curriculum fresh and customized for the student mix; the *teacher* sets the tone and presents the material in the classroom. In smaller programs, the director and teacher may be the same person.

Have a clear vision and high standards. Many Christian schools have a strong desire to help students develop Christ-like behavior and practice love in the trifles. A good protocol program supports this vision. Protocol is based on deference and the practice of kind, considerate behavior. It cannot change hearts, but it does influence character and habits, and a good program is conscious of this goal. Do not settle for a program which compromises standards. Advocate, without apology, etiquette as an excellent means of equipping children with a working knowledge of polite rules in table manners, dress, conversation, introductions, and other social duties of ladies and gentlemen.

For example, the Logos High School protocol program's vision statement runs as follows:

> The purpose of the proposed Logos High School protocol program is twofold. First, it should provide a dressy, semiformal, or formal social event for the students that is consistent with our desire to teach a thorough Christian worldview; in this case it is applying Christianity to culture. Second, in a culture that despises authority and submission, we want to teach our students about the importance of manners and deference. After teaching etiquette we want to create an enjoyable social event in which the students can apply and become comfortable with what they have learned. The goal is to equip them for social events in their future so they know how to behave in manner worthy of the gospel.

What is your vision, and how does protocol fit in with it? What are your goals and purposes? If you desire to equip children with kind social skills for their futures so they can behave in a manner worthy of the gospel, then protocol training is a good means to that end. But without a clear purpose and reason, such training merely becomes a body of rules that are either written off as silly and unnecessary or are abused to nurture pride and snobbishness.

Learn from established and successful programs. Don't try to reinvent the wheel; find a program you admire, learn its history and current curriculum, and adapt it to your situation. I have had the pleasure of being involved with the program of Logos School, which serves as a model and resource for much of the material in this chapter. Logos' annual week-long program was specifically designed to teach courteous behavior to their high school students. The program began when the school had a small number of students, so protocol classes included all high school grades together. Class training sessions were required but student participation in the special event was optional. To have required classes but optional events was a good idea, especially for a young program. It ensures that while all students receive training, skeptical parents and students can opt out of the event and thus cannot complain about its costs. It also means that the students who do attend the event (the vast majority) actually want to be there and have parental support, which allows everyone to enjoy themselves more.

Nancy Wilson, a secondary English teacher, initiated, organized, and directed the early Logos program. She established the clear goals cited above and drew upon the expertise of volunteer protocol teachers for the classes, thus keeping costs to a minimum. When school enrollment greatly increased, the protocol classes split into two groups: A beginning or junior protocol program for ninth and tenth grades, and an advanced or senior protocol session for eleventh and twelfth grades. (Note, for clarification, that junior and senior protocol do not match up with the junior and senior years in high school.) This allowed training classes to expand and include both semiformal and formal events for beginning and senior programs respectively. It also made transportation and dining arrangements much easier. Donna Grauke, the next director, steered the Logos program throughout growth transitions with innovative finale events. It was a pleasure for me to teach protocol under the directorship of both these ladies, and many of their guidelines are included below in the section covering a program director's duties. Today, Logos training classes generally occur in late March or April since May has a full school calendar. Recently the school has begun offering dress sessions in the fall, which I highly recommend because it gives students time for budget planning.

Programs such as this have extensive cumulative experience and those involved are usually delighted to help other schools start similar programs. Try to find a school comparable to yours in size and location (rural, small town, city), since it will probably have faced challenges relevant to your program's future, but be aware of the practices of many other different programs as well. Collaboration may go even further: in the past I have encouraged several small schools to join together to put on classes and or the finale event.

Training Classes

Beginning/Junior Protocol vs. Advanced/Senior Protocol

Freshman and sophomore students receive a minimum of five one-hour classes for Beginning Protocol. They are introduced to basic, semiformal etiquette, and the week concludes with a dressy or semiformal local evening event centered on a nice dinner. Some schools, in the first year of the program, opt for dinner only. The second year, some programs add an additional pre- or post-dinner activity for the evening such as a before-dinner party with hors d'ouvres and special adult guests, or an after-dinner dessert party.

Advanced or Senior Protocol offers a minimum of five one- or two-hour classes for junior and senior students. These classes build on the previous years' foundation but incorporate new and more advanced material, including formal etiquette. For returning students, this is their third and fourth year of protocol, but for few others it is their first year, so some review is necessary. Teachers can avoid redundancy in class material by using fresh presentations and introducing new information related to adult life and personal style development along with the review. The week-long classes conclude with a gala affair requiring tuxedos or tails for the gentlemen and formal evening attire for the young ladies. A formal dinner at a fine restaurant, private home, or club is followed by a special event such as a play or concert.

As you consider your program's development, determine exactly what you want the students to learn, given your resources. Determine how many class sessions are possible in the school's schedule, what the students can afford, and similar issues. No matter what your program choices are, all training is best concluded with a gala dinner event which allows students a chance to practice what they have learned and gives them confidence in their skills.

Curriculum Summary

Following is a general summary of what to teach in training classes. The actual material taught in these classes is given in the later chapters devoted to each subject.

Early Fall Class: Grooming and Proper Attire

The early class, "Grooming and Proper Attire," gives students instruction for proper public appearance. When possible, boys and girls should be instructed separately for this class. After my experience working with school programs, it became apparent that this class is best offered earlier in the fall, rather than with other protocol classes in the spring, because it allows students time to implement grooming and dress lessons into everyday habits, plan their outfits, and take advantage of store sales.

This session teaches students about dress codes and appropriate attire. Younger Junior Protocol students first learn about grooming issues and the categories of casual, dressy, and semiformal so that they understand different dress requirements for those specific situations. The Senior Protocol classes build on previous lessons, provide needed review, and introduce students to daywear and formal wear. Business wear is a helpful addition for the oldest students. Teachers can also design lessons to help them understand wardrobe differences and form their own flattering, personalized style.

Class One: Dining Etiquette

The Dining Etiquette class teaches the placement and proper use of dishes, utensils, stemware, glasses, and napkins for many dining situations. Teachers explain and demonstrate the art of eating "from soup to nuts" and present specialized dining etiquette for homes, restaurants, parties, and buffets. The upper-level classes receive additional lessons in formal dining. The table manners class is best given on the first day of the protocol training week, so that students have time to practice at home before the dinner event. This material may require two class periods.

Class Two: "The Right Moves"—Protocol Techniques and Escort Finesse

In "The Right Moves" class, young men receive "how-to" escort tips—opening various types of doors, assisting ladies with coats, chairs, stairs, and instruction about when such moves are appropriate. Young ladies learn about poise—and how to gracefully and properly receive assistance with jackets and coats, negotiate stairs, enter and exit vehicles, and observe seating etiquette. The instruction does not assume the context of dating and couples, but the training is certainly applicable to such situations. Teachers should tailor the class to whatever situation the students need for their scheduled event; they can include theater and concert protocol, for example, when applicable. After reviewing proper escort procedures, advanced students also learn about valet parking and gratuity standards.

Class Three: Social Navigation Skills

The focus of the next session is *conversation skills,* but it also includes other important communication skills. It helps students learn about proper conversation standards, encouraging thoughtful speech and keeping smoothly-flowing conversations, with specifics on what and when to speak (or not). Lessons include general conversational skills, handshake etiquette, RSVPs, social correspondence, and levels of appropriate speech for many everyday situations as well as special social events. A special area of focus should be the art of introductions. Learning how to be introduced and to introduce others can take a full hour or more depending on class size and practice time. This class may be separated into two classes, one on conversation and correspondence, and the other only on introductions. In beginning protocol classes, they are usually combined.

Class Four: Practice Session

The last class is generally devoted to review, questions, and practice in which all students rehearse the techniques of the "Right Moves" class and practice their dining skills. Customize your demonstrations and practice for the protocol event activity. One Logos Junior Protocol affair was scheduled to wind down semi-casually with milkshakes at an ice cream shop after their big dinner event. A "how to properly drink a milkshake" lesson was added to the practice session, and students got to practice with their own individual mini-milkshakes donated by a local café—such fun! Tailoring your practice session to the final event is an important aspect of successful classes and adds another enjoyable element to the program. The students nearly always look forward to the "hands-on" approach.

The practice session should answer last-minute student questions as well. Remember in *every* class to allow twenty to thirty minutes for discussion and questions, especially with first-time students. Don't be caught unprepared, however, if it happens to take much less time.

Building Support for Your Program

Once the goals, scope, and curriculum are established, you are in a position to secure support from the administration, parents, and students. Before getting parents and students on board, obtain the vital administrative approval and support. The administration and school board must know the specifics; a vague or sketchy program plan is unlikely to win broad approval, but a thorough and specific one is impressive and persuasive. Fortunately, school leaders are usually enthusiastic about a well-planned protocol program because it offers multiple benefits for everyone. They will still, however, have valid questions. Answers for many of these concerns can be found in this chapter and throughout the book.

Seek support in an orderly manner, respecting the school's authority structure. What is the administration's preference for the presentation of a new program? Do they prefer a written outline? An oral presentation? Try to anticipate questions, especially those concerning financing the program. (Logos's school office handles the money collection and bills, while some small schools allow the director to settle accounts and take money.) Present the goals, purpose, class topics, time required, special event suggestions, expected costs, possible dates, and possible candidates for the program director and teacher(s). Remember to include *who, what, why,* and *when*—the more complete the information, the better. Busy people appreciate specific information rendered in an efficient manner. They need a fairly complete program picture before they can confidently grant approval. Welcome their additional suggestions for the program's operation, and be willing to rework the program and present it to the board again if necessary.

After the administration and board give their stamp of approval, and basic plans are in place, then it is time to share program information with parents and students. Support from students is almost a given once they hear this program is approved and on its way. They eagerly look forward to the special dress-up event and classes where they will learn the manners of successful and social adults.

Most parents also welcome the program, but even so, timely communication builds better support. It also helps those few parents who feel a bit intimidated about having their child come home knowing more than they do. This is also why teachers remind students that it is unwise and dishonoring to bring any sort of superior attitude into the home—no smirks if parents or siblings commit a protocol error. Students may of course take home and share the information they have learned, but they need grace and wisdom in doing so. Teachers also encourage those students who have less-than-enthusiastic parents to patiently practice their manners. General and specific details matter. Parents appreciate receiving exact information ahead of time rather than hearing things secondhand.

At the program's launch and each year afterwards, advance general information should communicate the need and purpose of the program, answer potential questions, and allow everyone the chance to plan ahead. Budget is a main parental concern—"How much will this cost?"—so include prices in your first communication. A program director can expect to send two or three advance notices in which parents and students are briefed on developments as the program time draws closer.

Although it is rare, I am occasionally asked what a student should do if his or her parents are not supportive of protocol training. First, a well-written advance letter to parents will defend the program and put unsupportive parent's primary concerns at rest. However, should a lack of support still exist, it is unwise for students to lecture parents who resist the idea of good manners. Instead, the student should quietly and respectfully practice proper manners. Soon, a reasonable parent will be won over by their child's respectful and admirable behavior. If the parent continues to be non-supportive or ridicules the student, there are bigger issues involved, none of which actually have to do with protocol.

Take time to explain a new protocol program carefully to parents. The following letter is modeled on one that was sent to parents and students of the River Academy in Wenatchee, Washington, to introduce our new grade-school and high school program. The purpose of this general letter was fourfold: to introduce the new program, to dispel misconceptions about etiquette, to answer possible questions, and to establish cooperation and support for the program at home and in the school. I hope it provides some ideas about good communication with your students and parents.

Dear Parents and Students,

Most parents agree that our children are delightful. What in life is more enjoyable than these God-given treasures? Who among us, however, has not noticed these delightful bundles of spontaneous combustion seem to burst on the scene with a few rough edges? I know that my children were not born with immediate knowledge or skills in good and noble manners, especially at the table, nor were they able to properly dress themselves. Were yours?

These are learned actions. The proverb "Train up a child" tells us that children require training in how to live in a godly way. In pursuit of such excellent behavior, we at TRA are offering a helpful new program, protocol training, to equip young people in the art of kind and respectful social skills. The program will provide practical instruction in how to function skillfully and sincerely in our part of the civilized world.

Protocol, as Preferred Codes and Correct Behavior, Is a Means of Respect

Christians are admonished to "treat all men with respect" and protocol/etiquette is a tool towards this end. TRA recognizes that etiquette has a rich heritage from which we can draw. This heritage must not be neglected. This stands in contrast to some in the world around us who despise authority and submission, eager to cast off temperance and restraints.

Protocol is a means of equipping children for social events and future occasions, so that they know how to behave in a respectful manner worthy of the gospel. We want to teach every student, from kindergarten through the twelfth grade, the importance of good manners, deference, and the honoring of others. By implementing traditional protocol standards at TRA, we hope to equip God's children with a practical working knowledge regarding their social responsibilities. Habitual practice will eventually become a comfortable behavior pattern. Protocol provides life skills that are applicable outside school. The students are expected to be wise learners who apply the information diligently and usefully.

Protocol for Grade School

Children are happiest when they know what is expected of them, when it is expected, and how to fulfill those expectations properly. Wisdom promotes expectations in good behavior born of grace and kindness. Even Christ's youngest image-bearers are to reflect His light of love and grace—in all the details. We honor Him as we honor those around us in ordinary daily situations. Some call protocol "love in the trifles," but these become very important trifles as our children's souls develop habits, day in and day out. We think this program will support the good effort already begun in your children at home.

It is easy to incorporate etiquette's rules so they become a natural part of personal demeanor. It only requires consistent and diligent application at home and school, as well as student cooperation, to maintain the highest standards. Therefore, the program includes helpful guidelines that address students from the start, in kindergarten and grade school. In the early grades, the protocol program is part of the everyday classroom structure and involves teachers as well as students. Small, considerate courtesies involving words like "May I please" and "Thank you" become a part of the child's expected vocabulary. Standing in respect when addressing adults is expected behavior. Self-control and respect for others are the key components in this program.

What Is the Protocol Program for Older Students?

This spring, late in the school year, the River Academy will introduce a unique educational advantage. Ninth- and tenth-grade students will be able to participate in a two-part "protocol week" program. The first part will include a concentrated and specific program of classes designed for their age group. The training classes will conclude with the second part of the program: a special "semiformal" dinner in which the students may put into practice what they have learned during the week of protocol classes.

These older students are ready to embrace and apply protocol's finer details, so their classes will include detailed instruction in proper table manners, beginning social navigational skills including introductions, escort etiquette, and other protocol necessary for the special event. Two special early classes, one for young men and one for young ladies, will cover appropriate clothing categories, how to select and when to wear semiformal attire, and personal grooming tips.

Our Goal: Light for Living

The River Academy now has the distinct advantage of being able to present classes in traditional manners with training based on Christian principles. The unsurpassed brilliance of practical and applied Christianity is that it overcomes all darkness. Its light is available for every area of life. This is good news for the realm of social interaction, because the Christian principles behind most traditional etiquette are like a ray of light, granting practical assistance to walk more easily in a manner worthy of our calling—a manner with which we esteem and honor others more highly than ourselves.

Therefore we hope that this program will not only be a support to parents and a help to the children, but a continuation of Christianity's application to culture.

The Cost?

The training classes are required, but the second part of the program involving an evening dinner and event is optional. Students pay $50.00 for the optional special dinner and event, but the protocol training classes are provided as part of TRA's regular tuition fee. We do encourage all students to participate in the dinner and event so that they may put into practice what they have learned. Volunteer chaperones will attend either training sessions or a refresher course in order to set proper examples, and will pay for their own dinner and admission to the event.

Questions? Please give us a call. We anticipate this will be an enjoyable and beneficial program in your child's life.

Key People and Their Duties

Finding the right people for your protocol program is clearly a prerequisite for success. There are many capable people willing to share their time and organizational skills once a program is underway. The two necessary positions are that of *director* and *teacher*. While a single person might be able to fill both roles of director and teacher, it is better to involve more people and divide the responsibilities, because both jobs are time-consuming—even though they are "only" organizing one week-long program each year.

The Director

A high school program requires time, thought, and organized planning by a dedicated director to coordinate its many fine details. The director is in charge of scheduling the classes and activities, and thus has to juggle the schedules of the school, students, protocol teacher(s), chaperones, and those providing the dinner and evening activity. Strong organizational skills are required in order to arrange and coordinate all facets of the program.

The director also selects a qualified teacher or teachers well in advance of protocol classes and event dates. Other duties include finding chaperones, arranging transportation, communicating with students, parents, and others interested in or affected by the program, and planning dinner events that are suitable, enjoyable, and affordable. The director may ask others for advice or suggestions, but final decisions are best made by the director, with approval from the administration.

The director determines the formality level for the programs and plans a final evening where students can dress appropriately and practice what they have learned. From experience, I advise a dressy or semiformal event for beginner students (junior program) and a true formal affair for advanced students.

Many grade schools already have etiquette standards in place, but the director may also steer a grade-school program in the right direction. The program can be as simple as providing classroom teachers with recommended manners to add to their classroom rules, or the director may arrange for a special assembly, a party, or short program with etiquette training suitable for younger children.

The Director's Duties in a High School Program

Schedules certainly vary, but the following outline provides a suggestion for the director's tasks in a chronological order. Even in the same school, one year's schedule may slightly vary from another's. The crucial thing is to plan well in advance for a smoother operation and to avoid last minute disappointments and unnecessary complications.

*1. **Pray for Grace and Wisdom.*** "He who seeks good finds goodwill" (Prov. 11:27a). The wise director prays for God's blessing and grace upon this endeavor at the beginning, middle, and end. This advice may sound cliché, but Christians know its necessity. Seek God's wisdom, goodwill, and bountiful provisions. Pray that God will grant the students a desire to learn and apply protocol so that they might transform our culture. Pray for a qualified teacher(s) to present the material with wisdom in an enjoyable manner.

2. ***Plan Far Ahead.*** Ideally, the director selects the event and schedules a date for high school protocol week at least nine months to a year ahead of time. Planning may be done in less time, but it is wisest to allow this much. It allows time to coordinate all aspects of the next year's program with a good evening event, as well as helps students and parents plan ahead for the expense of the evening and any clothing or accessories they will buy or rent for the occasion.

Four aspects of the program must have dates that match. It is problematic if a scheduled event happens on the night when all the dining rooms in your favorite restaurant are reserved by another group, or when teachers are unavailable for classes or when the selected event is sold out for the scheduled week of protocol classes. In a small community, the relative rarity of plays, concerts, and other events means that the event date will determine the schedule, and the school should accept this. In any case, the director needs to coordinate the following:

1. The event.
2. The dining options.
3. The teacher(s).
4. The school class dates.

This requires a certain amount of cross-checking before submitting in formation for approval to the school principal. It also requires keeping all information in a file for easy future reference.

*3. **Event Selection.*** The director selects and arranges the program's pre- and post-dinner events. These activities should definitely be enjoyable and fun for all. Events should be compatible with the dinner plans and with the formality level selected by the director.

One resourceful director, when faced with a small choice of activities, arranged for her class full of athletic young men to travel out of town to see the Harlem Globe Trotters after dinner. Of course it was a hit! And the students created quite a sensation, receiving admiring glances as heads turned to see the well-dressed students enter the spectator seats. Another director, after the students enjoyed a white-glove dinner, selected tickets to a unique opera performance in which award-winning student opera singers performed interesting introductions to a variety of operas.

Every area offers plays, concerts, special performances, and other productions. Universities, community colleges, and community groups in your city or nearby cities sponsor many different types of potential events. Chambers of commerce and arts and theatre groups publish calendars of upcoming activities well in advance of performance dates. The director can request the school be added to various theatre and performing arts mailing lists so that advance notices of scheduled productions are sent to them for the coming year.

*3. **Dining Location, Menu, and Reservations.*** The director determines dining options and cross-references possible restaurant reservations with possible event dates and the school calendar. Ideally, the director works months in advance with the restaurant to secure needed reservations and selects the dinner menu appropriate for a semiformal or formal dinner. It is not unusual for catering facilities and popular restaurants with limited private dining rooms to book up to a year in advance. The director must be familiar with the chosen restaurant, noting their food and service—protocol night is not the time for trial runs. Catering managers and small restaurant owners alike offer personal service and are frequently very helpful and enthusiastic about your program.

Initially, the director chooses the restaurant or catering facility and makes reservations, with some "wiggle room" in the final number of diners, which allows adjustments in numbers closer to the reserved date. It is wise to obtain a written reservation for a large group confirming the date, menu choices, prices, and other details that may be forgotten in a few months. Keep this information in a file with the names of all contacts. Remember that the early bird gets the choicest meal—with less stress!

In making dining arrangements, pay special attention to time considerations, waiters, kitchen capacity, and gratuities. The director plans ample time for a leisurely dinner with plenty of conversation, which can take an average of two to three or more hours, depending on the number of food courses and waiters. Allow time for travel, for students to enter and exit cars and buildings, and for other various small tasks, such as checking and retrieving coats and accessories from cloakrooms. The schedule allows time for special needs such as riding on elevators (remember your whole group needs to use them!), parking facilities, and walking distances to reach the destination.

The director confirms the exact number of wait staff with the dining facility and determines whether it is adequate for the group's size. A formal dinner with multiple courses requires additional waiters and bussers. Too few waiters will result in service delays and interfere with the planned schedule. A general rule of thumb stipulates one waiter for every twelve to fifteen people and one busser for every twenty people.

The director also confirms the number of diners that the restaurant kitchen can accommodate for efficient, simultaneous servings. Most kitchens can serve small groups without delays, but larger group numbers require special banquet facilities. It will likely be necessary to offer a limited menu choice (two or three entrees) when accommodating large groups. Also remember to inquire about food options for students or chaperones whose beliefs or health conditions prevent them from eating the standard menu choices.

Don't forget that a fifteen to twenty percent gratuity will be expected. It is sometimes automatically included in the bill for large groups, so double-check the restaurant's policy.

4. Reserve School Dates. The director works closely with the school office to reserve the best possible dates for protocol week and the final evening event. It is easier to coordinate program activities with school dates when event choices are made months in advance of protocol classes. This avoids an overly full activity calendar at school, which can result in unnecessary complications and elimination of selected events. The director may make arrangements to dismiss classes early on the day of the gala event so the students have ample time to get ready for the evening out.

5. Resolve Conflicts. The director works with the school office to ensure that protocol class dates will not conflict with other programs that students might be involved in. Avoid scheduling events on school nights (if possible), church retreats, and times that conflict with other major school activities such as sports events or field trips. Particularly if your school is interdenominational, be sensitive to religious convictions that impact scheduling; Friday nights, for example, are difficult for Seventh Day Adventist families, and other families set apart the time from Saturday evening to Sunday evening. Not all conflicts will be resolvable, but the director needs to weigh all sides. A wise director also avoids scheduling any event with content that has potential to cause division or concern among the parents.

As the decisions on the program's dates and activities progress, notify the protocol teacher(s). Provide information on expected dress category, planned dinner and event, time, locations, and class expectations. The more advance information a teacher has, the better he or she can prepare specific information in addition to the standard instruction material.

5. Select the Right Teacher. Selecting the right instructor(s) is absolutely necessary for a successful program. As you might expect, finding the right people to teach protocol can take time, thought, and certainly some prayer. In some communities it may be very difficult to find a Christian teacher qualified in protocol. You may have to consider having someone trained specifically to take on your program. In any case, the search for a teacher should begin immediately upon program approval, and replacement searches should begin a year in advance. See the below section on "The Teacher" for more details.

6. Communicate with Students and Parents. As soon as the restaurant and event are secure—ideally, nine months to a year in advance—and after receiving the school's approval on program decisions, the director sends a letter to students and parents informing them of program dates, dress requirements, menu selection, and a response form. It is a good policy to submit this letter to the school principal for approval before mailing it.

Logos School often sends this letter nine months to a year in advance of protocol week, while other smaller schools send the letter several months ahead. The letter is a good opportunity to set the tone, so be creative and give it an interesting format. As discussed before, explain the event, category of dress, the approximate cost, when payment will be due, and transportation arrangements. Include the dinner menu choices and a permission/response form.

It is best to collect money and establish group size early, so the response form should be returned soon (within two weeks) after it is sent to students and parents. The form indicates the names of students attending the dinner and event. The director tallies the number of participants to finalize dining reservations and advance ticket purchase. Remember that, depending on your situation, it is often a good idea to require the (free) protocol classes but to keep the final evening optional—this should be clearly indicated in communications to parents and students.

Students write their names, phone numbers, and menu choices in designated spaces on the response form and return it to the school office with a check in the amount needed to cover the costs. (Restaurants and catering services find it easier to serve a large group when menu choices are limited. Some directors simplify the dinner process by offering the same dinner for everyone, but I prefer a menu choice of two entrees.) A short reminder may be necessary as the return date approaches. Keep all response forms in your file. Some schools require permission forms to be given to the office.

8. ***Appoint Chaperones.*** Chaperones should be appointed at least three months in advance. The director, protocol teacher, and their spouses are automatic candidates for the evening's chaperones. Depending on group size and school requirements, additional chaperones may be needed. Parents of protocol students appreciate being first on the list for chaperone duties. Parents frequently volunteer to help, but if additional chaperones are needed, the request for chaperones can be added to the response form with the dinner menu. The most difficult part of filling these positions is usually telling enthusiastic parents that the limited chaperone places are already taken. Limit the number of chaperones to keep a reasonable parent-student ratio, but there should be enough adults to easily help lead, organize, and possibly transport the students throughout the evening.

Chaperones need to know exactly what is expected of them. It is their responsibility to comply with the evening's etiquette. It makes good sense to require their attendance at a special chaperones' protocol session or invite parents to attend the student classes as a refresher course.

9. Reconfirm All Dates. Reconfirm all dates with involved parties about three months in advance. Remind students and parents of the event dates and any fees still due.

10. Have the Administration Contact Affected Teachers. The director confirms the dates selected for protocol classes with the administration office several months in advance. The administration can contact regular classroom teachers affected by protocol week classes so they can plan accordingly. The administration may stagger training class times during the chosen week to avoid interrupting the same class period every day, or schedule after-school classes (but this could interfere with other after-school activities such as sports practices or theater clubs). Most families appreciate the classes being scheduled during regular school hours to avoid scheduling headaches and extra trips.

11. Inform the Protocol Teacher with Details. At least two months before the selected dates, make sure the protocol teacher knows exact details about the event, menu, table setting, transportation, and schedule for the evening, so that class material will be tailored to the needs of the specific situation.

12. Finalize Transportation Arrangements. Life is simple when parents drop off and pick up students at the dinner location. This, however, is rarely the situation with larger groups or when the evening involves several destinations, which is usually the case. In this case, parents need only bring students to a common meeting area, which may or may not be the dinner location.

When the evening involves driving to other event locations different than the dinner site, the director determines drivers (unless chartered vehicles are reserved). Drivers may also be chaperones. Since the evening may end late, the director should plan a common pick-up location, or if possible have students taken directly home. All drivers should carry cell phones, and parents should have their numbers. Reconfirm driving arrangements with any involved parents at least one month in advance.

Group transportation should be arranged for several months in advance. Chartered transportation is best reserved many months ahead. A small group may enjoy a limousine to take them from dinner to the event, while a larger group may need a chartered bus. Any transportation expenses should be figured into the overall price per student.

13. Pre-evening Arrangements and Photo Time. A few weeks in advance, the director arranges and notifies students of the time and common meeting place where parents bring students before leaving for dinner. This meeting place also provides parents opportunity to bring cameras and take pictures. Depending on group size, a half hour is usually ample time for photos. Avoid bumps in the schedule by notifying parents of a definite start and finish time for picture taking.

The common meeting place provides opportunity for last minute instructions and announcement of which lady (or ladies) each gentleman will escort during the evening. The announcement made at this time eliminates discussion or requests for changes and adds another element of anticipation.

14. Finalize and Assign Escorts and Related Arrangements. One month ahead, determine escort assignments. The director predetermines who will be escorted by whom and pairs students together with complimentary discretion. One director tried pulling names from a hat to match students, but afterwards decided that assigning escorts was preferable because it more assuredly pairs Tim Taller with Tammy Tall rather than with Sam Shorter.

When assigning escorts, put students together who enjoy each other's company, but avoid the idea of "couples." This is not a dating affair. When the numbers of young men and young women are uneven, assign two ladies to one escort or vice versa.

Seating order in vehicles and at dinner tables depends on escort assignments and should be determined a minimum of two weeks before the event. The director determines table seating and may choose to make place cards to put on tables before students arrive in the dining room. Some directors assign different escorts in the vehicle than the escorts at the table so students have a variety of company during the evening. This is a good idea especially if escort arrangements are difficult or students might be uncomfortable with assigned escorts.

15. The Week Before. The week before protocol classes, the director sends notes to everyone involved in the program, reconfirming dates and times. Remind students and parents of the times and final arrangements in one last written reminder. A note with advance thanks to the teacher, chaperones, and other people involved in the program should be sent out also. It is wise to double-check with the restaurant or caterer, reconfirming menu choices and the final count of participants.

16. The First Day of Training. When possible, the director welcomes students for orientation time and introduces the teacher. The director may choose to attend class sessions, but if not, he or she should be easily available should a question or need arise.

17. Thanks to Those Involved. The director is responsible to send thank-you notes to teachers, chaperones, and others who helped with the protocol program. Many directors follow up by overseeing thank-you notes from students.

The Teacher

The teacher presents the actual class material and lessons in the art of protocol. The best-qualified teachers have teaching experience and skills along with a background in the subject. Well-presented lessons are largely dependent on knowledgeable, enthusiastic teachers who understand past and present standards of etiquette.

Qualifications

Select a teacher with interest and knowledge in protocol. Look for teachers with an enthusiasm for and comprehensive understanding of protocol in table manners, conversation, introductions, dress codes and any other etiquette included in your program. The candidate should also have familiarity with etiquette's regional variations. In other words, your candidate must demonstrate and possess a thorough working knowledge of the subjects taught.

Select a teacher who sets the right example. "We are all creatures of imitation: precept may teach us, but it is example that draws us."[2] Children and young adults constantly watch to see what is done, how and when. They are imitators as well as keen observers, so it is imperative the instructor sets a good example. Look for a person whose example includes a generally considerate character. In short, does he or she act like a lady or gentleman inside and outside the classroom?

As an example, the teacher must have courteous manners and a pleasant temperament. Does your candidate's life exemplify consideration and politeness? Does it reflect dignity and moral goodness? Does the candidate address and greet students respectfully? Does he or she consistently, even if not perfectly, practice kind etiquette? For example, if your lessons include speaking respectfully to others, and the instructor sometimes speaks with biting sarcasm, the message's credibility fails. No one likes hypocrisy, especially in an instructor. Teachers always set an example. It needs to be the right one.

Select a teacher with a Christian worldview matured by discernment. A person with a Christian worldview, accompanied by discernment concerning protocol in our culture, is a great asset to your students and the program. People with a firm grip on right behavior provide your students with light and

[2] J. C. Ryle, *Thoughts for Young Men* (Moscow, Idaho: Charles Nolan, 2002), 43.

truth. Anything taught apart from Christ and His principles is labor in vain. Protocol taught or applied for the wrong reasons produces superficial results.

Mature teachers usually come with a gift of discernment. Simply reading an etiquette book (and there are many) and then passing on the contents defeats the program's purposes. Far too many current etiquette writers ignore or compromise Christian standards. Some blatantly toss out good morals and offer new "protocol" advice on condoms for dating or how to have sex on a first date. A good teacher discerns such foolishness. Look for teachers who won't promote wrong principles, can distinguish Christian versus non-Christian perspectives, and will hold fast to what is good. The benefit to your program and community will be great.

Select a cheerful teacher who displays a spirit of thanksgiving. "Be of good cheer" is a powerful command, and so is "In all things give thanks." A happy temperament sets a much-needed tone in today's world of cynics, complainers, and grumblers, as does another quality that seems to accompany a cheerful attitude—thankfulness. Christians must cultivate a spirit of thanksgiving, beginning with the teacher in charge.

The subject of protocol tends to sound a bit stuffy with all of its do's and don'ts, but a cheerful teacher keeps the tone balanced. A happy countenance is more glorifying to God than a sober or rigid disposition in the classroom. This, with a good measure of dignified enthusiasm, is a testimony to God's goodness in practical matters.

Select a teacher with a friendly, professional appearance. Appearances are important. The teacher's demeanor and appearance set the class tone. Does your potential instructor's countenance include smiles and nice appearance? Your candidate's attire should be professional, modest, stylish and upbeat, without being loud or distracting. The way the teacher dresses is an important fact. Students give more respectful attention to a well-groomed, nicely dressed instructor than to someone who is sloppy and unkempt.

Finding Teachers

Some parents turn out to be excellent teachers when given the opportunity—after all, they have a vested interest in the students. Prior experience or certification has its benefits, but only if your candidate also possesses the other qualifications. Perhaps your candidate has attended etiquette or "finishing" school but hasn't taught before. A parent with polite social habits acquired from a home where proper manners were part of their everyday routine may also be among your possible instructors. A definite advantage of parent-teachers is that they may volunteer their services, especially if their doing so will make the program financially viable.

Don't rule out older people in your search for the right teacher. Respected, mature guest teachers can add variety and validity to class sessions. Consider a volunteer guest teacher whose gray hair hides a vast knowledge of past and current etiquette. Their experience may add new insights concerning skills that should be passed onto the younger generation. (Once in Spain I watched an artful demonstration of a nearly forgotten procedure to elegantly peel and eat apples and oranges, given by a very elderly lady who mastered the practice she had learned as a child. It was an object lesson in beauty to watch her graceful gestures.) Logos School, near the beginning of its program, found an older lady who had a rich background of protocol, spiced with plenty of humor and fun anecdotes. Your local senior citizens may have some wonderful information to contribute that can transform current protocol practices into an enjoyable art.

Consider a Christian man as a teacher. While work schedules make it difficult for many men to be instructors for all protocol classes, consider asking gentlemen to teach a class or two with the male students. Young men often do better under the instruction of a respected male role model. Last year I worked with a gentleman who was happy to take on the beginning-level boys' grooming and dress sessions. He possessed all the qualities just discussed, except a formal knowledge of some dress standards. After he was given the proper material, he was able to study it in a short time and did a marvelous job for the young men in his classes.

Also, consider people who are teachers already. A classroom teacher in your school may have experience and interest in teaching protocol and would make a good candidate. Certified protocol teachers may also be available in your community. If all else fails, consider training one of your parents or teachers to take on the role of protocol instruction.

The selection of the right teacher is a major component of a good program. Look for someone with the qualifications discussed and whom the students will enjoy. Don't skimp or rush the selection process—teachers matter as much as the material taught.

Teaching Matters: Duties and Suggestions for High School Protocol Teachers

New teachers will find the following suggestions helpful, while experienced teachers may wish to skip ahead. Recommended class material is discussed in separate chapters, but this brief section provides a few additional suggestions for the teacher in classroom presentation.

Greet your students. Put on a happy face. Be joyful! Remember to meet and greet your students as they enter the room. Smile. A cheerful countenance indicates a sincere instructor and establishes classroom tone. Personalities come with degrees of exuberance, but true cheerfulness nurtures a moderate tone balanced with respectful enthusiasm.

I recently spoke to a large group of high school students at a public school about art and design as part of career awareness. As students entered the room, some shy, some cool, I followed protocol's rules, greeting as many students possible, with a "Hello," a smile, and eye contact. The response was positive and the class enjoyable.

Maintain a professional demeanor and appearance. The teacher's attire is another important aspect in establishing a good tone. Demeanor and appearance should be professional, modest and upbeat, without being distracting. Be a person who inspires students to pursue excellence in their manners by remembering yours. The teacher's example is an important part of teaching presence and demeanor.

Keep the tone relaxed and enjoyable. The older students are usually excited but somewhat anxious about the event. The first year students, however, are nervous about everything, so set a reassuring, relaxed pace and tone. Don't rush. Experienced teachers know how to read their students, noticing each student's response to presented material.

Address concerns and answer questions. Take time to address student concerns and questions and be reassuring when presenting unfamiliar material to students. Soothe their anxiety or discomfort. The program is only successful when the students understand and embrace protocol. Students are usually enthusiastic—if they are not, the teacher needs to discern why.

Incorporate scriptures when appropriate. I like to include scriptures whenever applicable, so students understand how faith in action relates to their life outside the classroom.

Prepare students for the coming event. The teacher must prepare students to be competent and comfortable with all etiquette necessary for their gala evening. To do this, the teacher must first know what the director has planned. Where will the dinner occur? What is the dinner menu, physical layout of the facilities, and the type of event? Are doors double, single, automatic, revolving? Is there a coat check room? Valet service? Are there stairs? How are tables arranged? Where do students exit vehicles? It is the teacher's responsibility to know and teach the necessary details.

Understand regional protocol differences. A protocol teacher must be familiar with regional protocol. Area differences do exist, especially in dress. Basic courtesies generally apply anywhere, but life is always full of surprises and a wise teacher becomes familiar with variations before teaching the class.

Use discernment with selected books and materials. Discernment in the seemingly benign area of manners is a must. In newer publications, the "protocol" may not be the desirable norm and the information may even be incorrect! Some writers express opinions that are obviously wrong. One new "etiquette" writer's advice for mealtime manners counseled the reader who is called upon to say grace to avoid coarse language and revert to the following irreverent little ditty: "Through the lips and over the gums, watch out stomach, here it comes."

Other writers offer what seems common-sense advice at first glance, but when considered in light of established protocol and valuable principles, it turns out to be wrong. For example, one author, unintentionally undermining gentlemanly duties, said, "It doesn't matter who holds a door open—just get it open." Obviously, being in print is not a guarantee of correctness. A discerning teacher immediately dismisses such "expert" advice.

Most writers generally agree that kindness and respect are cornerstones of etiquette but may disagree on specific applications, so the protocol teacher has to wade through some conflicting details. Unfortunately books do not come with a "Teacher Discretion Advised" label. Information is clearer, and classes are stronger, when teachers refuse to be fooled or confused by current reinventions in protocol. I have included a list of books for your consideration in the bibliography at the end of this book. Today there are protocol writers who present good information and some who do not. As the proverb goes, "Eat the fish, and spit out the bones." This is the case with research in any field. Be especially skeptical of information found on the Internet.

Use visual aids and hands-on techniques. Make classes interesting by supplementing lessons with enjoyable presentations. Utensils for table settings, fabric samples, photos, slide presentations, cartoons, videos on dining, and other techniques keep lessons diversified and interesting. Give students opportunities for involvement and practice—hands-on demonstrations help students understand and remember the things being taught. Practice time is a very important part of this program. Students should not only be told, but shown, exactly what protocol applies and which manners are best at which times.

Because the same students receive protocol instruction several years in a row, the teacher needs to provide new teaching resources to keep the presentation of review material fresh and interesting. It is a good idea to maintain a resource file. I am constantly saving pertinent photos, news articles, and pictures of clothes, always thinking a year in advance so my presentation stays current.

Stories, historical facts, and humor are indispensable. A peek into the past is another useful teaching tool. Old etiquette books are entertaining and thought-provoking. Anecdotes from history (including your protocol program's history!) help maintain older students' interest. Numerous personal stories and examples reinforce the point of lessons, and every year new humorous stories occur. This year, one of my students laughingly shared about last year's dinner when she was asked if she would like soup or salad. Her response—"Sure"—left the waiter baffled. It turns out she thought he had said, "Would you like a super salad?" Students always enjoy real-life stories, so I am sure to sprinkle my sessions with them.

When students appear to grow weary with a too-long list of dos and don'ts, a bit of humor quickly regains their attention. Begin a "funny file" in your resource materials. It's amazing how many items you will find once you begin a file. Cartoons and humorous stories related to specific instructions make points memorable. Teachers need not be comedians, but humor is a very useful tool. It is like salt and pepper on the table, enhancing and seasoning the main dish.

Require note-taking and give handout materials. Students will learn more when they are required to take notes, and school budgets usually allow for printed handouts and photocopies of essential material. Handouts can be added to binder notebooks that students keep from year to year.

Encourage parental involvement. Most parents love protocol programs! Make use of their enthusiasm by welcoming volunteer help in protocol training, especially from parents of students currently involved in the program. The director can of course involve parents as chaperones, but there are other ways in which their participation adds to the program and lightens the teaching load. The table-setting class is one instance where willing parents can supply and set up tables with nice dishes, linens, and serviceware in the applicable category for practice. If the teacher is short of items for the dress session, he or she can ask parents to contribute interesting clothing items for the "trunk show," which will enrich the presentation without additional cost to anyone.

What about a Grade School Program?

Schools that establish standard manners for little ones reinforce good things taught at home and create more orderly halls, playgrounds, and classrooms. Grammar-age children like to learn facts, which means the best approach to teach protocol is filling young minds with straightforward "Do this, don't do that" instruction. This will be a ready resource for them later in their training, when discernment and flexibility play larger roles.

A strict program need not be underway in lower grade levels, but teachers and parents can still begin at this early stage to train children with a list of acceptable behavior tailored to the home and the school. In classrooms, playgrounds, or halls, on-the-spot, informal instruction and reminders are also effective. "Johnny, remember not to run inside buildings." "Class, please stand and say 'Hello' to today's guest, Mr. Brown." Impromptu protocol training reminds a child to be faithful in small things, fostering propriety, self-control, and kind behavior.

Classroom Rules

Classroom teachers can easily incorporate common courtesies as part of the expected behavior for young children. Training in manners instills respectful habits. Here are a few suggestions on the type of manners that should be the norm for every classroom.

- Do say "Hello" or "Good morning" and "Goodbye" when others first arrive or leave for the day.
- Do look people in the eyes when they speak or you are talking to them.
- Do speak in a respectful, quiet tone of voice, but speak clearly.
- Do wait your turn.
- Do use proper titles with last names or "Sir" and "Ma'am" when speaking to elders.
- Do stand up when an adult is speaking to you or enters the room for the first time.
- Do sit up straight.
- Do remember to say, "I'm sorry" if you accidentally hurt someone.
- Do wash and dry your hands before eating, after using the bathroom, or when dirty.
- Do turn your head away and cover your mouth and nose when you cough and sneeze. Do not sniffle; leave the room and blow your nose.
- Do help others when help is needed.

- Do not spit.
- Do not yell.
- Do not run in buildings.
- Do not interrupt other people when they are speaking.

One teacher I know posts class rules that consist only of a list of these passages: Philippians 2:3–4, 14; Matthew 22:37–40; Galatians 5:19; and I Corinthians 10:31.

These are a few of the many rules children need to know. But if I had to single out only one rule to insist upon as a part of a child's early manners, it would be "Always say 'Please' and 'Thank you' whenever you ask for or receive something." When students are trained to politely ask and receive, they offer respectful requests instead of demands, thus showing proper Christian gratitude. There is a whole kingdom of difference in asking, "May I please have such and such" versus "Give me such and such." Learning to say "Thank you" fosters an appreciative spirit.

Not long ago, while working with a group of young children at a large suburban school, a guest mother served a healthy fruit snack. One small face clouded over, complaining in louder and louder whines, "I don't want that. I don't like fruit!" Before long, other whining voices joined the chorus and complaints grew louder as the five-year-olds began demanding cookies. The inexperienced teacher chose to ignore this behavior and thus missed a perfect opportunity for impromptu instruction in thankfulness as well as table manners. It was an ideal time to instruct the small children in the rule of good table manners covering this situation—when being served something one does not want or like, no more than a smiling "No, thank you" is proper. This teacher allowed the children to multiply their complaints as if such grumbling was acceptable behavior. (Finally, the guest mother herself offered on-the-spot protocol instruction and all complaining ceased.)

Classroom protocol training involves principles of learning how to be faithful in "little things" as a preparation for faithfulness in bigger things. Faithfulness in being thankful and not complaining has major implications. You learn to see the glass as half-full rather than half-empty, which in turn establishes a more grateful heart. Don't underestimate this point. Young and old alike tend to take things for granted; we begin to think that tomorrow will always follow today's suit, bringing with it all the same comforts and gifts we have come to expect, and so on for the next day, and the next—ho, hum. Before we know it, our sense of gratitude has diminished to nothingness. "Please" and "Thank you" are necessary exercises for the healthy soul.

Classroom teachers are an amazingly creative and resourceful breed, and they have many opportunities to help build good character in students by presenting both a good example and interesting lessons. They can explain etiquette, assign art projects, plan parties, and do other activities that highlight good manners. Opportunity abounds for reading books on manners to the children. Most youngsters are eager to know protocol facts, and implement the "right thing" in their behavior. No one likes to do the "wrong thing" or embarrass oneself—especially young children. I know one kindergarten teacher who instantly rewards proper behavior in her classroom with a "big cheese" award. Her students eagerly seek opportunity to serve one another. Create an environment that exerts some positive pressure.

Other Suggestions for Grade Schools

The director can easily implement special training sessions or assembly programs about good conduct. One school had a manners-oriented assembly in the first week of school. Another introduced a weekly "Good Manners" series for their fourth-grade through sixth-grade students for one month. The material presented was basic and straightforward, and the class met outdoors in the late spring to make the sessions different and fun.

For younger elementary students, consider arranging a short training class with a guest teacher, and conclude with a "hands-on" demonstration and party. Parents and grandparents may be special invited guests. Visual aids are an important part of training for this age group—I use animal illustrations from a cute booklet called *Mind Your Manners!* by Walter Chandoha. At the River Academy, high school students have done protocol skits portraying the "Character Trait of the Month" related to biblical masculinity and femininity for elementary school assemblies. Students devised four scenes each for masculine and feminine manners. Their scenes showed wrong actions and right behavior in manners involving opening doors, avoiding gossip, dressing appropriately, and speaking graciously. What a joy to see older students teaching younger ones!

You will gain other ideas and approaches for a program as you proceed. I hope these few suggestions provide you with a good springboard from which to launch into your own training efforts for younger students.

Conclusion

Without question, our current generation of children has great need for practical training in Christian social arts. Teaching what is real, true, and right has great rewards. I trust that the Lord will bless your efforts and adventures in protocol's practical realm, and I hope that by sharing these few ideas and materials, I can help more people experience the joy, usefulness, and success of Christian protocol programs. It is comforting to be underway and on reliable paths, knowing that everyone involved will learn and grow as they go.

Your training endeavors matter greatly, not just to your children's edification and your school, but to the future growth of Christian culture. May the Lord grant you fruit that will remain to His glory.

Part III

Protocol Training Topics

5

Food for Thought: Notes on Table Manners

Surprising as it may seem, my table manners class usually ranks as a favorite among older students. Though younger children may not show much interest, by the junior high Dialectic and high school Rhetoric stages, students' interests and priorities have undergone a remarkable metamorphosis. They are suddenly anxious to learn what is proper and improper in what is to them the mostly uncharted waters of social navigation. Therefore our focus in this chapter is on teenagers (suggestions for younger children may be found in chapter 2).

Proper table behavior and a skillful dexterity with multiple knives, forks, spoons, and glasses can be daunting to a young person's confidence. This is one of the first areas in which they come to realize that they don't know quite everything yet. They want to know how to eat correctly for a variety of reasons—they don't want to embarrass themselves at social events, they want to come across as mature and graceful, particularly to the opposite sex, and they don't want to look clumsy and inexperienced. This makes them particularly receptive to protocol training.

After the earlier fall dress lessons, the table manners class is a good launching pad for the other protocol training sessions. It prepares the way for later instruction on the nuances of finer dining and social situations. Students enthusiastically (and nervously) anticipate the special dinner at the close of protocol training, and are naturally motivated to pay attention to this material since they know they will be attending this dinner soon. So expect a delightful, attentive response from your students—they are usually very willing learners at this stage.

Most people give only a passing thought to how they eat, and they eat every day! It is imperative that your students give this question some thought at the very start. So, before beginning technical instruction in table skills, it is wise to give young people an introduction that explains why these things should be important to them. This can be done whether you are teaching at home or in a school program. Though young people probably have a natural interest already, help them see that this is important not only to them, but also to civilization. Take time to lay a biblical foundation that will help them understand that God has made the table a central place for fellowship among His people. Time spent discussing this should help them realize the necessity and benefits of proper table behavior, and that they have a responsibility to use, daily and consistently, the training they are about to receive. Some teenagers may wonder if people nowadays really still care about polite dining etiquette, a shortsighted view which is based on their limited knowledge and experience at this early period in their lives. It is your job to teach them how valuable table etiquette is, and how it can benefit them in their day-to-day life—not just at the big formal occasions.

One main goal is that students apply the lessons they learn, making proper behavior and good manners a part of their everyday life. Show your pupils the advantages of using of good table manners. Remember, students enjoy anecdotes, stories, and real-life examples when you are teaching this material, so feel free to include your own, for they never fail to capture interest and make the points more memorable. Just as we set a table in preparation for dinner, a parent's attitude and teacher's orientation set the tone that helps students appreciate good table etiquette even on ordinary days.

If you have time restrictions that prohibit you from going into all of what follows in this chapter, try to incorporate as many of the following concepts into the regular table manners sessions as possible. Home training, of course, has the advantage of no time limits. Whatever level of detail you teach, remember that if young people do not understand the benefits and necessity of table etiquette, they will neglect its use daily. Their wrong eating behavior will turn into bad habits that will leave them ill-prepared for many situations.

Listed below are a few major topics to include in any introduction to dining etiquette.

Dining involves more than merely food consumption. Every one of us needs daily nourishment for body and soul together. When gracious manners rule at the table, we enjoy the simplest foods more and find our souls greatly satisfied. Dining provides an important opportunity for comfortable, relaxed fellowship where both soul and body find nourishment at the table. Young people have a responsibility to contribute properly to this fellowship by employing right manners at mealtime. Knowing the mechanics of how to sit, visit, and eat in various situations contributes to the kind of atmosphere that should prevail. Bad manners distract by their offensive intrusion and are as distasteful as spoiled food. A meal is not successful or enjoyable unless it includes both tasty food and tasteful conduct.

Once students are comfortable with table manners, they will lose their awkward, self-conscious concerns and will be able to give more attention to the other people at the table, instead of their own (mis)management of various foods and utensils. Their early hard work will yield fruit, adding good fellowship and polite manners to delicious food, and so rounding out a pleasant dining experience.

That dining is far more than physical nourishment is a time-honored concept. Consider Esther's extraordinary example of the importance of the dinner table as a backdrop for securing the king's favor. She served a delicious feast to set the stage to ask for Israel's deliverance, so that "The king's soul was pleased. . ." and a good thing, too. This was a state dinner with profound implications. No doubt Esther displayed perfect decorum at her fine banquet, employing exquisite manners in the presence of the king and her people's enemy. She had already obtained the king's favor, but the banquet was a place to secure it and to further please him. Her faith in God, prior training, and obedient practice of the rules of her times had equipped her for this serious situation, and she carried herself with impeccable protocol and timing. We may not face such grave situations, but many of us will find ourselves in a similar game with smaller stakes—a job or promotion, for example.

Good table manners promote an atmosphere of order and harmony. The importance of order and harmony often go unappreciated until they are lacking. A meal without them is an awful mess—hard on the digestion and hard on good fellowship. Mealtime should be a happy time. Proper table manners orchestrate order and harmony, and this contributes to a more enjoyable dining experience in which the possibility of strife is reduced. This dovetails with Proverbs 17:1, "Better is a dry morsel and quietness with it, than a house full of feasting with strife."

One current protocol writer correctly stated, "A person's behavior at the table really signals a certain sensitivity to other people." In other words, good manners are a way of expressing regard for others. Thus they eliminate obvious disorder like everyone drinking from the same glass or bottle, reaching for someone else's plate, taking extra-large or the last remaining portions, or spitting. Important dining "ordinances" are designed to encourage harmony and order by removing chaos and confusion.

The following descriptive illustration reinforces the point of order and harmony while encouraging students to grow up. Imagine dining with a group of unsupervised and protocol-illiterate toddlers, who lack a sense of appropriateness or order. If one toddler sets down an unguarded peanut butter and jelly sandwich, it may be lost to other, quicker little hands. The rule of grabbing and the concept of "mine" prevail. Drinks are spilled, and harmony disappears while tears appear from the hungry little sandwich owner as someone else gobbles up his lunch. Messy, sticky residue no doubt covers small hands, faces, table, and clothes. A resolution to the conflict of the disappearing sandwich is unlikely, leading to one or two hefty shoves. Strife, confusion, tears, and unhappiness reign. So much for harmony and order.

This reign of confusion is nothing new. Early medieval manuscripts report some free-for-all fights over pieces of choice foods by people much older than toddlers. This should remind us of Christianity's vibrant contribution to culture. Early Christian ideals were a great improvement over the Romans' (who threw food remains on the floor), not to mention the barbarians' even more uncivilized eating habits.[1]

Today, busy people find the practice of gracious table manners creates a much-needed atmosphere of calm and order that symbolizes mutual respect and esteem. Students who apply etiquette's considerate actions discover that they make a valuable contribution at the table.

People are judged by their table manners—or lack of them. Everyone knows there is a connection between who you are and what actions you display. The idea that the true person is revealed by outward behavior means that how we act, how we eat, how we look, what we do, and what we say are indicators of our character that other people use as measuring rods. Of course, impeccable outward manners can and do disguise a less than perfect character, and imperfect manners can obscure a good character, so our measuring

[1] One interesting early fourteenth-century manuscript cites the impact of Christianity on societies anxious to escape brutish, barbaric conduct. Written by Christian priests, the manuscript's instructions for orderly table conduct included eating slowly and sparingly, not grabbing or gulping food. These manners were considered "not small trifles, but matters of true significance expressing the spiritual grace of the person who displayed them." See Bridget Ann Henisch, *Fast and Feast* (University Park, PA: Pennsylvania State Univ. Press, 1997), 190.

sticks are somewhat flawed. The Bible teaches that while God looks on the heart, man looks on the outward appearance. Like it or not, we are judged by outward appearances, since most people believe that actions are an insight to what the person is "really like." Indeed, since we can't read minds, outward behaviors are the only way we gain insight into others. Actions can be revealing, especially when those actions fail to show foundational manners that keep selfishness and disrespect in check.

Throughout the centuries, wise people have maintained the proverb "Manners maketh the man." Aristotle quoted the then-ancient proverb in his *Ethics,* and the idea persists today. Another ancient proverb suggested, "You cannot know a man until you have eaten a peck of salt together." Learning how to properly "eat a peck of salt" together has advantages. Good manners always move us away from wrong, selfish, and ungrateful actions, and this has a good effect on our reputation. Our younger generation must clearly understand that wise people embrace and value a good reputation.

Table manners prepare young people for diverse dining experiences. Young people need to realize that different levels of dining exist, from formal dinners to casual outdoor picnics, but the same basic good manners preside over all. A table setting and its food courses can be simple, complex, formal, semiformal, informal, or casual. Good manners do not disappear with simpler meal courses, fewer dishes, or a casual and relaxed atmosphere. We still use napkins properly, chew with our mouths closed, do not talk with our mouths full, and so on. Good manners apply in every situation, day in and day out.

The regular practice of good table manners is foundational in every dining category and equips us for whatever dining event comes our way, whether in homes, restaurants, at private banquets, at picnics, for business, or special occasions. Training provides preparation for the future as well as equipping our youth with skills for today's different needs. Time and practice are required to master table etiquette. It can't be acquired at the last minute.

Good table manners foster refined, courteous eating skills. Pragmatically speaking, this means dining becomes an enjoyable art. Protocol's standards elevate the tone of behavior. This tone and refinement come with big benefits for those who use good manners. This common availability is in itself wonderful. Stereotypes aside, etiquette is not exclusively reserved for society's upper class or the very rich. There are no social barriers or limitations regarding etiquette's ownership, nor are there any user fees. Manners are free and available to everyone. And, although numerous rules exist, young people find that table manners are quite easily learned. While this should eliminate social inferiority complexes, it doesn't mean that everyone practices or develops good manners.

Money is certainly no guarantee of refined personal decorum. I once witnessed a surprising incident in a fine, upscale restaurant at one of the world's top resorts where prices reach beyond the average pocketbook. A mother, father and two sons were seated at a beautiful table complete with linens and flowers. The eldest son of about thirteen years old ignored his utensils and ate with his hands. As the meal progressed, he grew increasingly bored and restless. He pushed his chair back. He gradually slumped down until his back was finally flat on the chair seat with his legs and feet partly on the table. His parents never corrected him in spite of his big, dirty feet being on the tablecloth and the unsightly contortions he displayed during the course of the meal. This was a poor reflection on more than the son; his affluent parents, in spite of their riches, were poverty-stricken in a much more important sense, and their sons were heirs of their poor estate. They failed to train their son in the simple task of eating properly. How will he face future realities with such undeveloped life skills or the simplest compliance to good table manners? Who should correct this young man? First and foremost, his parents—and failing their duty, the restaurant manager was the next responsible person in charge who could remind the young man that his actions were unsanitary and improper in the dining room.

Good table manners help eliminate awkward and embarrassing moments. Nobody likes an awkward moment, least of all when one is the cause and center of it. Table manners grant us capability to reduce the likelihood of awkward times. Even more than adults, young people have a strong aversion to embarrassing themselves. They want to be accepted and respected, and table manners create a whole realm of potential embarrassment. We have all seen advertisements showing a young woman's disdain towards an escort who unknowingly reveals spinach on his teeth when he gives her a big smile at dinner. Aside from giving up spinach, young people want to know what to do if that really happens. Good table manners help us know what to do if this happens and how to avoid other social dangers. Protocol codes discourage dining mistakes and social catastrophes. Children trained in basic good manners are better prepared to avoid embarrassment at the table and better prepared to know how to handle awkward situations when they do occur.

A warning: Don't set impossible expectations. Some students have a tendency, once they understand the importance of table manners, to desire instant perfection from themselves (and sometimes from others) at the table. In reality, the world of multiple plates, forks, spoons, fingerbowls, and numerous food courses sometimes stumble the best of experts. Anyone can forget an infrequently used rule. Consistent practice reduces this possibility, but it takes time to learn the various applications. As discussed earlier, the practice of table manners benefits fellowship and a pleasant dining experience. We don't develop manners to feel perfect or superior to others, but we should feel comfortable and socially competent. Unrealistic expectations of rigid perfection or superiority are robbers of enjoyment.

All this new information can seem overwhelming, especially for young people with little prior protocol training. If they harbor unrealistic expectations about their performance, nervous discouragement can be the result. Parents and teachers can reassure beginners that practice will result in proficiency in the art of dining well. Precepts of respect, order and beauty are best maintained by observing them in our everyday habits. Conduct then becomes habitual and easy.

Practice makes perfect. Learning table etiquette is gradual; it takes time and practice to master the many details. Practice not only makes one perfect; it also makes one comfortable. Taking all opportunities to exercise what one has learned will prevent any nervousness. Habitual, second-nature practices will replace self-conscious concerns and worries that stem from lack of application. Apprehensiveness simply disappears—we don't have to worry about what glass, fork, or salad plate we should use. The payback is being properly prepared and comfortably equipped for real-life situations. We can then focus on fellowship with other people instead of our own manners. (Good table manners include appropriate conversation, which we will discuss later.)

Table manners empower us to make a gracious contribution towards a pleasant dining experience, and this alone is a significant reason for their use. Again, it is important to reassure your pupils that no one is expecting immediate or constant perfection in all the formalities. The art of dining takes time and practice, after which we expect consistent practice of good dining standards at all times, in all places—at home and away. Thus, we begin to explore the world of table settings and protocol for different dining situations.

Eliminating the Guesswork: Casual to Formal Table Settings and Foods

Familiarity with the terrain of table settings provides children with fundamental skills and competency when they sit at a table. The table provides the backdrop for different types of dining experiences—formal to casual, and so instruction must cover different categories' requirements in order to prepare young people for various occasions.

You would be amazed at the number of children who have never learned to set a table. It involves more than placing plates, glasses, and silverware in the right order. No matter the degree of informality, for example, the table must be clean, orderly and attractive. Every item has a place and function. A well-set table is attractively arranged not only with a place for every person and necessary tableware for the foods served, but also an appropriate centerpiece and other pleasing decorations.

Complex rules for table settings, believe it or not, have a real function and do not exist simply to trip up the ignorant and grant superiority to those "in the know." Proper settings aid the orderly rhythm in food course service, helping even the most elaborate dinner proceed smoothly. A formal meal, especially, has greater numbers of plates and silverware to accommodate the large number of food courses. Informal meals have fewer courses and don't require servants, so the place settings are appropriately simpler, but in both cases the settings and manners are functional.

Ideas for Table Setting Classes

There are several successful approaches for teaching about table settings. Foremost, the protocol teacher presents the information lecture-style along with hands-on demonstrations of actual settings. This is best for first-time students who have many questions and need practice time. Showing one of the many good instructional videos on table settings is another option and requires fewer materials.

A third method involves a table setting project assigned to students. My junior high and high school art class students have an assignment we all enjoy. After some introductory lessons on table settings, teams of one boy and one girl select a dining category and theme. They then design and properly set up an actual table for two, complete with full settings—serviceware, plates, and glasses—in the designated category of dining formality. They "invite" guests whom they would like to meet and make place cards for them. One team selected a tropical theme and invited Tarzan and

Jane. Another team chose a Japanese theme and invited the Emperor and Empress of Japan to sit at their beautiful table—their place cards were even written in Japanese. National, historic, and literary themes are favorites. No two teams are allowed to choose the same theme, so the first team to name their theme earns the exclusive right to it. The finished tables are later displayed at a school event to show off the students' creative ingenuity and mastery of properly setting a table.

Whichever methods you use, class instruction should include time for students to practice their eating skills and tableware handling techniques for themselves. For example, the instructor or helpful parent could provide paper plates, flatware, glasses, and snacks that are easily cut (such as fig bars or strawberry shortcake) so that students can practice and refine their eating skills. Students of all ages enjoy the treats, and the hands-on approach provides good practice time and helps answer questions.

Table Setting Categories

Informal meals are, for obvious reasons, customary in most homes even when guests are present. It is also the first category in which children need training at home, but your protocol training must help students understand the different dining categories. Young people need to realize, however, that differences in dining categories are only in table settings, foods, and dress codes—not in basic good manners.

The following information is based on my teaching notes from table setting lessons. Freshman and sophomore classes begin with the informal and semiformal categories, while formal dining lessons are reserved for older students after they are familiar with the informal dining categories. Lessons include instruction in eating skills and tableware management, which prepares them for the dining events in their respective categories.

Casual

Casual dining is easy, unfussy dining that includes potluck meals, picnics, barbecues, outdoor eating, and fast food drive-ins. Eating fast food in the car hardly qualifies as dining, but general manners still apply to eating on the run or at a picnic table. Disposable tableware fits into this category.

Informal

The informal category is comfortable and familiar terrain because most of our homes serve daily informal dinners. (Buffet meals and many receptions are also generally informal.) Table setting rules and protocol exist, but are

Typical casual, family-style setting with placemat. Spoon optional depending on menu.

Typical informal setting (salad served before entree). Salad plate not shown.

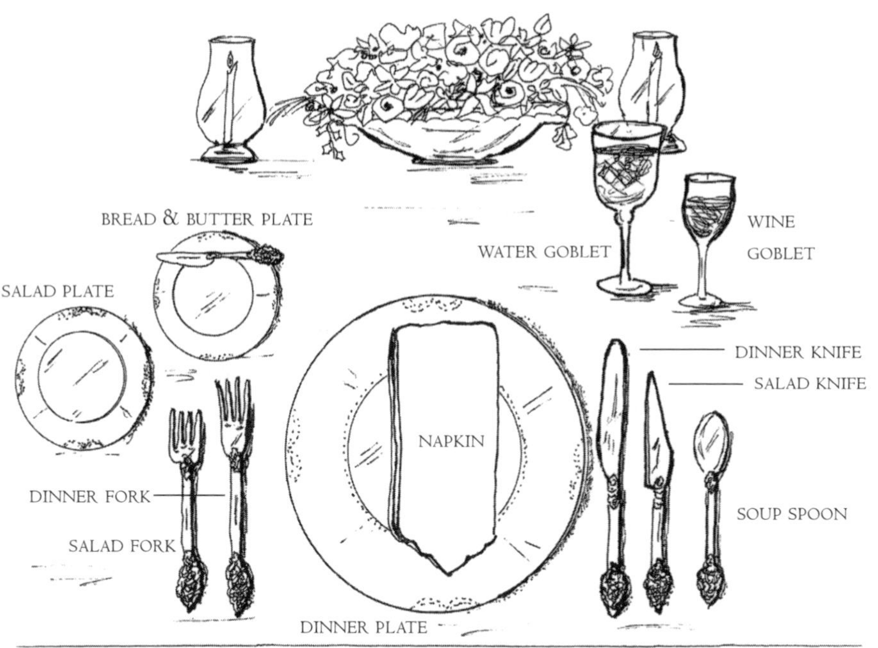

ypical semiformal setting with centerpiece and candles (salad before entree).

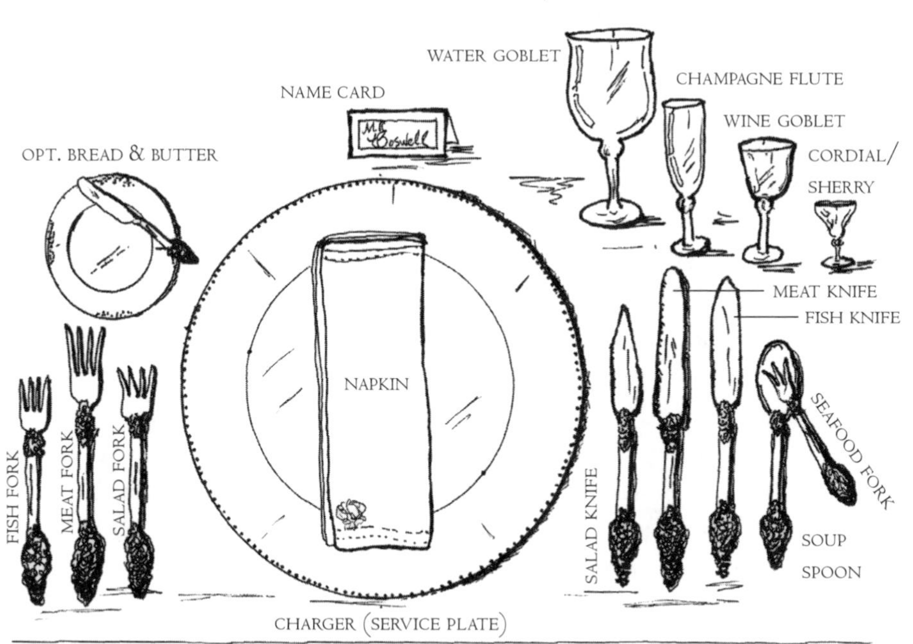

xample formal setting: seafood appetizer not pre-placed, salad served after entree or meat course.

clearly much less rigorous than those for formal and semiformal meals. The more relaxed rules fit easily into our busy daily schedules. Tableware may be less elaborate and more colorful, and invitations may be verbal or written on convenient fill-in invitations.

Stoneware or pottery instead of bone china is often used on an informal table. Colorful table cloths or placemats of cotton, linen, or blends are perfectly suited for informal tabletops. Napkins need not match the tablecloth and paper napkins may be used. Smaller nosegays or colorful, creative, and even unconventional centerpieces are common.

Informal meals, a relief to hurried (and harried) moms, usually involve three to five healthy food courses, some of which—like roast beef and potatoes—may be served on the same platter and eaten on the same dinner plate. All food, except dessert or possibly soup and salad, is served at the same time. It's an efficient way to serve food and perfectly acceptable in this category. Often soup or salad is eaten first, followed by a main entrée, vegetables, and/or fruit served together, finishing up with optional dessert or fruit, and coffee.

Today, meals served in most homes—with or without invited guests present—are informal. Guests expect to serve themselves as food is passed at the table. Remember, though, that the label "informal" does not mean we can abandon basic protocol. Good table manners are an important part of the informal meal.

Semiformal

When entertaining guests for a special occasion, dinner is frequently semiformal. Whereas formal events are grand, sophisticated, and impressive, they can be a bit intimidating and lengthy due to all the waiters, service, and procedures they involve. Not so a semiformal affair. Although some protocol experts resist its title, this category has its own festive aplomb—not truly formal, but still quite elegant. Hence, "semiformal" is popular for many special celebrations, including weddings, receptions, anniversaries, school parties, dances, and other special events, even birthday parties.

Semiformal table settings may use white or colored linens with fine china, crystal stemware, silverware, and a creative centerpiece. Often five courses are served, beginning with an optional appetizer course. Individual, separate salads may appear before or after the main entree.

Specific dress requirements for semiformal events rule out jeans and shorts. Here, as in the formal category, dress codes deserve respectful observance by guests. Semiformal invitations are usually handwritten on printed, filled-in invitations or note cards and a prompt response is expected. In restaurants which offer semiformal dining, take-home leftover boxes (a.k.a. "doggie bags") are not requested.

Formal

True formal dining has not quite disappeared, but it is reserved for rare events and is increasingly uncommon in homes not only because there are multiple food courses requiring a large, professional kitchen, but also because skilled wait and cooking staff are necessary. Formal affairs require a waiter for every six to eight persons—one never serves oneself at a formal dinner. As you can imagine, putting on a formal dinner is quite expensive and time-consuming.

Many government and state ceremonies are excruciatingly formal affairs. Guests are expected to comply with official state protocol and strict codes of deference to rank are respected. Knowledge and compliance with official protocol are part of the guest's responsibility at these special functions. Some weddings, balls and special parties are also formal events. The formal invitations, generally written in the third person and requesting "the pleasure of your company," arrive between two to five weeks before the event and specify the occasion, time, and dress requirements. They require an immediate reply. Dress codes are rigorously observed at formal affairs.

Formality is also reflected in how the table is set. Fine lace or damasks—traditionally white—with matching white napkins, cover a symmetrically set table and typify a formal event. Plates and silverware are precisely set one inch from the table edge. Only three pieces of silverware for the first three courses will be on each side of the plate. The waiter removes used tableware as each course is finished, and brings new sets as each next course is served. The first several courses' wineglasses stand empty, ready to be filled by the waiters, and later, additional glasses for each course are unobtrusively replaced as used ones are removed.

Whenever more than eight guests are present, which is usually the case at a formal dinner, place cards with abbreviated titles and last names designate seating places. Folded name cards go above the dinner plates while flat cards are situated on the napkins. Small menus may be set near each place. Tall floral or fruit centerpieces provide dramatic elegance. Silver candlesticks, fine china, and crystal grace the damask or lace tablecloth, making a formal event very special indeed.

Second portions are not offered because a formal dinner already consists of at least five or six, and up to fourteen, exquisitely prepared courses.

Yes, you read that correctly—the grandest of formal banquets can have as many as fourteen courses, presented one at a time by skilled waiters in a leisurely procession. Diners should spend time enjoying every small portion, while seeking to keep with the pace of the others, eating neither too fast nor too slowly.

The minimum sequence of courses is presented this order: (1) an appetizer of caviar, seafood cocktails, or shellfish; (2) clear or thick soup; (3) fish followed by sorbet; (4) a beef, pork, or fowl entrée accompanied by vegetables; (5) salad and cheeses (salad may also be served before the entrée); (6) dessert followed by coffee, liqueurs, and optional sparkling waters. Various wines accompany each food course. Little wonder the formal dinner is not an everyday occurrence—it takes hours to plan, prepare, serve, and enjoy such a meal. But it is an impressive dining experience!

Table Setting Components and Food Courses

It is essential for protocol teachers to describe and explain tableware thoroughly if they want young people to understand, and be comfortable with, each level of formality. Every item on the table has its place and use. I have found it best to begin at the beginning of the meal, with items used first, and proceed through the world of table settings in chronological order. As with all technical aspects of protocol, there may be slight variations in the following common settings. Remember that truly excellent manners allow for gracious adaptability.

Napkins

The napkin is the first item you attend to once you are seated. In a home, it is polite to wait until after everyone is seated at the table before taking your napkin. As a guest, wait for the hostess to take her napkin from the table before taking yours. In certain restaurants the waiter may place the napkin across your lap just after you are seated. When this is not done, it is best to immediately place the napkin on your lap. This is done before placing any food order, although a few experts say a napkin on the table signals the waiter that you have not yet ordered, so if you forget to immediately pick up your napkin, do so immediately after ordering, and certainly before you eat or drink any food. The napkin remains on your lap until the end of the meal.

For large dinner napkins, use your left hand to retrieve and unfold the napkin. Reach forward and pick it up by the upper left corner opposite of the fold and bring the napkin directly to your lap. Turn it so that the fold is facing your body. This is done without any waving, flapping, or shaking the napkin in the air. Gently lay it folded across your lap. Only if you are less than six years old is it acceptable to tuck a napkin into your clothes, and then only if there is no bib. Gentlemen have the option to place their napkin over the right knee, but the lap is preferable (and more secure). Smaller breakfast or luncheon napkins are usually placed fully open on the lap. Paper napkins, commonly used in casual and informal situations, are handled the same way as the cloth napkins.

Where is the napkin placed? At an informal meal, a cloth napkin is placed to the left side near the forks. Some informal table settings feature the cloth napkin in a goblet at each place. Paper napkins may be used in place of cloth at an informal table, but napkins at semiformal tables must be cloth. The napkin may be folded plainly and set to the left of the forks, or folded more decoratively, such as in a fan shape. In a formal setting, a twenty- to twenty-four-inch, square-folded, damask napkin will be placed on each individual's plate. If the first course is already on the plate before guests are seated, then the folded napkin will be placed to the left of the plate near the forks. Monograms on napkins are generally placed to show on the lower left of the napkin's folded rectangle.

What about napkin rings? Napkin rings originated at a time when family members or long-term houseguests each used the same cloth napkin for several consecutive meals. Today, it's common for hostesses to use their favorite decorative napkin rings for one-time guests, and so the napkin is not returned to its ring when the meal is finished. During the meal, your napkin ring goes to the upper left side above the plates.

How do I use my napkin? Use the napkin to gently blot or pat—*not* wipe—your lips in between food bites as needed. Use the napkin often before drinking so that food will not be left on the glass rim. A lady avoids leaving lipstick marks on a napkin by privately blotting lipstick on a tissue before being seated. The napkin is also used to remove food from hands and fingers. The open edges allow you to inconspicuously slide and wipe your fingers as needed. It is not polite to lick fingers or lips—that is the napkin's job. The napkin is not intended for nose blowing—that is a handkerchief's job. (For this reason ladies and gentlemen find it wise to always carry a hanky for the nose).

What if I need to leave the table? In a perfect world, you would not leave the table during a meal, but if you absolutely must, quietly say, "Please excuse me" and place the napkin on your chair rather than the table. This signals the waiter that you will return. The standard procedure, in a perfect world, is to leave the napkin on the chair seat or arm. If your world, however, is less than perfect, and the restaurant chair arms or seat are less than clean, then you may prefer to place the napkins on your chair's back. In an upscale restaurant, don't be surprised if the waiter replaces your refolded napkin on the arm of your chair or at your place setting. Return to your table as soon as possible (never an absence longer than fifteen minutes). Upon your discreet reappearance, return the napkin to your lap with your left hand once you are seated.

What if I drop it? If your napkin (or any utensil) drops to the floor, leave it there and simply ask for another one. If it falls where someone might trip or step on it, and you can easily slide it out of the way with your foot, do so. Do not get up and take a napkin (or a utensil) from another table. Do not create a distracting scene over this minor incident.

Where does it go after the meal? In a restaurant, when everyone is ready to leave the table after the meal, pick up your napkin with your left hand. Take it up by its center, placing it loosely (neither crumpled nor folded) to the left of your place setting on the table. Again, avoid shaking or waving movements. The napkin is never refolded, wadded up or placed on a dirty plate or in a glass. In a home, wait for the hostess to put her napkin on the table before retiring yours.

Silver and Flatware Service

The array of utensils can be overwhelming, especially at a formal table. Here are some rules and tips for using silverware and flatware:

- A formal table, no matter how many courses the dinner will have, will never be set with more than three forks and three knives at a time. Additional silver will be placed by the plate when the course is served. Dessert silverware is brought in with the dessert. When you are finished with each course, place the utensils at a five o'clock position on the course dish.
- Forks are set to the left of the plate, except for a small seafood fork, which goes to the right of the spoons.
- Knives are set to the right of the plate with the cutting edge of the blade facing toward the plate.
- Spoons are set to the right of knives. Teaspoons are used for tea or coffee. Soup or fruit spoons may accompany the soup or fruit, or may be set to the plate's right. Often, for semiformal and informal meals, the dessert fork and/or spoon are set above the dinner plate.
- Assume tables are set correctly and use the "outside-to-inside" rule.

It is safe to begin the meal using the flatware piece that is on the outside of the utensil group, the farthest one away from the plate. The soup spoon is on the outermost right side, the salad fork on the outermost left. Then use the next outside utensil and work your way in towards the center plate with each new meal course.

- Once you use a piece of silverware, rest it on the appropriate plate; never replace it on the tablecloth.
- Avoid scraping dishes or making other unnecessary noises with your silverware.
- As is the case with many other protocol doubts, if you feel uncertain about the use of silverware, watch the hostess. It's best not to call attention to your dilemma—distractions disturb a dinner's rhythm. Simply watching the hostess will tell you what to do next.

Bread and Butter Plate

The small bread and butter plate is seldom seen at very formal dinners and may even be absent from semiformal dinners. In those cases, crackers are served with the appetizer or soup on the service charger, and later, rolls (usually without butter) are served with the meat course. When a bread and butter plate is used, however, it is set to the upper left of the dinner plate, directly above the forks. A small, rounded, butter knife will rest on the bread and butter plate's upper edge at a ten to two o'clock position.

How do I handle bread and butter? Informally, when bread is served or passed, take a roll and place it directly on the bread and butter plate. A slice or two of butter is taken from the butter dish with your butter knife, and place a pat at a time on the plate by the bread. Do not put butter from a common butter dish directly onto your bread or roll. Many informal tables are not set with bread and butter plates, so if rolls are served with the main course, the roll may go on your dinner plate.

When a meal is casual or quite informal, individual butter knives may not be present. Your (clean) regular dinner knife may be used and then placed on the butter plate, blade towards the plate's center. In Europe, and for some formal meals in our country, butter may not be served with hard rolls accompanying roasted meats and sauces. It is also somewhat customary for the bread to be placed directly on the tablecloth at some European restaurants and cafés. This is a minor difference in customs—truly gracious people are flexible and undemanding.

Bread *slices* (rather than rolls) may be served at informal meals but not for formal occasions. During a formal dinner, rolls are presented rather than sliced bread. Do not break or eat your roll before the hostess or guest of honor has begun to do so. In finer restaurants, it is polite to wait until after your order is placed to begin eating your bread or roll, even when it is immediately brought to your table. Many people relax this rule in informal and casual cafés.

Break both bread and rolls into small, bite-sized pieces which are buttered and eaten separately. Do not butter an entire large piece of bread or single roll all at once. (According to one etiquette writer, "This custom dates back to medieval times when bread was broken at the table and each piece eaten separately so that the leavings could be given to the poor.") Hold your small bread or roll piece close to the plate with your fingers, not flat on your palm. An exception is allowed in the buttering procedure for hot rolls or toast, which may be buttered entirely at once so that the butter will melt easily.

Seafood Appetizers

Seafood cocktails may be shellfish or other seafood, such as shrimp or crab. They are most often served with a tomato-based sauce or in a chilled glass on ice, and are usually served as an appetizer. When they are served at an informal or semiformal dinner, they are in place on service plates or doilies before guests are seated. For formal dinners, the cocktail is served on a service plate and may or may not be on the table when guests are seated. When the cocktail is finished, the glass is removed but the service plate (charger) remains to receive the soup.

How is it different from a fish course? During a semiformal or formal dinner, the shellfish cocktail or oysters are served early as an appetizer, while the optional fish course comes later, usually after the soup, and does not generally include shellfish.

What's this little fork on the right side? Remember the helpful rule of using the farthest outside fork first (remember, forks are on the *left*)? There is one exception to the rule. When you sit down to dinner and observe a small fork partially resting on the outside spoon on the *right* of the plate, it's not a mistake; that is the oyster fork, which means it is the fork you will use first. The other helpful hint reminding you to look for the oyster fork is the fact that your chilled seafood cocktail, in a special glass, will already be on a service plate as you enter the dining room.

Use this fork to eat oyster, shrimp, and clam appetizers. Dip small shrimp in your sauce and eat them whole; larger shrimp are dipped in cocktail sauce and eaten a bite at a time. Sometimes clams or oysters will be served as the appetizer. Clams may be eaten whole, while some oysters are too large to do so. Hold the shell securely with one hand, using the fork in the other hand to lift the oyster or clam and dip in sauce before placing it in your mouth. Some experts say you may also drink the juice from the shell, but use common sense here. Risks of spills aren't worth the few drops of nectar. Another surprise: oyster crackers may be dropped whole into your sauce and eaten with the oyster fork.

The Soup Course

A meal's first course (after the appetizer, if there is one) is often soup, which is always served in a cup or bowl placed on plates, and is eaten with a soup spoon. When charger or service plates are used, the soup plate is placed on it and remains there until the soup is finished, when both will be removed. Between sips and when you are finished, the spoon rests on the soup plate beneath the bowl. When the soup bowl is large, it is permissible to rest the spoon in the bowl in between sips until finished. When a clear consommé or bouillon soup is served in a two-handled cup, one has the option to lift the cup and drink instead of using the spoon, but using a spoon is always correct. The spoon should never rest in soup served from a two-handled cream bowl or bouillon cup—place it on the saucer instead.

What is the best way to eat soup? Soup is eaten without slurping, inhaling or blowing on it. If the soup is steaming it means it is too hot to eat. It is wise to wait a moment and try some conversation until the soup appears cooler. Allow your first spoonfuls to cool for a few seconds while you hold the spooned soup over your bowl. A soup spoon is held the same way one holds a pencil or a fork, but with the thumb up. Hold the spoon sideways, its length parallel to the table edge. The soup is spooned away from you towards the bowl's center. The spoon may be touched slightly on the bowl's side to eliminate excess drops before lifting to your mouth. As you lift the spoon to your mouth, remain sitting upright, leaning from your waist and keeping your back straight. Do not strain from your neck or lower your mouth towards the bowl. Quietly sip the soup from the side of the spoon into your mouth. Avoid placing the entire spoon in your mouth, even when you are eating chunky soup with the appropriate smaller spoon. It is not proper to cut food in your soup with a knife.

What about crackers? And may I tip the bowl? Soda crackers are never crumbled into the soup. They are to be broken, like bread, and eaten in pieces. Your soup bowl may be tipped away from you in order to fill your spoon with the last few spoonfuls of soup remaining in the bowl.

The Fish Course

The fish may be presented in small pieces (relevées) or in a larger entrée size, depending on the host's preference. The small fish fork is placed at the far left next to dinner fork in the outside position. A fish knife will be at the far right on the outside of the dinner knife.

How should I handle a whole fish? When a smaller fish such as trout is served whole, cut off the head and tail and then cut the fish lengthwise. Lift the meat (the fillet) gently away from the entire skeleton (this is not as difficult as it sounds) and place the bones on the side of your plate. When you are in a restaurant, you may ask the waiter to fillet the fish.

What about bones? Chew small bites carefully in case of stray bones. If you feel a bone in your mouth, push it to the front of your mouth and then quietly place it on your fork. Do not try to swallow bones—they are a choking hazard. The discarded bone may be discreetly placed on the side of your dish.

The Salad Course

Salads are generally served on small plates that are placed directly in front of each person. In restaurants, salads are usually served by the waiter before the main entrée, but they may also be served after the entrée. Salads are eaten with the salad fork located at the outer left side of the dinner fork. It is smaller than the dinner fork but is held the same way. It is permissible to cut large pieces of salad foods when necessary. In the absence of a salad knife, use the dinner knife. Leave the used knife on your plate after using it—remember, dirty utensils are never placed directly on the table.

How are salads served in informal settings? For informal family dining, salads may be served from a large bowl and placed on a small salad plate, or more casually, on a larger dinner plate together with other food. During informal dinners with guests, first-course salads are often preset, just before the dinner seating, on individual salad plates.

What about formal and semiformal settings? Salads are served individually and set upon service plates. A salad knife should be provided for cutting certain food items into bite-sized pieces. Heart of palm, asparagus, whole leaves, and lettuce wedges are common examples of salad foods that usually require cutting. Between bites, the knife's resting place is at the top of the salad plate with the blade facing you. Place both the knife and fork in a five o'clock position when you have finished the salad course.

How do I handle difficult salad foods? When eating potentially noisy foods, chew small bites without chomping too hard or quickly. Here are some tips on how to eat different salad foods:

- *Asparagus.* Use salad knife and fork to cut into bite-sized pieces
- *Caesar salad.* If the leaves are large they may be cut with a knife.
- *Croutons.* Eat whole when possible. Lift with the fork rather than spearing.
- *Cherry tomatoes.* Often served whole. If they are small enough, eat them whole (make sure they do not shoot off the plate when you try to pierce them with the fork). Cut larger ones in half carefully to avoid squirting the insides on yourself or others.
- *Olives.* In a formal situation olives are pitted and so are eaten whole. If an olive is served in a salad, it is eaten with the salad fork, not with the fingers. When a large olive contains a stone and is served as a relish, it may be held in the fingers and eaten in bites. The stone may be transferred from your mouth onto a spoon before being placed on your plate or you may "kiss" the palm of your hand, allowing the pit to go there before discreet disposal on the side of the plate.
- *Lemons.* When the lemon wedge is not wrapped in cheesecloth, hold the lemon piece between the forefinger and thumb in one hand, and gently insert the fork tines into the lemon. Hold the lemon close to the food; slowly and gently squeeze the desired amount of juice onto the food. The squeezed lemon is returned to the side of the plate, not placed on the tablecloth.
- *Lettuce pieces.* Ease small pieces of lettuce onto the fork rather than spearing them with the tines, which is usually more difficult. Cut large pieces with a knife.

The Entrée or Main Course

The entrée is served on a large (often ten-inch) dinner plate centered in front of each person's place, one inch from the table edge. This plate accommodates the main dish, which is usually meat and vegetables. The large dinner knife and fork, also one inch from the edge, are placed on each side of the plate.

How do I handle the main course? The dinner fork and knife must be used to cut one bite-sized piece of meat at a time. It is incorrect to eat any meat, including fowl or chops, with the fingers during a formal or semiformal dinner. After placing the small bite of meat in your mouth, chew slowly and thoroughly before swallowing. Do not cut another piece of meat until the previous one is swallowed.

How do I cut my food properly? Take the dinner fork in the left hand, tines down. The knife is held in your right hand. A knife is best held by allowing one half of the handle to rest in your palm, with the remaining part of the handle resting on the index finger as you grasp and turn your hand over, so that your index finger is mostly on the handle and less than one inch on the top of the blade itself. To cut the meat, pierce the next bite with the fork. Cut with the knife about a quarter inch away from the fork. Draw the knife in one direction only, as a stroke, towards you. Do not "saw" the meat. Lift the knife after each stroke to repeat the cutting motion. Cut bites into small sizes, one at a time. If your bite is too large, cut it in half to eat separately. Do not run the knife blade in between the fork tines while cutting.

How do I hold silverware? There are two styles: the European (or continental) and the American. Either is correct but you need to be comfortable and consistent with your preferred choice.

- In the continental or European style, hold the knife in your right hand and your fork in the left, tines down, as described above. Once the meat or vegetable is cut, raise it to your mouth with the fork tines still down and eat it. Hands may remain above the table from the wrist up when they are not in use.
- In the American style, the food is cut in the same way. But after cutting, the knife is rested at the plate top, blade facing towards the plate's center. The fork is transferred to the right hand, tines up, and the food on it is eaten.
- A piece of bread or the knife in your left hand may be used to help push difficult, small foods (such as peas) onto your fork. This is allowable, but not preferable for every bite.
- The American style allows the fork to be rested occasionally, after two or three bites, for a short period of time to relax and enjoy the conversation and the meal in an unhurried manner.
- When finished with the meal, place the knife and fork in the five o'clock position. This signals the waiter that you are finished. (Unacceptable signals include pushing your plate away, burping, or saying things like "Wow, I'm stuffed" and patting your stomach as a gesture of satisfaction.)

May I ever eat certain foods with my hands? Yes, but only during casual or informal meals. Corn on the cob (only served in informal situations), chicken legs, wings, or ribs may be eaten by holding the bone in the hand. A disposable napkin or two will be needed in this instance. Other acceptable "finger foods" are crudités (cold vegetables), crisp bacon, French fries, pizza, pickles, fruits, cold sandwiches, nuts, and chips. Some etiquette experts rule out using the hand in place of utensils when eating any meat with sauces—anywhere, anytime. Some relax the protocol for ribs. Prudent advice is "When in doubt, don't."

Finger Bowls

Finger bowls, used for dipping and cleaning your fingers, are presented just before dessert at some formal and semiformal dinners, and often come with the dessert spoon and fork. (Younger children are less apt to receive invitations for more formal dinners where finger bowls are used, so beginners won't need this information.) The small finger bowl sits upon a doily and a dessert plate and is half filled with warm water. Flower petals or a lemon slice may float on the surface.

If your finger bowl arrived with the dessert utensils on a doily and plate, take the fork and spoon and place them to right and left of the dessert plate. Then take both the finger bowl and doily together, using two hands, and place them to the upper left of your dessert plate. After dessert, reach to your left, again using both hands. Pick up the finger bowl and doily in one movement. Set them in directly front of you. Barely dip one set of fingers on one hand at a time into the bowl. Dry them, then repeat with your other hand. When finished, leave the bowl there. The dessert silverware is placed together on the dessert plate. Your napkin is placed in loose folds to the left of the plate before you leave the table.

The Dessert Course

A sweet, tempting dessert by itself or with coffee or tea is often sufficient reason to inspire many get-togethers, but more often they conclude a dinner. Fruits and cheeses may be served just prior to dessert, with or after a salad; or they may be served as dessert itself.

Where is the serviceware for desserts? Your dessert plate will be brought to you shortly after the main course is finished. Your silverware's location depends on the dinner's degree of formality. If a dessert fork and spoon are not preset above the dinner plate (as in many informal dinners), then the proper silverware will be provided when the dessert course is served.

Where do I put my silverware when I am finished? When finished with your dessert, set your fork and/or spoon in the standard five o'clock position on the dessert plate to signal that you are finished. When there is no fork, as in the case of pudding or custard, place your spoon in the ten-twenty position on the plate when finished. If there is no dessert plate, then the spoon may be placed in the bowl when finished. This is also true whenever a companion dessert plate is too small to securely hold the utensils—place them in the bowl.

How do I eat desserts? First, respect the general rule to avoid eating anything with your fingers, because it also applies to desserts, with one exception: small, bite-sized pastries. If, however, this small pastry will leave food traces on your fingers (or face), it must be eaten with utensils. Second, respect the rules regarding silverware. Some desserts require only a fork, some require a spoon, and other desserts require using both a spoon and fork. The spoon is used for fruit desserts, puddings, and ice creams. The fork is used for pies and cakes. Cake slices are placed on their sides, not upright. Larger pastries such as napoleons or cream puffs should be cut and eaten with forks.

The proper method for eating desserts like pie à la mode (with ice cream) uses both a fork and spoon. The fork, tines down, holds the dessert in place while you push the food onto the spoon. The spoon is used, as needed, to "cut" the dessert and then lift it to the mouth. This takes practice, so it is often easier for younger people to use only a fork or spoon rather than both.

Whenever eating parfait, pudding, or ice cream, take one small spoonful at a time. If you don't have parfait spoons, iced tea spoons can be substituted. Whatever you put into your mouth from your spoon must not come out again—do not take a huge spoonful and "skim" the ice cream off the top. If cake is served à la mode, you may also use only a spoon.

Beverages

Beverage glasses sit on the right side of your dinner plate, above the knives. All drinks are served and poured from the right side. Good manners prescribe patting your lips with the napkin before you take a drink and of course having an empty mouth before drinking, which eliminates unsightly food residue in or on your glass. Take small sips and swallow quietly. Whenever drinking from a glass or cup, slightly lower your gaze instead of looking over the glass, but don't look into your glass.

Which one is my water glass? Water is usually served in the largest goblet or glass on the plate's right side above the tip of the innermost knife. The glass is filled about two thirds full and no more than one half inch from the rim's top. It is wise to be sure your lips are clean before taking a sip of water. You may take a sip of water when food is too hot in the mouth, if you must, but it is better to avoid putting such hot foods in your mouth in the

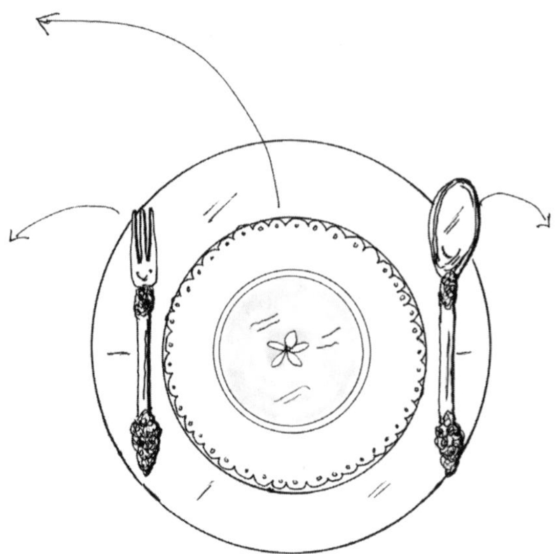

Formal dinner fingerbowl. The diner moves the fork and spoon to the table and places the fingerbowl above the fork. The plate is now ready to receive the dessert.

Typical glassware and stemware, from left to right: tumbler, juice glass, water goblet, red wine, champagne flute, sparkling beverage (saucer style), white wine, and iced tea/highball.

first place. It is impolite to squeeze liquids between your teeth or swish them around your mouth.

What about sparkling drinks, wines, and stemmed glassware? During informal dinners, wine and other drinks may be poured just before or after diners are seated, but always before eating begins. According to some experts, red wines are best served about an hour after the bottle has been uncorked and then poured into round, stemmed goblets about one quarter to one half inch from the top. White wines are uncorked and allowed a short "breathing" time, then poured in smaller goblets. Sparkling drinks, like champagnes, are poured into tall, flute-shaped goblets one half inch from the rim. When you drink from a red wine or water goblet, you may hold it by the base of the bowl. Goblets for chilled drinks are held by the stem to retain the beverage's cooler temperature. Generally, at an informal dinner, chilled and sparkling beverages are poured and served after guests are seated. Both red and white wines, however, may be poured before guests are seated. Some hosts prefer to pour the wine themselves at the table. At formal and semiformal dinners, several empty wine glasses (but no more than three) await guests. The drinks will be poured by waiters, and additional glasses will be brought as needed. For the student protocol dinner, of course, wine will not be served; instead you will have iced tea, sparkling juices, or another nonalcoholic beverage. Students should know, however, what to expect when they do come of age and why these glasses appear on a table.

Why are there different types of goblets? Wines and sparkling fruit drinks are served in glasses that are best suited to wine type, designed to bring the drink and our taste buds together as harmoniously as possible. For this reason, certain glass shapes provide better delivery of the beverage to the mouth, better concentration of its smell, better viewing of its color, and so on, resulting in a superior, multisensory drinking experience. A basic white wine glass is smaller and slimmer than a water goblet. The two main types of red wine glasses are the Bordeaux, which is taller and fuller than a white wine glass, and the Burgundy glass, which is even larger than the Bordeaux. The Bordeaux glass is used not only for Bordeaux wine but also other full-bodied reds like merlots and cabernets, and the Burgundy glass is obviously used for Burgundy wine, but also for similar reds like pinot noir. The champagne flute is designed to show off the bubbles and keep the drink fizzy longer. There are many other types of glasses and goblets for specific types of beverages, but these are the most common.

What about coffee and tea service? In a home, coffee and teas are traditionally poured by the hostess at the table or in another room after the meal. Cream and sugar may be added by the hostess, when the guest indicates such preference, or the guest may add these as they are passed to the left on a tray. You use your spoon to gently mix back and forth, not stir, the sugar or cream in the hot drink. The spoon rests on your saucer and not in the cup. When only mugs are used, rest your spoon on a napkin. At a formal or semiformal event there generally will not be a coffee cup and saucer (also called a *demitasse*) at the table until the end of the meal, when it will be brought to your place and filled, with or after dessert. It will be placed to the right above your spoon. In a restaurant, hot drinks are poured and served by a waiter or busboy. He will place your coffee cup to your right side.

Dining Etiquette at Home and Away

Teachers will normally introduce general dining etiquette after the young people are already acquainted with table settings, proper use of tableware, and degrees of formality. Training in general etiquette must include multiple, specific "dos and don'ts," but should also remind students that all these little rules exist to make mealtimes civil and pleasant whether at home or away. Once youngsters realize how offensive or repulsive manners spoil mealtime for other diners, they gladly embrace good manners. Noisy, selfish, disruptive, or unsightly behavior obviously does not have a place at the table. Many standards are more subtle than that, but they are still very important to learn.

Following is a list of standard, basic protocol practices, regardless of the dinner's degree of formality or location. Training in restaurant manners is also included in a separate section. When young people practice the following etiquette, they (and those with them) will remain comfortable in most dining situations. Parents who teach and practice these rules at home equip their children with a valuable social skill (see also the dining sections in chapter 2). School program students, however, should not preach to family or parents who may unintentionally break a rule or two.

Basic Rules for Daily Practice

- Remember to sit straight, with the head held comfortably upright. The body should be about a hand's width from the table. Lean slightly forward when raising a utensil to the mouth (this lessens the possibility of choking or of dropping food on the lap). It is always considerate to keep your feet near your own chair. No sprawling or tipping backwards allowed. This upright body position reflects attentive respect for one's fellow diners.

- Maintain a cheerful, thankful countenance at the table. No selfish scowling or complaints allowed.
- Keep your elbows off the table and your hands on your lap when not in use during the dinner. During a formal dinner, hands always remain on the lap, except when eating. This rule relaxes for informal and casual dining when the wrist and lower arms may rest on the table edge in between courses and after the meal is finished.
- Resist urges to play or make noises with silverware and tableware.
- Remember that ladies are generally seated first. Ladies are served before gentlemen and adults before children.
- Respect customs of grace by bowing your head and not picking up your napkin until after the blessing is asked.
- Wait until the hostess has taken her fork before picking up yours.
- Wait until everyone at your table is served before beginning to eat, unless otherwise instructed.
- Remember that food is served by waiters from the left side while plates, when finished, are removed from the right. Water and beverages are served, refilled and removed from the right side.
- Pass serving dishes only to the right (counterclockwise) when passing food around an informal table.
- Replace serving utensils in a convenient place on the side of serving dishes, where they are accessible to the next guest.
- Be willing to hold the serving dish for the next person if it is heavy or awkward.
- Take small bites. Keep your mouth closed as you slowly and quietly chew your food.
- Finish swallowing the bite in your mouth before adding another.
- Eat at a pace similar to everyone else so you are neither too quick nor too slow in finishing your food.
- Ask for something to be passed when you cannot easily reach it so that you are not reaching in front of other diners.
- Remember to say "Please" and "Thank you" when asking for anything on the table to be passed and when it is given to you.
- Don't ask for salt and pepper until you have tasted your foods.
- Pass salt and pepper shakers together, even when asked for only one or the other. They are a pair that travels together when passed.
- Use a toothpick if necessary, but not in public.
- Remain at the table until excused (unless there's an urgent reason to leave, in which case excuse yourself discreetly).

It is important that students know how manners play out in a meal's progression for their protocol dinner event and beyond. Of course, general manners that are always in place at home should also be used when away, but a few additional rules and tips are required for restaurant dining.

Reservations. Reservations are usually made by phoning the restaurant in advance and making the reservation under one name for a specific time and number of people. This is the time to request preferences or special needs such as a table by the window, a highchair, or seating in a nonsmoking section. Arrive on time for dinner parties and restaurant reservations. Many restaurants will not hold tables fifteen minutes past the reserved time, which is understandable. Just as a guest lets the host of a private dinner party know if he will be more than ten minutes late, so a considerate diner lets the restaurant know if he will be late.

Seating protocol. In a restaurant, the maître d' leads the way, followed by the ladies, then the gentlemen. Older ladies follow first with younger ladies next, gentlemen last. The youngest respectfully defers to honor the older persons in their group. When attending a semiformal banquet, the first order of business is finding the assigned table. The escort leads the way to the designated table. When place cards are used, they are never rearranged; each person sits in his or her assigned place.

If you are unhappy with the table given you, the time to request something else available is before you sit down at the table. Always use a pleasant tone of voice and remember "Please" and "Thank you." A better table may not be available if it is peak dinner time.

Ladies are seated before gentlemen. Usually the maître d' determines seating and assists the oldest lady with her chair. A gentleman may help another lady slide her chair into place but he remains standing until all ladies are seated. Here are some more seating guidelines:

- Whenever there are two people of the same gender and only one of the other, the latter is seated in between the two. Thus one man would be seated in between two ladies and vice versa.
- When being seated in a booth, ladies slide in first, facing each other, and men take the outside seats.
- Women are seated against the wall on banquet benches and men take the outside chairs.
- Items such as briefcases or purses are not placed on the table.

After being seated, it is certainly proper to give a prayer of thanks (grace) for the food. At a restaurant or large banquet party, follow the lead of the person in charge of the gathering. Stand or sit according to his direction. Take a hand if hands are extended. Refusal of a neighbor's extended hand for prayer, even when it is not your custom, is rude.

The next order of business is the napkin. Whenever there is a dinner host, wait to pick up your napkin, just like at home. Otherwise, everyone at the table places the napkin on their lap after they are seated. At banquets, wait until all people are seated at your table before taking your napkin. Other handling of the napkin is the same as earlier discussed in the tableware section.

The Wait Staff. The waiter's job is to take your order and oversee your dinner service. The busboy assists the waiter, pouring drinks and clearing plates. A well-trained busser does not speak or interrupt those whom he is serving. He will not ask, "Would you like more water?"—he simply refills the glasses at the table. Waiters and bussers are to be treated with respect—never rudely (even if there is a problem). They are often very busy, so do not to engage them in distracting conversation.

Menus and ordering. The captain or maître d' gives menus to diners after they are seated. Waiters inform diners about special dishes, and orders are given to the waiter. Until quite recently, it was customary for the gentleman to order for the lady. Today some couples continue this tradition, but it is perfectly proper for a lady to give her order directly to the waiter when asked. If a couple prefers the older protocol, the gentleman should be quick to order for both himself and the lady when the waiter asks for the order. The gentleman orders for her first, e.g., "The lady [or "My wife"] will have the salmon and I would like the veal" (He never says "she"). Otherwise, the waiter, like some protocol experts, finds it "ridiculous and confusing," especially when in a large group, if a lady gives no response to him after he has addressed her, instead turning to her escort so he may relay her order.

When people pay for their own dinners they may obviously order what they like and what they can afford. When dinner is hosted (paid for) by someone else, it is best to avoid ordering the most or least expensive item on the menu. It is polite to try a specific item if the host urges guests to do so. Some fine restaurants offer menus without prices listed to ladies and guests, and only the host has prices on his menu. If this makes the guests or ladies uncomfortable on behalf of their host's pocketbook, they may safely order a modest dish (such as chicken), rather than an obviously expensive item such as filet mignon.

Two common menu phrases are *à la carte* and *table d'hôte*. *À la carte* means that diners order from a list of individually priced items. *Table d'hôte* means that there is a set price for a complete meal. Sometimes drinks are priced separately and this set price is for the entrée and its accompaniments only.

Serving protocol. Food is served from the left side and removed from the right side. Ladies are generally served first, just as in a home. Everyone waits to eat until all diners at their table have been served. If there are more than six to eight people to a table, wait until the six to eight nearest you are served. In restaurants, informal buffets involve self-service, which has certain implications for other protocol standards. Several return visits to common food tables are the norm, so common sense tells us it is inconsiderate and unfair to expect men to continually jump up and down as a lady comes and goes from a table to the buffet. Instead, an escort and lady best go to the food line together for the first time and return to the table at the same time. On return, he puts his plate down at his place and then helps her with her chair before taking his own chair. The escort stands and assists a lady with her chair again whenever she needs the help.

Today's etiquette realistically requires thoughtfulness on the lady's part when she is at a restaurant buffet or brunch with gentlemen. To those kind gentlemen who feel duty-bound to stand when a lady approaches or leaves, even at the most casual brunch, she should immediately say, "Please don't get up" so their meal is as undisturbed as possible. Of course, some truehearted gentlemen still prefer to half rise as she comes and goes, presuming she will not make an excessive number of trips so they may eat without too many interruptions.

When something goes wrong. Manners are particularly necessary when things are not going as smoothly as one would wish, particularly in a public place like a restaurant. Here are some guidelines:

- *Coughing or Sneezing.* Simply turn your head away from others to cough or sneeze while covering your nose and mouth with a hanky. George Washington's comments on table manners still apply: "Being set at a meal scratch not, neither spit, cough nor blow your nose except there is necessity for it." Do quietly say, "Excuse me" should any noises escape from your body.
- *Spills.* Etiquette discourages distractions at the table. Minor spills are not a major faux pas, especially if they are not the result of wild behavior or other protocol breaches, so avoid overreaction. A good waiter should notice the need for help after a minor accident. A napkin may be used to cover the spill and prevent it or a few ice cubes from running amok. When cleanup can wait, it is best to continue dinner without interruption. If the spill is major and the waiter fails

to notice the need, the escort should catch the waiter's attention and ask him for help. Cleanup is the waiter's job, not yours. Apologize, thank him for his assistance, and continue enjoying your dinner. It is an important mark of good manners to be gracious when accidents happen. Once a waiter spilled a tray of salad as he passed the table where my husband and I were sitting, spattering white salad dressing all over the back of my husband's jacket. The waiter was horrified at his clumsiness, but my husband, having a gracious spirit, a sense of humor, and good manners, was undaunted and calmly reassured the waiter all was fine. After returning from the men's room where he wiped off the dressing, a joke about baptism brought smiles and dinner proceeded as usual. My husband declined the restaurant's offer to pay for cleaning but he did accept dinner on the house and thanked them for a delicious meal and again reassured the pale waiter that all was fine. Accidents happen to everybody, so take them calmly, without annoyance, blame, or constantly referring back to it. If you should happen to spill on someone else, apologize and pay for any dry cleaning or replacement costs. (A halfhearted, "politeness-only" offer to pay is likely to be just as politely brushed aside; be active in making it right.)

- *Drops and Breaks.* When a piece of silverware or a napkin slips onto the floor at home or in a restaurant, if it falls out of the way, leave it where it falls. If it is where someone might step, gently move it out of the way with your foot. At a convenient time, quietly inform the waiter and request another one. Unsanitary items from the floor are never reused, and bending over to retrieve them creates an unnecessary distraction. If a person breaks an item while a guest in someone's home, he apologizes and sends a replacement as soon as possible. In a restaurant, breakage is an unlikely event, but if something is broken, the patron apologizes to the waiter and offers to pay for damages. It is likely payment will be refused, but the offer should be made. As with a spill, the waiter is in charge of cleanup, not the diners. A good staff can unobtrusively remove debris in seconds.
- *Food in Teeth.* Most loosely lodged foods can be removed by a drink of water (don't swish it). When water fails, turn your head slightly away from others. Then hold the napkin up over the mouth with one hand while quickly and discreetly using a finger tip on the other hand, under the napkin, to remove the food. Stubborn foods require privacy and a toothpick or floss. If your neighbor has food in teeth or

mustache, discreetly inform him of it—it is somewhat awkward but saves him embarrassment later on.

- *Removing Objects from Mouth.* Remove inedible objects like bone or gristle from the mouth promptly and discreetly. One protocol expert says it is permissible to remove a bone from one's mouth with a forefinger and thumb, while another authority prefers the more traditional method of discreetly expelling it by same means it entered the mouth—on a fork or spoon. Teach children and students that spitting onto the plate is not an acceptable way to remove such objects.

The bill. When dinner is finished the waiter brings the bill. If the waiter is delayed, the patron may request the check. The escort then settles the bill. (This is an appropriate time for a lady to excuse herself if she wishes to go to the ladies' room.) When the bill is presented on a tray or in a folder, the money or credit card is placed on it and the waiter takes care of the transaction, bringing back change or a charge slip to sign. When a signature is required, the customer copy is retained by the host patron. The one who pays should avoid showing other people the total. A nod to the waiter is appropriate if the waiter fails to notice that a card or cash has been placed in the folder. If the exact amount including tip is not given, the host patron awaits his change before leaving the tip.

Once the check is presented, be sensitive to the restaurant's need for their table if it is peak dinner time and do not linger at the table. In casual cafés, the gentleman may pay the bill on the way out, after he has left a tip on the table. The lady stands aside out of other patrons' way. There are times when a lady plays host and pays the bill. If she is with gentlemen, she discreetly makes arrangements beforehand, informing the maître d' that she is responsible for the bill. Some ladies give their credit card number in advance, so all they need do is quietly sign the slip before leaving.

Tipping. Tips should be merited by services rendered. It is rude to under-tip normal service, but it is also incorrect to over-tip when it is undeserved.

- In a nice restaurant with good service and cloth napkins, the general tip is twenty percent of the bill. The tip is split by the head waiter, servers, and bussers, who all depend on tips as part of their wages—so please don't under-tip.
- In cafés or ordinary family-style restaurants, the tip is usually about fifteen percent for good service. When paper napkins are used, ten to fifteen percent is the norm. Never leave less than ten percent.
- At banquets the tip is usually prepaid by the hosts.

- In a cafeteria or self-service diner, tips are not left unless a busser brings your tray or performs an extra service. Then a small tip of (currently) fifty cents to a dollar is optional.
- Tips at brunches or smorgasbords are ten percent. The tip may be left in cash on the tray or added to the charge slip at the end of the meal. When change is returned to the patron and it includes coins, the extra change is left on the tray in addition to the tip amount.
- When you are hosting a large group or banquet, and if the maître d' has provided you with exceptional courtesies and service, it is currently appropriate to tip him ten to twenty dollars. Fold the bill in half twice so that the number shows and slip it into his hand with an appreciative "Thank you."
- Cloakroom attendants currently receive a dollar per coat and any other items such as an umbrella.
- To keep tipping smooth and trouble-free, stock your wallet or purse with small bills before going out.

When may I leave the table? Traditionally, it is the lady's prerogative to place her napkin to the left of her place, look inquiringly at her escort, and prepare to rise, after the bill has been settled and the meal finished. If the escort suggests they remain a while longer, she may do so. When they leave, he stands first and assists her with her chair.

Conclusion

Good training prepares young people for most dining situations in and out of the home, and it does so well—*secundum artem*! Learning artful customs grants our children poise and skillfulness. Again and again, teach children that gracious table behavior is mandatory as part of their everyday life. It's a basic step in the course of "Living Well with Other People 101."

6

Social Navigation Skills

> Let your speech always be with grace, seasoned with salt, that you may know how you ought to answer each one. (Col. 4:6)
>
> The heart of the righteous studies to answer, but the mouth of the wicked pours forth evil. (Prov. 15:28)
>
> A man has joy by the answer of his mouth, and a word spoken in due season, how good it is! (Prov. 15:23)

The verses above are necessary and wonderful directives that guide a Christian's manner of speech. From them we learn that appropriately spoken words are extremely important. We are to speak words that fit the occasion. We also learn that we should speak with wisdom and that our words should be filled with grace. Like salt, our words should have a quality of preservation that protects from spoilage and the quality of seasoning that enhances pleasure. In other words, our speech should have a moral and aesthetic impact on the listener. There are many other verses advising us to speak suitable words with wisdom, but these verses are a good springboard to guide us in our discussion of conversational habits.

But what does it actually mean to speak appropriately? How does it play out in our associations with other people and in protocol? First of all, it means that we forsake all silly speech, insincerity, arrogant boasting, backstabbing gossip, and vain flattery. It also excludes unresponsive, icy silence, coarse or crude language, and a mean or shy downward glance.

The command to know how to answer every man can seem like an overwhelming task, and so reminds us of our need to ask for divine assistance. Speaking wisely takes a lifetime of prayer and practice, so the sooner our children learn guidelines, the easier practical application will be for them. When we remember that James called the tongue the most unruly member of the body, it is obvious that we need help to be obedient. So teaching our children methods for developing sound speech will be immensely useful to them, making them comfortable in any social conversation.

Here, as in all categories of manners, traditional protocol gives us some good, practical rules to follow. The following general information is especially helpful if your school training program includes a time during the gala evening with special guests, when students have opportunity for conversation with the adult guests and with one another. Consider inviting local leaders and other interesting adults in the community as your special guests to meet the students on the night of the event, at a special pre- or post-event dinner party, when it fits in with the other event plans. Though this might make the students a bit nervous, it is a great way for them to test their conversational skills.

Encourage them to think beforehand about appropriate topics for conversation, from local sporting events to national news. If they are particularly timid, they can practice talking about the topics at home and with friends beforehand, which lessens the intimidation factor. Special guests add a dimension to a protocol event that is mutually beneficial, giving everyone the opportunity to interact beyond their usual peer groups. Students' good conversational skills will open doors to new acquaintances among their elders who may have valuable insights for them. At one such pre-dinner party in a large private home for Logos junior protocol, the mayor demonstrated his verbal skills and sincere interest in the teenagers with his lively, fascinating conversation that made a valuable contribution to the students' understanding of city government. At such events, even small talk becomes an occasion to flavor our words with grace and salt as we attempt to interact with people in a worthy manner of the gospel.

Individual parents, of course, whether they have access to a formal school program or not, can teach their children these skills in their own homes during daily family dinners or when they practice hospitality. Parents may even plan a nice event—anything from a special dress-up dinner to an informal brunch—with special adult guests to give their children a chance to practice social and conversation skills. And of course they can practice these skills in restaurants as well, learning how to carry on edifying conversation at the table and speak properly with the wait staff.

If you are teaching a protocol class, expect some nervous anticipation among the students regarding this type of social event. Remind students that this class and all social events are meant to be enjoyable. Reassure them that they can function competently if they follow the conversation rules, and though there may be some discomfort at first, confidence and enjoyment in meeting new people will come with practice.

Conversation Guidelines

Students need to realize that social conversation is basically an *exchange* of words and thoughts. Successful conversation is like tossing a ball—it involves more than one person, and so requires plenty of give and take. We don't "hog" the ball, and neither do we drop it; we toss it back and forth as skillfully as possible. Likewise, good conversation involves each person present in the immediate group. Each person in the group has a responsibility to contribute to the exchange in discussion—conversation is "bounced" back and forth just like a ball.

In various classes, after assigning a conversation topic, I have taken a real ball and tossed it to different students in a group circle, while asking a question to which they must give a sincere and appropriate conversational response. Then they ask a question and toss the ball to someone else. Everyone in the group's circle must be included. This active, hands-on game illustrates the point of conversation. (You need to establish a few rules ahead of time if you play "conversational ball toss." For example, toss and don't throw the ball; everyone has a turn; and the remarks must be appropriate and on topic!)

Now let's consider a few conversational guidelines to help young people learn the art of communication.

- Stand up as a person approaches you. Men always shake hands with other men when a hand is offered. In social settings, a man should only shake hands with a woman if she offers her hand first. (The protocol for handshakes is covered more thoroughly in the "Right Moves" chapter, but its mention here is to remind students of proper behavior that sets a good tone for conversation.)
- Use first names in greeting friends and peers: "It's nice to see you, Brock." (Introductions are covered later in this chapter.)
- Speak clearly, concisely, and loud enough to be heard, though not so loud that your voice carries across the room and draws attention, or disturbs other groups.
- Smile! Your facial expression is important when speaking. Body language communicates attitude.

- Stop, look, listen. Pay attention to the other person. It is polite to look at their eyes as they speak, but do not stare. Listen attentively to what they say. These are signs of respect. Someone once said, "When God gave us two ears and only one tongue, it was His way of encouraging us to work twice as hard at listening as at talking."
- Practice give-and-take conversation. Seek to include all in the group, but don't focus too strongly on one person if he or she is visibly uncomfortable.
- Learn to ask good questions to draw the person out. When dealing with a shy person, questions that can be answered with a "yes" or "no" will not get you far. Likewise, when you are asked such a question, be willing to add some comments to your "yes" or "no" to stimulate conversation.
- Don't brag or otherwise center the conversation on yourself.
- Learn to be tactful. Say what you mean in the best way possible. Do not use coarse or crude language, and remember to use acceptable subjects for all conversations.
- Do not participate in gossip or speak unkindly about other people.
- Remember to say "Please" whenever you make a request and "Thank you" when something is done for you or a compliment is given to you. If you are offered something, and you don't want it, simply say "No, thank you."
- Do not interrupt. When two people start to talk at once, be the one to defer, especially if the other person is your elder.[1] If you inadvertently interrupt someone else who is speaking, simply say, "Excuse me" or "I'm sorry" and allow them to finish talking.
- There are times for silence: when someone else is speaking, and during plays, concerts, sermons, public addresses, and speeches. It is disrespectful to the speaker or performers and annoying to those around you when you try to engage in conversation at these times.
- Some retorts are best left unsaid. It is better not to have the last word if it is a mean last word.
- "Pardon me" is a polite expression when you pass in front of people, or bump into anyone, or spill something.

1. From an old children's book, *The Goops:*

> *Don't interrupt your father when he's telling jokes,*
> *Don't interrupt your mother when she's entertaining folks,*
> *Don't interrupt the visitors when they have come to call—*
> *In fact it's generally wiser not to interrupt at all.*

- If you hurt someone or their feelings, quickly apologize. It is usually a good idea to be the first to say you are sorry with friends during a misunderstanding.
- When you make an obvious mistake, don't overreact or underreact. Don't try to hide your mistake or draw attention to it. Rather than making long excuses, be willing to sincerely and quickly say, "I was wrong."
- Wise people practice grace. When someone says, "Please forgive me," immediately and ungrudgingly do so.
- Don't change the subject if people are enjoying the current conversation, even if it doesn't excite you personally. Small talk is a good way to connect with other people and establish friendships.

Levels of Relationships

A word fitly spoken is like apples of gold in settings of silver. (Prov. 25:11)

Learning to speak fit words is a lifelong challenge. If we desire children who speak thoughtful words, we will teach them what to say and how to avoid extremes of presumptuous chatter or disinterested silence. One of the most helpful aspects of appropriate conversation involves knowing and respecting the type of relationship you have with the other person, and understanding what topics are suitable for your level of association with that person. We want to respect the conversational boundaries of each category.

Some people seem to understand relationships intuitively, but others do not. However, even if we are unaware of distinct category boundaries, we usually know when they are crossed. "What happened to your hair!" and "Are you as rich as everyone says?" are obviously shallow, presumptive questions. While we might tolerate such social trespasses coming from a toddler, we are less apt to do so with adults who should respect etiquette's boundaries. A considerate person will "read" the person he is talking to by watching his facial expressions. When you see any discomfort, disinterest, or distraction, react appropriately by changing the subject or ending the conversation.

The following information contains the levels of associations and a few suggestions for safe topics. (In a class, these four levels may be presented all at once to your students, with reviews given each year; or the categories may be divided in half, introducing the first two levels to the freshman and sophomore grades, and then adding the last two categories for the junior and senior classes.) Give students this following information, on a handout with pertinent Scripture verses, for their notebooks. This provides a reference and helps them realize the practical application of Scripture to this subject.

Acquaintances

An *acquaintance* is someone we have just met, or have limited contact with and do not know very well. When meeting new people, smile and maintain a cheerful countenance, giving special attention to their names—it is easy to be distracted in the introduction process and completely forget a name just said to you. Remember the name, repeat it, do not shorten or change it, and include it throughout your conversation. Apply rules governing titles and address; older people are addressed as Mr., Mrs., Ms., Dr., or other appropriate titles until they grant you permission to address them otherwise. As always, think before you speak, be a good listener, and show respect.

Appropriate subjects for conversation with an acquaintance will revolve around general questions that provide information about the other person. "How did you choose to live where you do?" "What is your favorite thing about your hometown?" "Where were you born?" (Not when!) "How did you choose your career or college?" "What is involved in your work or study?" Ask about interests, travels, hobbies, favorite sports, pets, musical instruments played, opinions about places to go or where to shop, and so on. In talking to different adults, one astute young man made it a point to ask each what he considered important advice to pass onto young people. Another fellow asked adults what they considered keys to successful living. Both gleaned some thought-provoking answers.

Though it is appropriate to ask questions, don't fire them so quickly that you appear to be drilling or interrogating the other person. Questions should be woven into conversation in an easy, relaxed, and interested manner. Of course, be tactful. Avoid personal or potentially embarrassing comments and questions, such as "How *old* are you?" "How much do you earn?" "How much do you weigh?" "What did your suit cost?" or "What is the matter with your leg?"

The term *social pleasantries* is particularly relevant to good conversation, because talk should be pleasant and it is an important aspect of successful social interaction at all levels of relationships. Conversation is made pleasant when questions and their answers are appropriately and cheerfully offered. Good conversation is one of the only ways we can connect with other people. Never underestimate the importance of sincere "small talk"—it is a building block with good rewards, leading to better relationships.

Casual Associations

Casual associations include people you see on a fairly regular basis, like classmates, people at work, or fellow church members. While you may share many things in common, you still don't know them intimately or well. If you want to see this relationship grow, you will have to show interest and respect for the person by your inquiries and conversation. A common situation requiring conversation with casual associations is with hosts or fellow guests at a dinner. Try to visit for a short time with everyone near you throughout the meal.

Topics can include personal experiences, vocational interests, and future plans, though questions may be more specific than for an acquaintance. Safe topics of conversation include family, background, church affiliation, future plans, various activities, sports, events, interests, and other semi-general information. Ask their advice in areas of their expertise. What features do they suggest if I want to purchase the latest laptop? How do they prepare and study for Mr. Hardteacher's upcoming final?

Conversations may lead to deeper discussions, but because you are still getting to know this person, learn to listen and respond tactfully. In social situations, avoid sensitive topics and heated discussions. If someone seems to get upset during a conversation, turn the talk away from that topic.

If someone in this category shares a personal problem with you, encourage him and keep his confidences. It is good to know how to speak encouraging words without presuming to offer solutions or pry into personal affairs. For example, if Sally Sad says, "Please forgive me [for being late, for appearing distressed or downcast, etc.]. Before I arrived I had a unpleasant situation to deal with." It is better to respond sympathetically with "Oh, I'm sorry. I'm glad you are here now. I hoped to see you," rather than "What happened?" If she doesn't offer the information, don't ask.

Close Relationships

Close relationships involve friends and probably some family members. These are people we know and like well, and may include schoolmates, coworkers, neighbors, or close relatives. These associations are usually based on shared interests or mutual goals.

Because you greatly value this relationship, speak praise and encouragement to your friends. We feel comfortable with these people because we have usually known them for some time. Conversation may be more personal as we grow to know the person better. We trust these people so we can share some opinions, and even gently exhort them to do something better or differently. Mostly we should enjoy the gift of friendship. A good rule of thumb is not to repeat gossip or involve people in problems if they are not part of the solution. Close relationships do not take the place of family, counselors, and intimate friends.

Conversation should be lively but respectful, involving subjects about family, home, travels, sports, hobbies, pets, animals, interests, activities, accomplishments, educational topics, goals, future plans, current events, and possibly personal and spiritual matters. These topics can be approached with more specifics and shared background than when talking with acquaintances. We may share interests or have mutual friends to discuss (good conversation means no ridicule, gossip, or bearing bad tales about others). Respect and enjoy these relationships.

Intimate Relationships

Intimate relationships are our associations with longtime friends and close family. These are the permanent people in our lives, the people we love. Immediate family members are of course in this category: fathers, mothers, grandparents, sisters, and brothers, as well as a special relative like a cousin, aunt, or uncle. Our closest friends will be in this category.

With intimates we have a sense of loyalty, commitment, and trust toward one another, no matter how frequent our personal contact and in spite of occasional problems or disagreements. These are people whom we confide in and have open discussions with on almost any topic. Conversation may include encouragement, comfort with problems, and exhortations. Conversational subjects are numerous, from lighthearted to serious. There are also times of comfortable silence in intimate relationships, times when words are not necessary.

We must always show as much respect, by our words and actions, to these people as we do to others. Our words have great impact on these people because of the closeness of the relationship. There is potential both to edify and wound, so our responsibility is greatest in these relationships. We should guard against the tendency to become lax in familiarity or to take these relationships for granted.

Social Conversation to Avoid

Forethought to conversational topics ("*think* before you speak") reduces the chance of improper remarks. Try to initiate topics that others will find interesting, and remember in all levels of associations you should be *attentive* and use *respectful* language. "There is one who speaks like the piercings of a sword, but the tongue of the wise promotes health" (Prov. 12:18). "He who guards his mouth preserves his life, but he who opens wide his lips shall have destruction" (Prov. 13:3). Wrongly spoken words and cutting remarks wreck havoc in relationships. Though we cannot erase our words once they are spoken, we can give careful thought beforehand to what we say and how we say it. Good conversation is an art that involves being an interested listener and a responsible, considerate speaker.

What follows is a list of specific topics and habits that a responsible speaker does well to avoid.

- Potentially upsetting, angering, or sensitive subjects. A considerate guest will not spoil a party's celebration or social atmosphere by unfriendly, extremely argumentative talk. Lively conversations and discussions that include difference of opinion are permissible, but not arguments or heated debates. A good guest will steer conversation in better directions if it begins to upset others. Interruptions are more tempting during discussions, so make an extra effort to avoid them.
- Topics that might embarrass another person.
- Self-centered talk (*me, me, I, I, mine, mine*), which includes not only bragging but also constantly demeaning oneself.
- Questions of personal financial status.
- Physical problems of others ("Is that a birth mark?") or oneself ("The doctor said my kidneys . . ."). Talk about death or gruesome details of illnesses or surgeries can be upsetting or distasteful to others.
- Negative, critical, or demeaning comments about others or malicious talebearing that degrades a person ("Did you hear about her? Well, let me tell you what she did . . .").
- Cursing, swearing, crude jokes, mocking, and racial or ethnic slurs. Such language obviously reflects badly on one's character and intelligence. "A wholesome tongue is a tree of life: but perverseness in it is a breach in the spirit" (Prov. 15:4).
- Complaints and grievances.
- Whispering secrets in company of others. A mark of maturity is realizing we don't have to say everything we know or think.

- Insincere compliments or flattery.
- Personal or disagreeable discussion in close public places (elevators, buses, theatres, etc.).
- Personal discussions with strangers.
- Slang speech and phrases. Say "Yes," not "Yeah"; "Hello," not "Hey." Also avoid patronizing or empty words like "Is that so?", "Right," "Ya know what I mean?", "Really?", and "Gotcha."
- Loud, boisterous talk, or monopolizing the guests of honor or the hosts with lengthy conversations.

Other Conversation Tips

Ending a Conversation

Just as it is always proper to greet people with "Hello," it is polite to say "Good-bye" when someone leaves. It is also courteous to close a conversation when you have to leave, rather than just walking or wandering away. You can eliminate any nervousness or awkwardness about this disengagement by learning how to end conversations in a definite and considerate manner, which makes everyone comfortable. For example, a simple "I had better go now, but it was nice to talk with you" is a comfortable and respectful signal that it is time to end the visit.

This courtesy especially applies to group parties where people frequently move from group to group. The need to end conversations may be due to time constraints, introductions, or other situations. In situations like this, short conversations prevail, so breakaway times are normal and necessary. To merely "fade away" is awkward and inconsiderate; never leave without giving closing comments such as "I've enjoyed meeting and talking with you"; "I hope I am able to talk to you later, but I need to find my escort. Brad is waiting for me at the punch table"; "This has been a wonderful evening. It has been good to talk with you, but my family is ready to go now"; or "Please excuse me. I need to say hello to those people who just arrived. It was nice chatting with you."

If you need to break away, yet want to continue your conversation, simply invite the other person to accompany you. "Have you had hors d' oeuvres yet? Let me show you the table. Brad is waiting for me there and I know he would like to say hello to you."

Showing Respect to Elders

Because body language speaks volumes about attitude, standing in the presence of elders is one of the first signs of respect that young gentlemen and ladies learn. If seated, young men rise whenever an elder, or lady, enters the room for the first time. Considerate seniors often encourage young people to be seated after a greeting is exchanged.

Young people show respect by looking *at* an older person who is speaking, not looking down, away, or disinterested. This means that they are giving their full attention to what is being said. It is proper to ask questions regarding the topic at hand, and then listen to the answer. A cheerful countenance and tone of voice should be used at all times. Young people do not interrupt an adult who is speaking, unless it is an emergency, and of course elders should not strain children's patience by ignoring them.

When more than one adult is present, young people yield to their lead in conversation. Many elders are not hasty in speaking, so a slight pause before engaging in conversation is polite. Deference to elders also means allowing those who possess greater wisdom from age and experience to speak without challenge. Polite and refined young people willingly contribute to, but do not monopolize, a conversation. Responsible older people have a wealth of knowledge and wisdom, so it benefits young people to learn from them.

Regarding specific topics, it is appropriate to ask one's elders where they were born (not when), where they have traveled, and about their career, interests, hobbies, or family.

Compliments

Compliments are a form of praise, approval, admiration, or congratulation. Words are sincere and appropriate rather than overdone. I am reminded of a remark by Emily Post: "A compliment is baloney sliced so thin that it is delectable. Flattery is baloney sliced so thick that it is indigestible." While I disagree that sincere compliments are "baloney," her point about flattery is right. Sincere compliments are nice thoughts spoken aloud. All students of protocol should know how both to give and receive compliments.

If you always look for the best in others, it will be easy to extend genuine compliments. Show respectful admiration when appropriate, but don't overdo it. For example, if someone makes a humorous remark that lightens a situation, it's fine to give a compliment later: "Your good humor back there rescued the situation." But it would be inappropriate to slap him on the back and say, "You are really funny. I mean *really* funny. You should be a comic. It's great you are so comical!" In the same way, if someone's dress looks very nice, it is usually permissible to say, "That dress looks very nice on you." But it would be over the top to say, "Wow, you look so awesome, you could be in Hollywood!" Flattering exaggerations make people uncomfortable, while genuine remarks affirm a person. Compliments may also be given in a secondhand manner, followed with a question. When it is sincere, this technique aids conversation as well as edifies the people involved. "Brock told me how much he enjoyed your playing the piano for the school program. He said you performed very well. How long have you been playing?" Or, "Tyler said you looked beautiful in the new outfit you wore to receive your award. What kind of award was it?"

A proper response to a compliment can be as simple as saying "Thank you." Thanks are appropriate whenever a favor, help, or a compliment is given. Skill in expressing gratitude is something we can cultivate. Encourage young people to say "Thank you" appropriately throughout their conversations. Children of all ages need to know that when they receive a compliment, they should express gratitude with these two words *at least,* and they may add an appropriate comment. For example, after being complimented on clothing or hairstyle, they could add, "Thank you, I'm glad you like it—I do, too." Express appreciation for the compliment, not dissatisfaction. For example, a rude response to "What a nice dress!" would be, "Oh, this old thing! I don't like it at all," or "I've had it for years." This sort of brushing aside devalues the other person's judgment and turns his compliment into a negative reflection on his taste. Presumption is equally rude. If the compliment were for an accomplishment, one does not respond with, "Yeah, I know. I deserved it." Nor would a person accept credit for something they did not do. If the compliment is for an achievement that involves other people as well as yourself, it is polite to mention their involvement when thanking someone for the compliment. "Congratulations on winning the tournament!" "Thank you. Our team worked hard and everyone played their best."

Telephone Manners

School protocol training does not necessarily include proper telephone etiquette, but parents often request that it be part of the program. I have included a few guidelines here in case your program schedule allows for it.

Handle phone calls respectfully and efficiently. Answer the phone with a pleasant tone of voice. A simple "Hello" is standard and correct, but many parents prefer identification of the location and speaker: "Hello, this is the Smith residence," or "Hello, this is the Jones's house, Robert speaking."

The caller should then properly identify himself and name the person he wishes to speak to. "Hello, this is Mrs. Caller. May I please speak with your father if he isn't busy right now?" If the caller doesn't identify himself, it is permissible for the child to ask, "Who may I say is calling?" The young person should then say something like, "Just a moment, Mrs. Caller; let me check to see if he can take a call right now." Then Mrs. Caller is informed, "Yes, he will be right with you."

If the parent isn't home or is unable to take the call, it is correct to say, "Father can't come to the phone right now. May I take a message?" (Or, "Would you like to speak with my mother instead?") When a parent isn't available, a message should be taken. The young person has the responsibility to write it down with the caller's phone number, and then repeat the message and the number to the caller. Then he should say, "Thank you for calling. I will give him [or her] the message." And, of course, the message should be given to the parent as soon as possible.

It is rude for children or teenagers to tell an adult caller, calling for business, to call back if they have call waiting and are on a line with another young person on a social visit. Adults should not be told to call back unless it is absolutely necessary.

Common sense phone etiquette applies to young people as well as adults. It is wise not to make or accept calls during mealtimes, so avoid calling people between five and seven o'clock. As a rule of thumb, do not call after eight o'clock in the evening, or before eight o'clock in the morning, unless it's an emergency, or you know the person you are calling very well, and the call will not be an interruption to their schedule. Other rules to keep in mind: do not eat while talking on the phone; do not make rude or prank phone calls; do not monopolize the phone with long personal conversations when someone else in the home needs to use the phone; and finally, office phones are for business calls, not social calls.

Cell phone use in public common areas, such as in a store, at church, a play, a concert, a restaurant, or an office is distracting and rude to others. Turn phones off. When you do take or make a call don't try to have a conversation with anyone else but the person on the phone.

Benefits of Proficient Conversation

> How can a young man keep his way pure? By keeping it according to Thy word. . . . Thy word I have hid in my heart, that I might not sin against Thee. Blessed art Thou, O Lord; teach me Thy statutes. With my lips I have declared all the judgments of Thy mouth. (Ps. 119:9–13)

Words are powerful! James warns us the tongue is the most dangerous member of our body. By treasuring and mimicking God's word, we safeguard the purity of our own words. It is wonderful to watch young people become proficient and gain confidence as they develop good conversational skills and right speaking ability. Seeing their unique personalities develop with "golden" conversation skills is a reward in itself. Training the tongue to speak respectfully and thoughtfully prepares children for future interaction of greater importance. Every generation needs ordinary yet able and sincere representatives of God's truth. The youngsters who apply simple conversational rules excel in fitly-spoken words having both "salt" and grace, and they reap the rewards of peaceful and fruitful relationships.

Introductions

Introductions disturb the comfort zone of many people, no matter what their age, so learning how to introduce others and how to respond when being introduced is very useful. Understanding the rules makes everyone's social life easier and more enjoyable.

The importance of introductions cannot be overemphasized; they are absolutely mandatory for any protocol training program. Why? Because proper introductions leave no one standing ignored as an outsider or stranger. Introductions do more than acquaint people with one another; they acknowledge identity, presence, and a person's value. Even an imperfectly-performed introduction is better than no introduction at all.

Everyone at one time or another has the duty to make an introduction for two or more people who have not met. On other occasions you may be the newly-introduced person. In both cases, you have obligations to fulfill. For example, since initial actions are part of a "first impression," a smile should always accompany introductions. Smiles have the power to set a good tone and produce a cordial first impression. Without a cheerful look, a sober mood prevails. Children should be taught the basics of making introductions, which includes smiling and saying "Hello" when introduced, even when they are first learning to talk. Obviously, teenagers are ready for more comprehensive instruction. Whatever the age, all should learn how to respond respectfully to other people, whether performing the introduction or being introduced.

Using an outline describing what to do in various real-life scenarios is one way we can simplify the complexity in learning about introductions for students, and handouts are a helpful tool for reference and practice. Schedule short practice sessions while you are covering this material so the students can become comfortable applying the rules. This gives them opportunity, with guidance, to prepare for future social introductions.

It is easy to make this practice time fun and interesting. One of my favorite practice methods, inspired by Emily Post and Judith Martin of *Miss Manners* fame, involves using clever or unusual names for practice introductions. I often surprise my students with interesting names for their practice time. Students may pick a name out of a hat (or have names assigned if our session time is limited). The students then "assume" that name during our rehearsal of introductions. I might use historical names, such as Cleopatra or King Henry, or silly names like Cinderella, Humpty Dumpty, or Polly Perfect. Other times I use names of famous contemporary characters (real or fictional) like Batman or Queen Elizabeth. Young men enjoy assuming the names of their favorite heroes, including musicians and actors. Whatever the size of your group, students enjoy the surprise of this relaxed approach.

Just like a coin, there are two sides to introductions, both equally important to know and practice. The following sections cover both introducing others and being introduced yourself.

Introducing Others

Knowing how to introduce others is the responsibility of the person who knows the other people present when they do not know each other. Here are a few important rules:

1. Make the introduction at the earliest moment possible. The longer it is put off, the more awkward it becomes.
2. Use full names.
3. Say the most "important" name first—that is, address yourself initially to the more important person. This is a key point to remember in making proper introductions. We properly defer to people based on sex, age, or rank. This means the name of the oldest person (the most "important" one) or the woman's name is said first.

The person with lesser rank in life is presented or introduced to the one with greater rank, so we say the "important" person's name first. (This doesn't mean the people are assigned different values of worth according to their different ranks, positions, or places in life; respect does not degrade the one who respects, but shows honor. A father, by his age and position, has a position of rank greater in life than that of a teenager, and his rank should be respected.) The key point is that the person responsible for the introductions presents the "less important" (name said last) to the "more important" person (name said first). To summarize informal introductions: The younger are "presented" to the older, friends are introduced to parents and other relatives, men are "presented" or introduced to women, and other people of high position or rank are introduced to others of lesser rank. This might still be a bit confusing, so I have included several examples below.

4. Again, smile. Introducing people is not painful, and we are not at the dentist's office. A pleasant countenance is a compliment—and comfort—to others.
5. Provide a small bit of information about the person. This provides new acquaintances with a starting place for conversation. A student introducing a friend to his father may say something like, "Dad, this is Sam Smashing. He is on the lacrosse team."
6. Do not introduce someone as your "friend" when introducing two people who are both your friends. Do not order people to shake hands—they can take care of that themselves.

Sample Introductions

Traditionally, protocol dictates that the gentleman is always presented to a lady, so her name is said first. In an *informal* situation, one of the following examples would work.

"Maureen, this is Tyler Terrific. Tyler, this is Maureen Marvelous."

"Maureen, allow me to introduce Tyler Terrific. Tyler, this is Maureen Marvelous."

"Maureen, I would like you to meet Tyler Terrific. Tyler, this is Maureen Marvelous."

When you are the person being introduced in an informal introduction, you may simply respond with "Hello," or you can add a bit of appropriate information: "Hello, I'm glad to meet you. I saw your team play yesterday. What a good game!"

In a *formal* situation, proper titles are used in the introduction. Formal introductions are used with dignitaries and officials at formal events or state occasions: "Mayor Uptown, may I present my brother, Mr. Nearly Perfect?" Dignitaries include elected officials, religious officials, or visiting statesmen. An exception to this rule of the "most important" or prominent name first is that no woman is ever presented to a man unless he is a church official, head of state, royalty, or an older man in a recognizably high position. As stated earlier, these introductions usually occur in more formal situations. Here are some more examples:

"Mrs. Serious, may I present Tyler Terrific. Tyler, this is Sally Serious."

If Mrs. Serious is older, Tyler will use her title in reply: "How do you do, Mrs. Serious." He will not call her Sally.

He will wait to see if she offers her hand first before extending his. The rule applies in all social situations. It is the same during informal or formal introductions when a gentleman is presented or introduced to a younger woman.

"Miss Marvelous, may I present Tyler Terrific? Tyler, this is Maureen Marvelous."

When introducing an older gentleman to an older lady, again, the lady's name is said first: "Mrs. Years, may I present Mr. Ben Older? Mr. Older, this is Lotta Years."

Young people should always use titles and last names when introducing their elders. "Mr. Proper, this is Daniel Dependable." Mr. Dependable then addresses Mr. Proper as such, unless Mr. Proper indicates otherwise. This no-first-name rule also applies to persons of higher rank (i.e. elected officials), business situations, clients, customers, and professional service people (i.e. doctors, accountants, etc.) unless they ask you to use their first name.

When introducing two people of the same sex, the younger person is introduced to the older person, so the older person's name is said first.

"Mr. Older, I would like you to meet Stan Sixteen. Stan, this is Ben Older."

"Mrs. Years, I would like you to meet Fanny Fifteen. Fanny, this is Mrs. Lotta Years."

When introducing people of the same age, gender, rank, and position, introduce the one you know less well to the person that you have known longer and better. For example, assume you are introducing your acquaintance Ned Newcomer to your good friend Tyler Jordan:

"Tyler, I'd like you to meet Ned Newcomer. Ned, this is Tyler Jordan."

Introductions of Family Members

Now here is an exception to the rules. Even though family members are more "important," they are introduced *to* others as a matter of courtesy. When you are introducing your friends to your parents, make a deliberate effort to bring your friend to your parents and give your parents some information as a conversational starting point.

"Faye, I would like you to meet my parents, Mr. and Mrs. Perfect. Mom and Dad, this is Faye Fabulous. We are on the knowledge bowl team together."

Students will also introduce family members to teachers.

"Mrs. Letters, I would like to introduce my mother, Mrs. Nellie Perfect. Mom, this is Mrs. Belle Letters, my literature teacher."

Some people might question this ranking because the parent is the most important person in your life. However, honor and respect are given to the instructor as an educational representative appointed by the parents as well as from tradition in common courtesy.

Group Introductions

At a large group gathering (such as a formal reception) it is not necessary for the hosts to introduce everyone. However, at a smaller party, the hosts should introduce as many people as possible among those who do not know each other.

Whenever one new person needs to be introduced to several people at once, it is preferable if a gentleman who knows the new person performs introductions to the group. Ladies in the group are given social preference of rank, so women are named first, beginning with the eldest lady.

"Mrs. Lotta Years, this is Mike McMarvelous. Susie Sensational, this is Mike McMarvelous." If the group is large, he need not repeat the last name over and over unless some did not hear.

Take your time with group introductions and do not feel pressured. The most important rule to remember is to introduce everyone so that no one is left out or unknown. Next, continue to respect the traditional ranking in the group. Turn to the older men before younger men.

The young man in charge of introductions should say, "Mr. Grandfatherly, I would like to introduce Mike McMarvelous. This is Greg Grandfatherly." Then he should turn to the next person in the group and continue in like manner: "And this is Ned Next, Ted Third, and Leonard Lastly."

Upon conclusion of introductions, something of interest about the newcomer (in this case, Mike McMarvelous) should be included: "Mike has just arrived home after several days of snowboarding on Mount Everest." This gives the group a jump-start for conversation.

If Mike really is Marvelous, he will not monopolize the talk or bore others with long tales of his epic adventures. He will cheerfully answer questions, but before interest wanes he will begin asking questions, turning the attention to others in the group by using "toss the ball" conversational skills. At some point the large group will probably form into smaller conversational clusters. At appropriate closing points, people say their farewells with "It was nice to meet you."

Party Etiquette and Introductions

A good guest stands ready to introduce himself at parties or gatherings when hosts are busy or occupied with other guests. It is the guest's responsibility to mingle on such occasions.

Whenever hors d'oeuvres are served, with standing room only, drinks should be held in the left hand, which makes it easier to meet or greet people with a free right hand. Keep a napkin handy. Always take time soon after arrival to meet the hosts, any guests of honor, and chaperones, even if you must introduce yourself. Then, try to meet and mingle with other guests. Don't expect to engage in lengthy conversations. A good guest circulates in order to acknowledge and engage others in the room. Some use the terms "socializing" or "working a room" for this activity. I personally don't like these terms, but they get across the idea of a guest's responsibility. It is a pleasure and a privilege to meet new people; it shouldn't be termed "work," even if it is a duty.

Memory Lapse

Everyone has memory lapses. If your mind goes blank and you forget a person's name, don't panic. There are several ways to handle this situation. First, pause and allow the other person to speak first. Remain silent a few seconds on the chance the people who don't know each other will step forward and give their own names.

Secondly, try just saying the name of the other person whose name you do remember to the person whose name eludes you: "Oh, have you met Mandy Moore?" This is a tactful clue that help is needed. Hopefully the mystery person will offer her name immediately: "Hello, I'm Sarah Savvy." If she is not savvy and fails to give her name, the situation is more awkward but not hopeless. As a last resort, simply say apologetically, "I'm so sorry. Help me remember your last name so I can introduce you properly."

People understand that everyone has forgetful moments. However, don't try to be too clever. I know one fellow who forgot the name of a casual acquaintance when he needed to make an introduction. He sought for a clever way to cover his memory lapse and said, "Tom, I would like you to meet, to meet—your last name is so difficult, how do you pronounce it?" When the acquaintance said "Jones," they all had a good laugh. Humor always helps awkward situations.

When you are the person being introduced, and the person forgets your name, be ready to "jump in" and help that person—they will appreciate your help. Never put someone on the spot—for example, by saying, "You do remember my name, don't you?"

When You Are Introduced

This brings us to the other side of the coin—what to do when you are introduced. The following points cover the basic, polite responses.

1. Look at the person(s) being introduced as they are named. There should be no wiggling, fidgeting, or looking down at your shoes. The focus should be on remembering the new person's name and standing tall. (On remembering names, see below.)

2. Shake hands. It is common and polite for a gentleman to the shake hands when another man is introduced to him. Hugs are not acceptable at introductions. A true gentleman waits to see if a lady first offers her hand (and a younger lady waits for the older lady to offer her hand first). But if a gentleman does offer a lady his hand, she should not refuse to extend hers. Today, handshakes are acceptable social greetings for all, although higher protocol still defers to traditional ways regarding ladies.

3. Stand up for introductions. Men always stand when being introduced. Though an older woman is not required to stand when being introduced to a younger person, she may do so if she is in a business situation or when she is being introduced to an older person or to a dignitary. Standing is a way of showing respect and interest.

4. Generally, after being presented to someone, it is best to wait for the other person's response and then say, "Hello, I'm happy to meet you," or "It's nice to meet you" with a smile. In more formal circumstances one can use the older, traditional responses of "How do you do?" "I am pleased to meet you," or "Pleased to make your acquaintance." These remain valid, proper, and respectful in spite of their quaintness. When time is short or there are multiple introductions in progress, it is permissible to simply say "Hello" with a smile.

5. After introductions, and when the conversation ends, polite protocol recommends the acknowledgement of any introduction by again saying, "I'm happy to have met you" or "It was nice to meet you." A smile should always accompany these remarks. And of course, the other person may respond, if he feels the same, with "Thank you. It was nice to meet you too." Otherwise he can simply smile and say, "Thank you."

We must not forget that other formalities exist in many parts of the world. My husband and I once had the privilege of hosting a reception where a leader from a foreign country was a guest, and many of our other guests were also from his country. As they met him, they bowed and showed deep respect for his position. I had not seen such courtesies since my childhood and was reminded of the respect and deference shown by these powerful symbolic formalities.

In a formal situation, your clue for a stricter, formal response is the manner in which you were introduced. For example, if you are introduced to the President, after the introduction you would say, "How do you do, Mr. President? It is a pleasure to meet you." This is the proper formal response. Smiles are always in order during formal introductions. Gentlemen always remember a courtesy smile while shaking hands. In a reception line, time is limited so lengthy conversations are not expected and in fact inappropriate.

Handling Names

It is all too easy to be distracted during the introduction process and not pay attention to the other's name. Make a point of understanding the name and repeating it back to ensure that you have it right. Try to use it immediately and throughout the conversation to help your memory. Use other memory aids, such as letter or word association, such as "Mike from the Marines."

If someone introduces you by your first name only (they may have forgotten your last name), be ready to say, "Hello" or "It's nice to meet you" followed immediately by your full name. Smile and enjoy meeting this person regardless of any improper introduction procedure.

Sometimes we are introduced with incomplete or inaccurate names, or we are thrust into situations where there is no one present to introduce us, or someone fails to make introductions, assuming everyone knows each other. These are times when it is proper to introduce yourself. This is the easiest introduction to perform. All you need to remember is your own name. Simply say, "Hello, I'm [your full name]."

If your name is pronounced incorrectly, or wrong information is given about you, simply correct it immediately and in a kind tone: "I know it can be confusing, but my name is Brad Boswell, not Buzzwell."

At Banquet Tables

When you are meeting new people at a banquet, try to make introductions or introduce yourself to those who will be seated at your table as soon as possible. Ideally all introductions are made before everyone is seated and begins the meal, but they may be made after people have taken their seats. It is a gentleman's responsibility to take charge of introductions. He introduces the lady he is escorting and himself at the first convenient moment.

Give each guest a cordial acknowledgment and a smile as the opportunity arises. If there are other people at the dinner party you want to meet, but haven't met prior to the seating, do not interrupt guests at other tables while they are eating—usually there will be a chance to meet them after dinner. Standard etiquette requires that you converse with everyone sitting near you throughout the dinner.

"Sidewalk Socializing" and Informal Introductions

What about introductions at a mall, or when you are with one friend and run into other acquaintances or friends in an unplanned, unexpected meeting? In this case, as soon as possible, when someone stops to talk, the people who know one another are responsible for the introductions of those who do not know each other. Remember, it is best avoid the phrase, "This is my friend," when introducing two friends. This informal introduction has the same rules already mentioned.

Responding with Titles

Young people always use titles for older people (Mr., Mrs., Miss, and Dr.) unless they specifically give permission to call them by their first name. (Some dignitaries have special titles, so prepare yourself beforehand to use the correct one.) There is a respectful trend in some circles today to recover the traditional custom of teaching children to say, "Yes, Sir" or "No, Sir" when responding to a man and "Yes, Ma'am," "No, Ma'am" when speaking to an older lady, which trains children to show respect to their elders. It is a custom still honored by different regions, social circles, and in the military.

Introductions: Conclusion

Introductions are not difficult. Protocol's rules for introductions help make them easy, respectful, and orderly. The most important rule is always to make introductions so that no one is ignored or forgotten. Young people who understand the importance of introductions will be faithful in this essential social duty and their friends will appreciate the courtesy. It starts relationships off on the right foot and keeps them running smoothly.

7

The Right Moves

In the class I call "The Right Moves," students learn techniques and refine skills that help them move and act with poise and competence. It covers basic protocol for escorts, toasts, handshakes, and good posture, and includes guidelines for home, restaurant, vehicle, and concert settings. This class reduces awkwardness in these common situations, so that the conduct of both ladies and gentlemen can reflect self-control, grace, dignity, and certainty.

The "Right Moves" class provides students with practical training as well as practice time. In order to grow up acting like ladies and gentlemen, young people need to know what ladies and gentlemen do and how they act. These uncomplicated, visible, timely movements not only make life better, but also distinguish those who use them as young ladies and gentlemen. Some call this *refinement.* It's not just that young people know the protocol of when to stand, sit, or offer a helping hand, but also that they can do so with poise and dignity.

Right Moves and Gender

In this class, instruction is given about who does what, as well as when and how. The best programs are those going with the grain of masculine and feminine differences. When this is rightly taught and taken to heart, it can produce high levels of poise, dignity, and confidence. And, young people gladly embrace social duties customized to their gender. American protocol, as well as western world culture, uniquely respects and honors women. True, the largest burden traditionally falls upon the gentlemen, but that is why God gave men big shoulders.

Gentlemen

For men, this means they should consistently display charitable conduct reflecting noble, gentlemanly character. Contemporary protocol author John Bridges further describes this masculine character in his book *How to Be a Gentleman*:

> A gentleman never makes himself the center of attention. His goal is to make life easier, not just for himself, but for his friends, his acquaintances, and the world at large. Because he is a gentleman, he does not see this as a burden. Instead, it is a challenge he faces every day . . . it is what you do and who you are—an accumulation of gentlemanly behaviors over the course of a lifetime—that makes a man a gentleman.

When a boy's shoulders are big enough to handle manly duties, protocol assigns him duties, such as offering a helping hand to elders and ladies. He may offer to carry a heavy package, open a door, or simply stand to show respect. Through protocol he begins to think beyond himself. He soon learns that a gentleman is a pleasant, considerate, and unselfish man who performs duties cheerfully and patiently. It takes a strong, secure man to take on the role of a servant this way.

Here are a few of the most rudimentary social moves for gentlemen:

- He always maintains good posture: he stands, sits, and walks straight and upright.
- He always demonstrates self-control.
- He does not spit in public or use coarse language to "prove" his manhood.
- He always looks another person in the eye when speaking.
- He immediately stands up when a lady approaches him.
- He always stands up when a lady near him stands.
- He always helps a lady with her chair at a table when she sits or rises.
- He always helps a lady with her coat or wrap.
- He always offers his chair to a lady or elderly person when other chairs are not available.
- He always retrieves dropped items for a lady or older person.
- He always treats other people respectfully.
- He always holds open a door for ladies and elderly people to pass through first.

- It is always better for gentlemen to pass behind people rather than in front of them.

In these basic "right moves," we see that much of the purpose of gentlemanly protocol is assisting others. Traditionally, protocol recognizes that each gender has different duties. Thus, a gentleman's faithful attention to his duties radiates quiet command and strength worthy of respect and admiration.

Ladies

Protocol tutors girls in polished social behavior, which means they ought to enjoy behaving like young ladies rather than unrefined, boisterous teenagers. Good training also helps young girls better recognize decent men. Protocol training raises the standards by which girls value and appreciate the men who demonstrate honorable intentions with courteous behavior. True gentlemen are "servers," not selfish "takers." Protocol awareness provides higher values and expectations for social conduct. This increases appreciation of the type of man worthy of respect and admiration. Those two small words, *servers* and *takers*, are a universe apart, with profound implications for society's morality as well as a young lady's future.

This ties in with another necessity for today's girls: becoming a virtuous woman. I always share Proverbs 31 with young ladies in training, and first-time listeners find this chapter of biblical wisdom quite enlightening. No matter what a virtuous woman's work, duty or activity, she is intelligent, maintains high moral character, and performs social graces well. This is not a wimpy woman: "Strength and honor are her clothing," and she's nobody's fool, for she displays wisdom in her words and decisions. She is sincere, industrious, and ably serves others.

It is reasonable that a virtuous woman also practices the art of deference. She is not pushy or presumptuous. In this way, she is distinctively different from some contemporary women. She respects the rules of good conduct and she respects gentlemen by resisting the urge to seize their responsibilities. She does not rob a man of his place to prove her own strength or capabilities, and her refusal to run over or downgrade men is an honorable mark of distinction in today's world. A lady moves and speaks with gentle graciousness; she learns to control her tongue in both its content and the volume level, eliminating sassy, cutting remarks as well as gossip, nagging, and presumptuous or disrespectful retorts.

Protocol rightly specifies deference towards older people, and women are no exception. Girls should defer to older women in many situations: a young woman allows an older woman to pass through a door first, to take a chair first, and often, to speak first.

Deference in protocol serves another important purpose. It fosters gratitude, which in turn cultivates the virtue of humility. The loveliest ladies I know possess a grateful and unassuming nature. Their character is beautifully enhanced by their gracious, appreciative attitudes. Arrogance and pride are not beautiful. Humility is a strong remedy against the "little princess" mentality, which can spoil the best of girls. It protects from selfish arrogance that often accompanies the many privileges lavished upon this generation. The danger of becoming arrogant is very real for those young ladies who come to expect (and demand) attentive courtesies without returning humble gratitude. Humility is clear-sighted, undemanding, and unpretentious. It is a wonderful quality.

A young girl can demonstrate graciousness in the following ways:

- She accepts proper offers of assistance with a smile and "thank you." (She need not accept assistance from strangers.)
- She always maintains her sense of poise and dignity whether or not good manners are observed by others.
- She always stands, walks, and sits gracefully.
- She remembers to sit with her head held upright, legs straight or crossed at the ankles.
- She always allows an escort to offer her assistance with doors, chairs, steps, coat, or wrap.
- She always keeps her purse, glasses, and handkerchief off the table.
- She always speaks quietly and thoughtfully.
- She remembers that grooming is done in private.
- She does not play or fuss with her (or a friend's) hair and clothes in public social settings.
- She refuses improper advances in a firm but polite manner.

Exceptions

Because life is full of twists and turns, children need to realize there are times when right moves are wrong. Rules can sometimes be difficult, awkward, or even inappropriate to apply. When we teach this subject, we should attempt to instill propriety and common sense—not blind, unthinking rigidity—in our pupils. We teach protocol because we want young people to have considerate, unselfish, and undemanding traits woven into their character. So when rigidly insisting on a certain rule interferes with the goals of humility and deference, it is unsuitable in that circumstance to observe the rule. This discernment increases with wisdom and maturity.

Developing common sense and discernment takes time, but it is important nevertheless to make young people aware of propriety. For example, after protocol classes, several sweet young girls, in their sincere (and eager) quest for ladylike behavior, became overly concerned regarding the men's duty to open doors for them. My zealous young pupils refused to open their own school doors if a boy was anywhere within eyeshot on the school grounds. The girls were exasperated with the boys, and the boys were exasperated that the girls were exasperated. Obviously, I had failed to communicate the heart and soul of the matter—*appropriateness*. Not only should ladies be more concerned over their own behavior than the behavior of others, but they also should never insist on courtesy toward themselves. There are many times when they must open their own doors, and it is perfectly proper and suitable to do so.

On another occasion, during a protocol dinner, *all* the young men at *all* the dining tables in the entire banquet room rose respectfully when one lady had an urgent need to leave the dining table. Of course, she was embarrassed by such a grand gesture and having all the eyes in the room upon her. Although my favorite Miss Manners would applaud the men's chivalrous actions,[1] I had failed to impart to the girls that a lady should excuse the nearby gentlemen of their duty during dinner, and that only her escort need rise for her discreet departure. In that case most of the other people in the room would have been unaware of her departure and the rhythm of the dinner would have remained uninterrupted.

With that said, let's look at how these valuable "right moves" play out in various situations. Properly applied, these rules equip our children for living well, so they fit comfortably into the scheme of life, and, more importantly, they become a blessing to others by their considerate actions.

General Escorting Moves

Walking

- Gentlemen generally walk on the left side of a lady and on the street side of sidewalks. Pedestrians pass to the right. Men should take care not to walk too fast. A lady will follow the gentleman's leading pace.

[1] *Miss Manners' Guide to Excruciatingly Correct Behavior* (Warner Books, 1983), 102.

- In necessary instances, such as rain, snow, or uneven terrain, a gentleman offers his right arm to the lady he is escorting.
- Should a lady (or older person) ever slip and fall, a gentleman immediately offers his assistance. He may relieve the embarrassment with a calm, reassuring smile and few words. A witty remark may lighten the moment if there is no injury.
- When a lady or an elderly person drops an item, a gentleman immediately retrieves it.
- When a gentleman accompanies two ladies, the oldest lady is on his right side, and the other lady is on her right. The gentleman helps both ladies with doors and chairs in the same order.
- An escort is prepared when "stepping out":
    - He has an umbrella when necessary.
    - He carries a clean handkerchief in his pocket in case it is needed.
    - He always has some spare cash (including change and small bills) in case of unforeseen needs or emergency. He is never caught short. He may carry his cell phone inconspicuously in a pocket, but it is turned off.

In Vehicles

The escort's duties include safely helping ladies in and out of vehicles. He opens doors for ladies and extends a helping hand when needed. He always assists matrons first.

- Younger women graciously step back while the gentleman helps the older lady. The same rule applies at doors in buildings. These small acts demonstrate respect for elders.
- The driver does not leave until he is assured that all passengers are safely inside his vehicle.
- Passengers enter and exit vehicles via the curbside door. One escort slowly and firmly shuts (not slams) the car door after all limbs and garments are safely inside the vehicle. He then proceeds to the other side door to enter the car. The lady does not slide over in the seat, unless there is a third person or the other door is located on a busy street which makes it unsafe for the escort to go around.
- When entering a car, turn with your back to the seat, lower the body onto the seat, then turn and pivot both legs together into place. Passengers fasten their own seat belts.
- When riding in a limousine, doors are opened and closed for ladies and gentlemen by the limousine driver.

- When exiting a vehicle, the escort opens his door first, pivots his legs together and steps outside. He goes to the other side of the car and opens the door for the lady who is waiting for him. It does not damage a lady's spirit to wait for this assistance whether or not she needs it. It reaffirms her womanhood. She allows a man the opportunity to act as a gentleman. He may extend his hand should a lady need help exiting the car.
- The lady unfastens her seat belt as the escort comes around to her door and slides toward the door. While still in her seat, she pivots towards the open door, places both feet on the ground and stands up on both feet. If she has a package she gives it to the escort to carry before she exits.
- The escort should give assistance to others who need help. The lady with him stands back toward the inside of the sidewalk to allow him room to fulfill his duties.
- When there is more than one man present upon entering a van, one gentleman, not necessarily the driver, slides the back door open. When the front seat passenger is a lady, the driver usually assists her while the other gentlemen help passengers take back seats.
- When a group is traveling together in a van, it is best for one younger fellow to first enter and take a seat in the rear row. He takes the very back seat that is most difficult to reach. Often several gentlemen will take the third row seats in the back. Common sense prevails regarding the seating order that is most convenient.
- Next, the ladies enter, while one gentleman remains outside the van by the door. Ladies enter gracefully by turning sideways and facing the van's front. One foot at a time is placed on the running board before taking the next step into the van. If necessary, she slightly lifts her skirt to avoid stepping on the garment. She is mindful of her posture and keeps the upper body as straight as possible. She enters the van in an erect position with her head up, then sits, turns as in a car, then slides over to the far side of the seat to make room for the next passenger. Ladies do not hop or jump into vehicles. She waits for the lady ahead of her to be seated in place before trying to enter.
- After all ladies are seated inside the vehicle, the last gentleman enters, shuts the door, and takes the last seat nearest the van door or the nearest seat in the last row.
- When exiting a van, one or all gentlemen exit before the ladies, then stand by the door to steady each lady's arm as she steps down.

- "Heaviness in the heart of man makes it stoop, but a good word makes it glad" (Prov. 12:25). Conversation should be lighthearted and cheerful during travel, but it is rude (not to mention dangerous) to distract the driver. Silent intervals are often welcome.
- Do not leave garbage on the vehicle seat or floors.
- Headphones should be left at home.
- Passengers thank the driver when they leave the vehicle.
- Doorman/Valet Parking
  - If there is a doorman, he will assist the ladies and driver first. Ladies wait for him to open and close the door.
  - Say "Thank you" as you depart.
  - Tips to doormen are not obligatory, unless they has performed a special favor or help (e.g., hailing a taxi or removing luggage for the bellman, in which case a tip of one to three dollars is expected).
  - Give a gratuity to the person returning your car to you at pick-up time (currently a two- to five-dollar tip). The escort is in charge of the tipping, which is why gentlemen always keep spare small bills on a money clip or in the pocket.
  - Limousine service tipping is handled when you reserve your limousine. If the fifteen to twenty percent gratuity is not added automatically to your bill, request that it be added. When service bills include tips, additional tips are not necessary.

Doors

- A gentleman shows honor and respect towards women by opening and holding doors for them to pass through first. When there are several men in a group, only one need hold the door for the group, allowing four to six people to pass through. Everyone should pass through without lingering.
- When a larger number of people arrive at the door at the same time, the first gentleman opens and holds the door. After six or eight people pass through the open door, another gentleman, midway in line offers to hold the door. This courtesy relieves the first man so he can proceed to his lady waiting inside.
- When approaching double doors, the gentleman opens the door on the right side. It usually swings open toward the inside. If there is a second set of interior doors, the lady stands aside so that the gentleman can pass by her and push the second door open, allowing her to

go through. When a door is wide or heavy, it is permissible for him to go through first and hold the door with his back against it, rather than straining awkwardly to lean forward and hold it with his arm. Whenever a group approaches two sets of doors, one gentleman should hold the exterior door while another passes through to hold the interior door. This prevents a group of ladies from clogging the space between the doors while they wait for a gentleman to come and open the interior door.

- Ladies smile and say "thank you" as they pass the gentleman holding the door.

Stairs

On single or narrow staircases, the lady walks up first, but the man is first going down. At the bottom of the stairs, he stops, turns, and offers his hand for the last step or two. On doublewide stairs, the couple may walk together, lady on right. They both walk on the right side of the stairs.

Coats

- Remove coats and wraps in the restaurant's entrance lobby. (Inside a home, coats are removed by the escort or host and hung or placed where designated.)
- A lady may keep her coat or wrap if she wishes, but a man removes his outer dress coat.
- Most better restaurants have a cloakroom, and it is best to take advantage of it. Coat check service is usually "complimentary" with a tip tray nearby. Currently the standard tip is one dollar minimum or, if there are multiple garments, fifty cents to a dollar per garment. Men are responsible to keep claim tickets and to take care of the tip.
- If the lady wishes to keep her coat with her but not wear it, the escort helps her out of the coat before going to the table; then he drapes it over her shoulders, and they proceed to the table following the maître d'. The coat or wrap may be kept on the shoulders or placed over the back of the chair so it will not touch the floor.
- A man should not take his dress coat or hat to the table; he checks them and places the receipt in his suit pocket. Otherwise, he hangs the coat in a designated place. A man always keeps his suit or tuxedo jacket on when dining.
- At a banquet or group gathering the same procedure applies. Upon entry, the man finds the coat rack, and coats are removed near the

rack. The gentleman helps the lady first and then hangs her coat before removing his coat.

- Men leave hats and gloves with their coat.
- Men always remove hats when inside buildings and when talking with ladies.

Dining Situations

Approaching a Restaurant

- Ladies and gentlemen enter rooms with dignity and poise. No one is loud or boisterous.
- Once inside, a pause of a few seconds gives newcomers time for a quick preview of new surroundings. Avoid barging into a room.
- The gentleman in charge approaches the host or maitre d'. After acknowledgement from the host or maitre d', the gentleman gives the name of his party and states the time they were expected.

Approaching the Table

Restaurant

- The maitre d' always leads the way to a restaurant table. The group quietly and promptly follows his lead with ladies following first and gentlemen last. The eldest members of the party proceed before the younger, although young children may hold their parents' hands.
- When a group passes by a table of people they know, no one in either group stops to visit. A low-toned "hello" or "good evening" said with a smile, is sufficient acknowledgment from anyone in both parties. Dinner interruptions or stopping people who are on their way to a table is inconsiderate and impolite just as it is impolite to interrupt someone eating.

Private Banquet Room

- When ushers lead a group to the table, ladies follow first.
- When ushers are not present in the private banquet room, it is the escort's duty to lead the way and find the assigned table. Ladies follow behind.
- It is permissible to have a short conversation with friends in the room if they are not seated and preoccupied.

- Politely await the arrival of the other table guests before taking a seat, unless they are late.
- Considerate gentlemen stand to greet latecomers unless this creates a distraction for a program in session. In this case, a partial rise from the seat and a smile are sufficient acknowledgement to latecomers.
- When table partners do not know each other, each escort introduces his lady, then himself, to new guests. Preferably, this is done before sitting down. While introductions are best made before taking one's seat, it is permissible to make introductions at the table. Gentlemen stand for introductions.
- Dining chairs are entered from the left side. As usual, gentlemen draw the chair for the lady on their right. This is most helpful because chairs can be awkward for a lady to manage when she is dressed in formal or semiformal attire. As always, ladies acknowledge this kind assistance with a sincere "Thank you."

Seating

- In a restaurant, guests are usually seated upon arrival.
- The maitre d' usually assists the first lady with her chair.
- All men at the table remain standing until ladies are seated, just as they do in a home.
- Men assist the lady on their right as the first lady is being seated.
- Ladies are generally given the best view or seat in a restaurant, but they should take the first seat offered to them.
- The lady approaches her chair from the left side. She grasps the chair seat with her two hands to help pull the chair into desired position as she sits down. The gentleman stands behind the chair and gently slides it into position. He carefully avoids pushing the chair too quickly or hard.

Standing

- There's truth in the proverb, "If you don't rise to the occasion, you will sink in the estimation of others." Men demonstrate their good manners and respect by standing up to greet or welcome people, for introductions, to acknowledge elders, and for the approach and departure of ladies. Ladies may remain seated at tables during these times.
- During dining occasions, all men best remain standing until each lady at his table is seated.

- Gentlemen have the obligation to rise when a lady at the table leaves or returns. (No one should leave the table once the dinner service has begun, except for an emergency.)
- Should a lady urgently need to leave her table, she mustn't interrupt others during dinner. Thus she instructs her escort and the other nearby men to excuse her, but please not to stand. Her escort still rises to help slide her chair while the other men respect her request, ignore the distraction, and she inconspicuously slips away.
- Upon her return, her escort may choose to half rise or stand while he makes a courtesy gesture with his arm on her chair as she slips back into place. Other nearby gentlemen may also extend a half-rise courtesy.
- When a gentleman must leave the table, he quietly excuses himself and slips away at a convenient moment. No one stands for his departure or return.

Receptions and Parties

Acknowledgement of Hosts

- Receptions often have a receiving line where guests are greeted by hosts or dignitaries. Welcome acknowledgements and short introductions are made in reception lines, but lengthy conversations, which inconvenience everyone, are inappropriate.
- At parties, guests always seek out and speak to the hosts soon after arrival and before greeting or speaking to other guests, if possible.
- The hosts extend brief welcomes. Briefness is expected at large parties and open houses because the hosts have many other guests.
- Hosts and guests circulate at a large private party.
- Considerate guests spend a few moments with the hosts but never monopolize them or the guests of honor in lengthy conversations.
- Considerate guests circulate, mingle, and meet with many people. Eye contact, smiles, and proper and congenial conversation are important.
- At these types of parties, guests are expected to move freely in the common, public areas. You should train children not to explore private rooms or to open closed doors in a home.
- Guests leave near the specified time. Before leaving, each guest briefly thanks the hosts for the hospitality. Children should individually express their thanks as well.

- Arrive and depart at the given times. Open house events permit guests to come and go between designated times.
- After escorts assist ladies into the room and then away from the main traffic path, they help ladies remove coats and wraps before removing their own.
- The gentleman always offers his lady refreshments before getting his. The lady may choose to accompany him to the serving table.
- Hors d' oeuvres, finger foods, and dips are served with a small plate and a napkin, which should be used as intended.
- Use proper serving utensils for serving food. Do not use hands.
- Do not eat at the refreshment table. Take food or drink, and then find another place to stand, out of the way.
- Place dip on a plate. If plates are not provided, one dip only with a piece of uneaten food is permissible, but do not double dip.
- Toothpicks from food go on your plate. If there is no other convenient disposal, it may go in the napkin.
- Dispose of dirty plates and napkins only at a designated area, not on the main table.
- Don't take both plate and drink at the same time when standing to eat—it is awkward to handle both, especially when also meeting people and shaking hands.
- Don't talk with the mouth full.
- Use a napkin to blot mouth before taking a drink.
- Hold drink in left hand so right hand is free, warm, and dry.
- Remember polite body language: maintain good posture, stand straight, keep eye contact, and smile when visiting with other people.
- Always thank the hosts before leaving.
- Gentlemen retrieve coats and wraps.

Handshakes

Handshakes symbolize friendship, peace, and goodwill in social and business situations. Among men, shaking hands has been a time-honored tradition when meeting someone. Social handshakes occur during introductions, arrivals, and upon departures. (And "Let's shake on it," of course, signifies a friendly pact or agreement.)

The traditional rule for handshakes is that ladies are not obligated to shake hands, and men wait for a lady to first offer her hand before extending theirs. (Some protocol authors abandon this rule regarding handshakes between ladies and gentlemen, but most still acknowledge the option.) Likewise a younger lady waits for the older lady to offer her hand first. In any event, it is rude to refuse an extended hand, regardless of who offers the hand first.

How to shake hands:

1. Start with the hand extended, fingers together and thumb pointed up. Ladies and gentlemen may keep gloves on when shaking hands outdoors. The gentleman may remove his right hand glove when time allows or he wishes to do so.
2. Slide hands together until they meet at the base of the thumbs so the action will be a handshake and not a finger-shake.
3. Use enough pressure for a firm, confident shake, but not enough to cause discomfort. Gentlemen should refrain from bone- or ring-crushing grips when taking anyone's hand, but especially a lady's.
4. Handshakes are brief, lasting about three seconds with two or three up-and-down pumps. When trying to free your hand from someone who won't let go, try giving a final, stronger squeeze while increasing your eye contact. Then smile and withdraw your hand firmly so the other person knows it is time to stop.

Toasting

The glad custom of speaking kind words and raising a glass to a happy occasion or an honored person is known as *toasting*. The toast gives special recognition, best wishes, praise, or congratulations to the honoree. Some occasions for toasts are weddings, birthdays, anniversaries, bachelor parties, christenings, and engagements. Toasts are also in order at dinner parties or holiday feasts, and always make the occasion memorable.

A toast should be a very short speech of sincere and complimentary words. It may be humorous or serious, but never an embarrassment. Remember that the honoree is to be *honored* by your words. Don't use the occasion to score points for yourself, however subtly, at his or her expense. Don't turn a toast into a "roast."

When?

Toasts generally happen partway through or toward the end of festive celebrations, weddings, and special dinner or party occasions. At public dinners, such as a convention, toasts are proposed at the end of the meal, before guest speakers take the podium. The toastmaster (or master of ceremonies, aka emcee) generally proposes the first toast. Honored guests may propose the next toasts, but others in the large group audience do not. Toasting at a smaller informal dinner usually occurs anywhere from midway in the main course to after the main plate is removed, but before dessert is served, and may be proposed by anyone at dinner. One exception is when a toast is given as a welcome to a guest of honor. In that case a toast may be made at the beginning of dinner by the host. Guests rise only if the toaster stands.

Preparing for a Toast

Glasses are usually filled or refilled before the toast. Often champagne or other effervescent drink is poured, but any beverage is acceptable. Children and those who do not drink alcohol may raise a glass of juice, milk, or soda to join in the toast. After glasses are raised, a sip of the drink is taken. Standing toasts for high-ranking dignitaries, such as a country's president, are traditionally consumed until the glass is empty. In other instances, more than one toast may occur, so we keep our sips small.

Proposing a Toast

The gentleman proposing the toast first gains the attention of his group. If he is seated, he stands by his chair. In a large group he stands in a prominent location. He does not whistle or yell. He may *gently* tap his water glass once or twice to gain everyone's attention. This is a signal for group's attentive silence. He waits for everyone near him to look towards him.

After securing attention, the one proposing the toast stands with filled glass in hand, turns towards the person he wishes to honor, and speaks a few, sincere sentences. He then raises his glass towards the honoree. This signals everyone in the room, including young people, to raise their glass towards the honoree as the toaster raises his glass. People may quietly offer some polite response such as, "Hear, hear," "Cheers," or simply a nod in agreement as they lift their glasses. It is appropriate for gentlemen to rise as they raise their glasses to the honoree, although for informal toasts, when the host proposes the toast and remains seated, gentlemen do likewise. Ladies may remain seated in most instances. Again, high-ranking dignitaries receive standing toasts.

Length and Tone

I once read somewhere that "toasts are like a woman's skirt. They should be long enough to cover the subject, short enough to maintain interest, and always be in good taste." Succinctness eliminates the need for remarks to be read. Any prepared remarks are best not read because toasts should sound genuine; besides, reading prepared remarks indicates a lack of effort and sincere confidence which defeats the purpose of preparing them in the first place. Toasts should be succinct and sound spontaneous in delivery even when they have been prepared beforehand. When a person feels nervous about a toasting duty, such as at a wedding, then a prepared toast may reduce the jitters. It will likely contain additional sentiment due to the forethought, but again, deliver it naturally and do not read it.

Purpose and Content

A toast may be made to "health, wealth, or well being": "To your good health"; "Salud"; "To Bud—happy birthday! May you enjoy many more happy birthdays to come." It may also contain a few words of honor, praise, or recognition: "Your wonderful friendship is a blessing to all of us here."

Wordier toasts are permissible, but they should still be succinct in nature: "To Bud—happy birthday! You deserve the best of wishes. May your troubles be few, your blessings be more, and nothing but happiness come through your door."

Toasts are occasions to express thanks and may be made to more than one person: "To this happy occasion and to our hosts, Sharon and John—thank you for this fine evening, for your generous hearts, the wonderful food, warm fellowship, and loving friendship. You have enriched our hearts and souls."

Toasts can express appreciation as well as recognition: "To dear Nancy, without whom none of this is possible. Your encouraging words and caring friendship is a constant example to all of us, young and old. Here's to a wonderful person who brightens our days with her good words and deeds."

Toasts can express congratulations or best wishes for achievement or service: "To Donna—congratulations on another successful program. Your energetic dedication and talent has given us this unforgettable evening. Here's to our program's outstanding director."

Toasts may be witty and humorous. This example was reportedly given at dinner in the White House for Nobel Prize winners: "I think this is the most extraordinary collection of human talent and knowledge ever gathered here, with the possible exception of when Thomas Jefferson dined here alone." Another clever example: "May the winds of hardship and adversity follow you in life—but never catch up with you."

Clinking Glasses

The tradition of clinking glasses is accounted for by several theories, the first of which says that drinks transferred to another's glass by pouring with clinking sounds gave reassurance that beverages did not contain poison. Another account attributes the action to a medieval belief that alcohol contained "spirits" who were chased away at the sound of clinking. Today, touching glasses is symbolic of goodwill rather than safety.

Clinking glasses is one of those areas in protocol where we find conflicting opinions. First, in large groups, practicality dictates glasses are only raised towards the honored guest during a toast and not clinked together. People in small groups, conveniently situated near each other, may gently touch each other's glasses, but in doing so the glass rims should barely touch each other. When in doubt as to the host's preference, don't be the first one to clink. Follow the host's lead. A dear friend of mine and fellow protocol teacher made a good point when she once said, "I prefer not to have guests clink my Waterford crystal." Lastly, author John Bridges says that true gentlemen "will clink any other glass extended towards his." Of course, a true gentleman does so very carefully. And he doesn't throw the empty toasting glass down when finished. In all cases, raising a filled or partially filled glass is the accepted protocol—never raise an empty glass.

When a Toast is Given in Your Honor

When you receive a toast, remain seated and smiling. Do not take a sip of your drink. One does not drink a toast to oneself, though he may put a hand on his glass. Whether you receive a toast at the start of dinner or before dessert, it is proper to return the toast. After the toast, when all the others have taken a sip from their glasses, the honoree, if a gentleman, may rise and say "Thank you" with a few additional words. A lady returning a toast has the option of remaining seated, simply saying "thank you" with a smile, and raising her glass towards the group; or she may stand and give a reply if she wishes. In mixed company, ladies generally do not lead the way in proposing first toasts out of respect for the gentlemen present, but some circumstances today make this rule flexible.

Stepping Out: Theatre, Opera, Ballet, and Concerts

Adults attending live events such as plays, operas, ballets, and concerts usually take them seriously. They have purchased tickets and devoted their time to see a performance and they want to enjoy the event without distractions or rude behavior from others. This section provides tips for properly enjoying such events and allowing others to do so as well.

Tickets

Advance ticket purchase is wise in order to secure preferred dates and seating arrangements. The escort is responsible for holding the tickets, which he keeps in a convenient, safe pocket. Always double-check possession of the tickets before going out for the evening—few things spoil an evening more than missing an anticipated and possibly expensive event because tickets were forgotten at home.

Dress

Although a few people may dress improperly for live performances, it is still best to dress up and dress appropriately for plays and concerts. An evening event requires dressier clothes than a matinee, where daytime clothes are suitable. Day or evening, comfortable clothes are needed for sitting. Ladies avoid wearing very full dresses, hoops, or hats, all of which cause distraction or are difficult to maneuver in narrow seat aisles.

Arrive Early

Protocol stipulates early arrival for all live theatre productions. This protocol is different from home dinner party etiquette, which discourages guests from arriving early. At a theatre there are obvious advantages for early arrival even with reserved seats; young people especially may be unaware of this. Foremost, many theatres and concert halls do not allow seating after the performance begins, except during intermissions. Second, in dark theatres latecomers face a safety issue, as well as creating a disturbance that can distract the audience and performers. Third, an early arrival allows for relaxed entry to seats, reading the program with full lighting, and noting when the movements or breaks will be. It also makes the anticipation of the performance more enjoyable.

Should a late arrival be unavoidable, it is best (and often required) to wait for a natural break in the performance before entering. Even with the lights dimmed, late entry disturbs other people, and it is more challenging to find seats in the dark.

Ushers and Seating

Many production theaters have ushers to help with seat location. The escort shows the row tickets to him. The lady follows the usher, and the gentleman follows the lady. The lady enters the row first; gentlemen always take the outside seat. "Please" and "Thank you" are in order when ushers direct you to seats.

In the absence of ushers, the man leads the way to locate the seats and the lady follows. When they reach their row, the man steps aside to allow the lady to enter. When several couples have seats together, ladies follow the gentleman with the seats furthest into the row. If there are more than two couples, it is best to follow in order of seating, with those on inside seats going first. In this case, the gentleman with the farthest inside seat enters the row first.

If people are already seated in your row, you must pass in front of them. Traditional protocol suggests you face the people as you enter or slide pass. Some experts advocate facing the stage, but it is harder to see obstacles to avoid, and it is more pleasant to face others rather than turning your back on them. In either case, avoid bumping people and watch for feet to eliminate tripping. Also avoid bumping those in front of you. Of course, "Excuse me" and "Thank you" are spoken to those you pass or disturb.

If the performance has not started, then gentlemen should stand and lean against their folded seat when others enter the row to allow them to easily pass and reach their seats. When the aisle has enough room, ladies may turn sideways. Avoid causing people to step over your legs. When the performance is underway and there is room for people to easily pass, turn legs sideways so they may do so. If space is limited, you must stand and quickly sit down again so the people behind you can see.

If someone is seated in your seat, double-check your ticket first; then gentlemen may inquire politely as to their seat number. If there is a problem, the gentleman gets the usher while the lady waits to the side.

Basic Rules

- Keep ticket stubs for assigned seats.
- Sit straight and keep feet on the floor once seated.
- Show dignified, spontaneous laughter or surprise when appropriate.
- Applaud when appropriate (see section below).
- Use perfumes and colognes sparingly in case someone near you suffers from allergies.
- Show consideration for performers and those around you.
- Turn off audible rings on cell phones and beepers. Do not take calls during performances.
- Do not talk once the performance begins.

- Do not eat, drink, or chew gum while seated.
- Do not make noises such as rustling programs or lozenge wrappers.
- Do not cough or blow nose repeatedly; leave if you must do so.
- Do not talk during an overture.
- Do not leave the theatre during the performance.
- Do nothing that distracts others or the performers.
- Do not kick or bump the seats in front of you.
- Do not sprawl into your neighbor's territory.
- Do not obstruct your neighbor's view.
- Do not wear hats.

Handling Rude People

Most people are polite and often any rudeness is unintentional. If someone nearby causes a problem or distraction, give the situation a moment to change, then try to deal with it as quietly and politely as possible. Once, as people next to me kept talking loudly after a performance began, I waited a few moments but they failed to quiet down. I then glanced over at them, hoping they would take the hint to cease talking. They did not, so a moment later I quietly whispered in an unthreatening tone, "I'm sorry, but I can't hear when you are talking." They apologized and the problem vanished. If, however, a problem persists or the disturbance seems potentially threatening, the best solution is to call the usher or find another seat.

Emergencies

Just as leaving the table during dinner is impolite, it is rude and discourteous to leave during a performance. Intermissions are the appropriate time to leave a seat. If a departure is unavoidable, such as with uncontrollable coughing or something more serious, do so with a minimum of disturbance at a convenient break in the acts. Quietly say "Excuse me" as you quickly pass in front of others. Open the exit door as quickly and quietly as possible. Don't let it slam shut. Then wait to return until a break or intermission.

Intermissions

A person may remain in his seat or go to the lobby for intermission. Those in the lobby should return quickly when the signal is given. Intermission is a good time for refreshments, which may be offered in a lobby or reception area. This is also the appropriate time to use the restroom. Remind students to take care of this business *before* fetching refreshments. I also encourage them to do a mirror check of teeth and hair. Remind students not to linger so that they may return in a timely manner to their seats.

There will be a signal telling the audience when to return to their seats. The dimming of lights or ringing bells or chimes for symphonies is usually about five to seven minutes before the performance resumes.

Applause

Everyone knows what *clapping* is, but polite *applause* consists of holding one hand steady and semi-cupped while striking the other against it. Ladies use their finger tips to clap against the steady hand; gentlemen may use their entire hands. Of course you may clap heartily when you greatly enjoyed a performance, but avoid wild movements.

It is important to applaud at the correct times. At a play, the audience may applaud the opening of the curtain when the star first walks on the stage. Applause is generally withheld until the end of an act (rather than a scene) and of course at the end of the play or performance. When a guest soloist or conductor walks on stage, the general rule is to applaud their appearance. Jazz soloists are usually applauded after a solo within a longer piece of music.

The strictest applause rules apply at symphonies and other classical, chamber, or orchestra concerts. There is no applause between movements of a larger work. The conductor keeps his baton raised. At an opera, symphony, concert, or ballet the conductor is applauded as he takes his place on the podium and when he leaves. During operas, applause is usually given after an aria. Individual performers are not applauded when they come on the stage.

Be aware that there are also a few special traditions connected with certain works. For example, when attending a performance of Handel's *Messiah,* everyone in the audience stands for the "Hallelujah" chorus. These things are learned by experience and by following the lead of those around you.

At the conclusion of the evening, if you loved the performances give the performers a standing ovation. You do not have to applaud if you feel angry or insulted by the content or if you are displeased with the performance.

In musical performances, one encore is typical but two are rare. By the end of a long performance, the musicians (not to mention the audience!) need a rest, so requesting any more than two encores is inconsiderate.

Conclusion

The "Right Moves" session gives young people the tools they need for many social occasions, but there are other milestone occasions when young people need more specific training in what is expected from them. Balls, weddings, and funerals are three important areas in which children need very specific guidance and instruction before the event, but those are beyond our space limitations here. More exhaustive etiquette books such as those by Emily Post and Amy Vanderbilt contain helpful suggestions for these situations.

8

Public Appearance

Young people have a contagiously invigorating enthusiasm about a good appearance that makes them eager for training in dress protocol. The Rhetoric stage in classical Christian school protocol programs is devoted to teaching students how to act and appear in public by polishing their poise and self-presentation. This is a good time to further refine your teenager's manners at home, too.

Learning about styles, fashion, colors, and what is appropriate at different occasions intrigues most teenagers. Their natural interest and enthusiasm about personal appearance goes a long way toward their receptivity to dress standards. But this session is not simply about dressing, grooming, having fun, and looking good, but also how to do so *well*—that is, with decorum, discretion, and good taste. When approached in an upbeat manner, the subject of personal appearance is a joyful tonic for everyone. The class isn't only a tonic, though; it can be a remedy. Have you ever felt a pang of sadness when you observed the demeaning, immodest, or unnatural appearance of some poor teenager trying to be "cool?" Without direction, their enthusiasm goes astray and can manifest itself in some strange ways, often to their detriment.

We adults should embrace our children's enthusiasm, for it provides us with an opportunity to train them in their Christian responsibility to dress appropriately and thoughtfully—in manner worthy of their calling. The goal of this subject is to equip young people with some practical instruction in how to perform their responsibilities well and to live circumspectly, right down to the color of socks they wear. Our manner of dress is one way of expressing and giving form to the magnificent content of our life in Christ.

Of the various protocol sessions, however, "Dressing for the Occasion" is the one with most potential to ruffle a few feathers. If this occurs, parents and teachers need to realize that most objections—if there are any—are not serious threats, just disturbed consciences. Any ruffled feathers are usually caused by a couple of basic issues, which we need to approach with a good sense of biblical balance. They mostly originate from a bit of defensiveness about immodesty, insecurity about looking "uncool," or the almighty right to "do my own thing." We've all heard people insist, "Well, I'm dressing for *me*—if others don't like the way I look, tough! That's their problem, not mine."

Many teenagers (as well as some adults) who are still developing discernment do not understand the difference between good, bad, and ugly. Then, too, we live in a generation increasingly preoccupied with our own "rights" more than personal responsibility and duty towards others, and this self-centeredness carries into the realm of fashion. Impressionable teenagers have all manners of opinion about what they should or shouldn't wear, and influences from peers, marketing ploys, and the entertainment world add to the confusion. The result is that too many young people do not know how to dress appropriately for different occasions. Party dress is not the same as school wear, and day clothes are far different than "after-five" fashions. Regardless of fashion trends, denim is casual and satin is formal.

Far too many parents remain ignorant or silent about the importance and rules of dress, so misguided voices fill the void and bully aside respectful social duty and reasonable restraints imposed by dress standards. Many trendsetters frequently fall short in aesthetics and good taste, ignoring or mixing and matching categories at whim, without regard for propriety and occasion. Children are not immune to these voices or influences. Christian principles, though, will protect and add beauty to our children's wardrobe. How wonderful that this class has the ability to ruffle and rearrange little feathers into a lovelier image, promoting good public appearance!

Ignorance about appropriate dress standards and a nice public appearance show up in the most unexpected ways. I was reminded of this when I once saw a large professional wedding portrait. The bride had her back to the camera. Her tight, white bridal dress was cut so low in the back it nearly reached below her waistline. She was posed to cast a sidelong glance towards her father, who with his shotgun pursued a reluctant runaway groom.

This marriage photo illustrates poor taste and a faulty understanding of good conduct and culture. Today far too many youth are poorly trained, like this young couple who clearly lacked proper parental instruction. In fact, parents are often the ones promoting indecency. Obviously, our era of abundant wealth and satin gowns is no guarantee for good taste.

Misunderstood and forgotten standards need recovery. Many protocol traditions developed from gentler times when people more artfully considered and maintained Christian principles. Such principles are too important to be forgotten or ignored by a society that desires beauty, decency, and order. Standards do not nullify or compete with fashion changes and design savvy; it compliments them, guiding and challenging styles to offer appropriate beauty in new ways. Beautiful standards encourage good grooming and honorable dress. Demeaning clothes, reflective of low standards, have no legitimate place in the Christian closet.

Personal Grooming: The Proper Foundation

A training session in public appearance and appropriate dress is a welcome remedy with practical helps that offer a lifetime of benefits to its students. However, training in public appearance is incomplete for younger students if it neglects instruction for good grooming. The old adage "Cleanliness is next to godliness" reminds us that good grooming habits are not only crucial to appearance; they reflect on our character as well. As one writer stated, and almost every protocol authority agrees, "Without good grooming, nothing is fashionable or right."

A good public appearance involves more than merely looking good or wearing the right clothes. It goes beyond style. Good grooming is foundational. It is included as part of protocol training because dirty ears and messy clothes don't bother young children (and some older ones)—good grooming is not something they learn on their own. They need to be taught how to properly care for their growing bodies and how to maintain their clothes. Please don't assume that your older children or teenagers automatically understand good grooming basics—they don't. I recently heard a college student describe his dorm living conditions as "rancid" because his sports-active roommate neglected showering—sometimes for more than a week. This fellow didn't realize the necessity of frequent showers, if only for the sake of those a nose away.

This section has suggestions for children and young teenagers. Lessons best begin early in childhood at home. Of course many conscientious moms and dads provide basic grooming instruction at home, but not all homes are created equal. For whatever reason, some children reach teenage years without grooming instruction, and others seem to develop memory lapses around the junior high years, so this class is more necessary than you might expect.

Two- and three-year-old children can learn basic grooming habits. Bath time is the obvious place to start. Fortunately, most youngsters love baths and showers. Toddlers can learn to wash head to toe, pat dry in upward motions, brush teeth regularly, wash hands after using the toilet, and place their dirty clothes in a designated basket or hamper. As a part of his toilet training our grandson learned to avoid soiling the toilet rim and to put the seat back down as a courtesy to the ladies in his family. He needed a few gentle reminders, but by the time he was three, the habit was formed and the ladies were pleased. Washing his face and hands before meals also became routine business.

Twelve- to fifteen-year-olds, in transition from childish interests to more mature ones, are also dealing with rapidly changing bodies. Experience proves that a short grooming lesson for this age group is time well spent. Reminders to bathe regularly, keep hair and nails clean, brush teeth three times a day, and keep clothes neat and clean are essential. In a group program, offer separate classes to young men and young ladies so that specific issues can be discussed in a more free and dignified way. For home lessons, too, remember that boys' and girls' needs are different—mom is usually best suited to instruct daughters, dad to instruct older sons.

For program classes, the director might consider having some how-to information presented by a special guest speaker. As a highlight for one group of girls, I arranged for a friend who sells cosmetic products to give a demonstration of facials, manicures, and makeup tips. In another class for older girls, arrangements were made with parental permission to travel to a local beauty school for facials, manicures and hairstyle advice. This activity usually takes a full afternoon. It is not always possible, but when it can be arranged it is a great success.

Ideally, the young men's instructor in a school grooming program is a mature gentleman, but this is not always possible. Certainly a woman with maturity and expertise can also do the job, but talks on masculine subjects like proper shaving techniques and tie knots have greater authenticity when they come from a seasoned gentleman whose knowledgeable involvement also provides a manly example and shows that grooming sessions are not just for girls.

Whether you are a parent teaching your children at home or a teacher with a roomful of students, you can cover most of grooming basics in an hour or so. The library is full of books with additional information on manicures, pedicures, make up and good grooming tips. Demonstrations are helpful in this very basic class. Grooming guidelines cover proper bath and shaving techniques, body odor solutions, and how-to tips for nail, hair, and facial care. Everyone appreciates information tailored to their needs. Handouts and short demonstrations, such as overviews of professional manicures, are helpful aids. Instruction tailored to your young people's needs is what is important. For example, when several students have acne problems, offer ideas for proper diet and skin care.

Teach the basics from head to toe. I particularly like, and have adopted, Emily Hunter's quiz approach in my grooming classes, combining a handout quiz with other grooming information. After students have filled out the quiz, we go through the list together. Students need not share answers or scores. This method quickly conveys information, as well as individual progress, in a comfortable and relaxed manner. I always add some humor with this subject and incorporate lessons into the answer review, which puts my students at ease. Following is the quiz format I use to introduce grooming and certain manners to young teenagers who may or may not need training in this area. You never know whether certain points are needed or not until after it is administered. Many times students have approached me and said, "I never knew that," or "Will you please talk more about bathing and deodorants? So-and-so smells bad and I want him to get the point." You can count on this age group to be honest and enjoy learning facts.

Junior Protocol Personal Care Quiz. We have all seen people whose manners and grooming hurt their public appearance. Here's a quiz to check grooming, attitude and appearance. Check through these questions to see how you are doing. How do you look? How are your manners?

1. Am I clean and well groomed when I go to school or out in public?
2. Do I bathe or shower, using soap, once a day?
3. Do I keep my nails clean?
4. Do I wash my face morning and evening?
5. Do I use deodorant regularly?
6. Do I remember to bathe or shower after vigorous activities?
7. Do I keep my hair clean and shampooed frequently?
8. Do I brush my teeth two to three times daily?

9. Do I use mouthwash when I have eaten food with strong odors?
10. Do I shave as needed?
11. Do I keep my clothes clean, neat, and wrinkle-free?
12. Do I wear clean white, or are my clothes or collars dingy white?
13. Do I prepare my clothes for special occasions a day or two in advance?
14. Do I put on fresh underwear daily and for special occasions?
15. Do I tuck all tags and facings inside my garment?
16. Do I replace missing buttons or repair torn spots on my clothes?
17. Do I clean and polish my dress shoes prior to wearing them?
18. Do I allow plenty of time to get ready?
19. Do I speak too loudly with others in public?
20. Do I scratch my head or body in public? Do I play with my hair?
21. Do I pull or tug at my clothes or undergarments?
22. Do I pick my teeth in public or carry a toothpick in my mouth?
23. Do I extract an undesirable object from my mouth with my fingers?
24. Do I stand or walk pigeon-toed?
25. Do I bite my nails? Do I chip at my nails?
26. Do my legs go all directions and "spraddle" when I sit? Do I slouch?
27. Do I pick at my face, nose, or ears?
28. Do I try to bring attention to myself most of the time?
29. Do I hold a grudge if someone offends me?
30. Do I sulk and pout? Or lose my temper?
31. Do I remember to say "Please" and "Thank you"?
32. Do I whine and complain?
33. Do I interrupt others when they are speaking?
34. Do I try to make the best of even difficult or unpleasant situations?
35. Do I crowd or push?
36. Do I purposely spit, burp, or make other embarrassing noises?
37. Do I leave the room if I have a gas attack?
38. Do I try to be helpful to others?
39. Do I talk with food in my mouth?
40. Do I tilt back on my chair?
41. Do I carefully hang my good clothes up when finished with them?
42. Do I launder my clothes after I wear them?
43. Do I check myself in a full mirror before leaving the house?

Rating yourself: Score 40–43 correct answers: Congratulations. Keep it up. 30–39 correct answers: Good. You're getting there, but have some rough edges. 0-29 correct answers: Stay awake—you need this class.

Preparation and Time Management

Another tool I offer freshman and sophomore students is a handout on time management for their notebooks, which helps them achieve punctuality without a stressful last minute rush. Some students don't know what is involved in getting ready to arrive on time for a big event. Other ideas and approaches exist for time management, but this is a useful example. Whether or not this is part of your home or school program depends on your students and their needs. The following section is taken from the suggestions I hand out to students to help them prepare for the big night.

Preparation Handout: As Christians we hope to please Christ in everything that we do—that includes our appearance and our comings and goings. "Whatsoever you do, do all to the glory of God" (I Cor. 10:31). We do not have to "dress down" or be dowdy. Nor do we need to overdress. We can enjoy the beauty of good design and colors. Christians should dress with good taste and discretion (I Tim. 2:9–10). Our manner of dress is important; it says something about us as people.

Months to Weeks before the Event

- **Plan far ahead.** Decide what you will wear for our special dinner event as early as possible. Shop for semiformal attire or suits well in advance for good selection and budget savings. Early decisions about clothes will save you time and money.
- **Choose appropriate clothes. Dress for the occasion.** Styles and fads come and go, so consider flattering fashions with classic styling: "Be not the first by whom the new is tried, / Nor yet the last to lay the old aside" (Alexander Pope). Choose some trends and ignore others. Don't be afraid to reject styles that compromise your standards. Decide on a complimentary style and what works best for your body shape. The dinner party is a time to dress up. Base your decision for your outfit on the event's degree of formality. Invitations usually state the degree of formality in attire: casual, business, after-five, semi-formal or formal attire. It is generally better to underdress one category down in formality rather than overdress for an event. This is why the basic black business suit and dress are popular—they easily move up or down a category with the right accessories. Party dresses and semiformal attire are appropriate for our upcoming dinner evening. Among high school guys, this usually means a dark suit or sports coat, tie, and slacks. For girls, it generally means fancy tea-length or ankle

dresses with high heels. Shorter, fancy party dresses and after-five clothes (not floor length) are also perfect ladies' apparel for this special evening out.

- **Avoid Extremes.** Extremely short dresses and skirts, extremely low-cut necklines, and strapless dresses are not always in good taste or practical. Neither are wild, brightly colored suits for men.
- **Jacket or coat.** A ski coat or parka is wrong for dressy or semiformal occasions. A shawl, wrap, beaded sweater, dressy jacket or long dress coat is appropriate. Borrow one if you don't own one. Consider putting an evening shawl or jacket on your "wish list" for Christmas or birthday. A gentleman's suit jacket, with or without a vest, will be sufficient unless the weather is extremely cold, in which case he may also want to wear a dark dress coat (usually knee-length) and gloves. Escorts may need to provide an umbrella.
- **Hosiery.** Ladies need a slip, sandal-toe panty hose, and dress shoes. If you wear an open-toed shoe, current trends allow for perfectly groomed feet without hosiery. If you think you will be cold, wear seamless hosiery designed for sandals. Ladies should also carry a small evening bag, preferably with a chain, shoulder strap, or handle. Short gloves are optional. Gentlemen need dark, mid-calf dress socks (also known as hosiery) and black dress shoes.
- **Jewelry.** Ladies must decide beforehand what jewelry they want to wear. Pearls are always appropriate for young ladies. Slightly larger-scale jewelry is acceptable for evening events.
- **Hair.** Decide which hairstyle compliments your face and outfit. For ladies, an "up-do" is always appropriate for special evenings, and special hair accessories may be worn. Keep in mind you may need to make an appointment days in advance if the event is on a busy night. Gentlemen also should schedule any necessary haircuts for several days ahead of the event—do not wait until the last minute.
- **Small talk forethought.** Take a few moments to think about subjects for your conversations. Be well-informed about local, national, and international current events.

Several Days before the Event

- Make sure you have ample grooming supplies at home. Avoid last minute runs to the store for items like hairspray or aftershave lotions.
- If you want your skin to look its best, avoid chocolate, sodas, and greasy foods for several days before the event. Drink more water.

The Day before the Event

- Have all your clothes clean and ready to wear. It's wise to try on your outfit again to make sure everything fits and hangs properly.
- Press any clothes so they are ready to put on tomorrow.
- If you do your own hair, depending on your hair type and schedule, this might be the best day to shampoo your hair.
- This is the best day to trim and manicure your nails.
- Again, think about who will be at the event and what good topics of conversation would be appropriate.
- Ladies, place these items in your small evening bag: a cloth hanky, your lipstick, a small mirror, small comb (if you need one), and several quarters and a dollar bill (and/or phone card) for emergencies.
- Gents, place a clean, pressed handkerchief in your suit pocket. Is your tie wrinkle- and spot-free?
- Don't stay up late. Make sure that you get a full night's sleep so you won't be tired for the special event.

The Day of the Event

- Enjoy a nourishing breakfast. Avoid excess sugar throughout the day.
- Shampoo your hair early (if not done yesterday).
- Ladies, touch up your nails—a top coat freshens your polish.
- Ladies, about two to two and a half hours before you are to depart, shower or bathe. Gents can wait as long as an hour before, but no later. Use lotion on your arms and legs. Use moisturizer on your face. Apply deodorant. Do not use perfume or shaving lotion for deodorant. Avoid antiperspirants. Put on fresh undergarments, but don't dress yet. Save your outfit for the last item. Gents, wait to put on your suit jacket until ready to leave.
- Ladies, about an hour before you need to go out the door, apply makeup if your parents approve. Brighter makeup is best for night.
- Finish hair.
- Dress about thirty to forty-five minutes before you are to leave.
- Check your appearance in a full-length mirror. Ask your parents how you look. You should now be on time. Of course, your folks will want to take pictures.
- Enjoy your friends and the event. Have fun!

Dressing for the Occasion

Dressing correctly for any occasion has obvious benefits, the foremost being practical and aesthetic *appropriateness.* Classes about dress etiquette and categories promote appropriate choices for different situations, which in turn create responsible attitudes about public appearance. Young people reap lifelong benefits in how they look and how they are treated by others when they dress respectfully and responsibly. As in everything, teachers and parents must set good examples as they impart information about public appearance.

After this class, no one can realistically say, "Clothes are not important," or "Hey, times have changed; categories have relaxed, so it doesn't matter what I wear," or "I have the right to wear what I want whenever I want." The other extreme of prideful overdress or outlandish attention-grabbing garb should also be discouraged. As John Calvin once pointed out, "Where is our gratitude towards God for clothing, if we admire ourselves and despise others because of our own sumptuous apparel? Where is it, if we prepare ourselves for unchastity, with the elegance and beauty of our dress?" This builds upon Peter's exhortation to develop the imperishable inner qualities of a gentle and quiet spirit rather than mere external adornments (I Pet. 3:4). Such exhortations do not, however, mean that we should avoid nice clothes; those who embrace extremes dig a hole for themselves. This class keeps our children on level ground. Pitfalls are less appealing to young people who have been taught how to dress correctly.

Dressing for the occasion involves appropriateness, personal style, dress codes, thoughtful savvy, and budget. Appropriateness obviously involves occasion, modesty or decency, age, and place—fussy overdress is as wrong as sloppy indifference or attempts to look strange or outlandish. Basic dress codes provide safe general perimeters fitting to function and occasion, but confident personal styles are trickier and take time and maturity to develop, regardless of quirky fashion trends. The same styles do not look good on everyone. Flattering personalized styles, fitting for the occasion and respectful of dress codes, are important. Frumpiness is not flattering and neither is immodesty. Thoughtful savvy includes awareness of trends, discernment in designs, modesty, and cultivated taste, balanced by respect for dress codes and an ability to say no to the trend when necessary. This respect isn't bound by rigidity but adapts to personal style and preferences, considering appropriateness and budget as well.

Young people need to know about boundaries. They often recognize fads, but know little about criteria for what is lovely, flattering, or appropriate—and when. When dress codes and categories are understood, it's easier to apply the higher standards. In this class, it's best to start with categories that pertain to student lifestyle and activities. Practical training provides good standards that eliminate confusion about what to wear when. This prepares students for a life filled with subtle distinctions and statements in dress. It also helps them to plan a versatile wardrobe that will allow them to participate comfortably in life's various occasions—unwise or faddish purchases are hard on the budget and limit wardrobe versatility.

Because life is so multifaceted, filled with a variety of occasions, a person's wardrobe has many needs. Common sense dress codes take this into account. Different activities require certain attire, suitable to the situation. As obvious as it might seem, some students do not realize that certain occasions are more special than others, and that dress codes respect and reflect this fact. This is why young men need dress shoes, as well as a dark sports coat and dress slacks, or dark suit, in their wardrobe, and why young ladies need a party dress and nice daytime outfits. Dress protocol matters, helping our children move confidently into the arena of adult life.

When young people discover that clothes (and grooming) fit into distinct categories for specific times, they avoid mistakes like dyeing their hair blue or wearing a sweatsuit to a wedding. Good training means closets are wisely stocked with several versatile outfits and accessories. This affects wardrobe planning and budget. It requires quite a bit of valuable time to locate versatile items that compliment budget, lifestyle, and different figure types.

Lastly, this session's training offers important psychological support to our teenagers when they shop. Some young people (even girls) do not have mothers who shop with them. Numerous young ladies have mentioned their discouragement when they try to find clothes becoming to a virtuous woman. This class provides encouragement, direction, and accountability.

In order to help students begin thinking about dress categories, the following questions encourage a thoughtful approach to wardrobe selection, rather than a simple reaction to store displays or temporary fads. Thus inappropriate choices and shopping mistakes are more easily avoided. Ask students to consider the following points:

- What type of clothing best accompanies this occasion or activity? Sporty? Casual? Dressy? Informal? Formal?
- When will this event happen, in the daytime or the evening?
- Did my invitation specify a dress requirement, such as "white tie" or "black tie"? What category of attire do the hosts expect or desire guests to wear?
- In what season of year does the event happen? What are the weather possibilities? (Coats and jackets should be in the same category as the outfit. A formal event in the winter necessitates a formal jacket or dress coat.)
- What is considered customary or proper in this region or locality? What dress codes apply?
- What current styles best fit my figure type?
- Will I outgrow my clothes in the next few years?
- Does this garment look good on my body type and fit me properly? Do I need a size larger or smaller for a better fit?
- What is my budget? What style is the best choice for my budget? Trendy? Classic? Is this a garment I will wear often? If not, should I buy a classic style so I will be able to wear this more than once in the future?
- Does the garment show quality construction? Will it last?
- How will this garment perform or function for the event? Is the fit comfortable?
- What will the outfit say about me as a person? Is it appropriate for my age?

Most of these questions have obvious answers. Function, however, is an aspect that is not always considered. In order for clothes to be suitable they must function well, and comfortably, for their intended purpose. Some examples:

- In sportswear, an athlete considers the performance of his clothes for the competitive edge.
- A casual picnic requires comfortable clothes for bending and sitting. Durable clothes that aren't ruined by grass stains are the best choice.
- For a formal ball, a full-skirted gown is better than a slim, tighter fitting gown so that dance steps remain unhindered.
- An excessively low-cut or strapless gown can prove to be an unsuitable choice for several reasons. On the dance floor, it may mar a young lady's poise since she has to constantly tug at her dress to keep it in place. Such dresses may also fail the criteria for those concerned about

modesty. As one protocol teacher said, "Strapless gowns for dinner can leave a young lady looking somewhat undressed when all that shows above the centerpiece on the table are her head, neck, and bare shoulders." Strapless dresses do not belong at the dinner table without a jacket, just as a shirtless young man does not. And, practically speaking, the lady will face shivers and goose bumps if the temperature in the building is too low.

- Comfort is an important aspect of function. This is why men should avoid one hundred percent polyester suits—it is too hot and uncomfortable. The new microfibers and blends are a great improvement, and many are wrinkle resistant.

Sense and sensibility matter in dress. Good instruction at home or school broadens the common sense approach to clothes selection. There is more to wardrobe purchases than impulse buying. After one dress class, several high school young ladies sensibly passed over trendy, colorful, semiformal dresses and instead opted for versatile, tasteful, basic black party dresses that would offer future wear in classic style. Their dollar-wise choices will serve well for years to come.

Dress codes underscore appropriateness. Most people recognize that pajamas are not appropriate for shopping, but there are less obvious distinctions that our young people need to learn. For example, a girl might wear capris or stretch pants when going to the mall or grocery store on a quick errand, but she would not wear these same "everyday" pants to a morning shower brunch because the shower represents a special occasion in honor of another. A fellow might wear khaki cargo shorts and football shirt to a friend's house, but not to a funeral. Our children don't know about appropriate dress if we don't tell them. One university student once said to me, "I feel like my generation has been robbed because no one told us about these things until now." Despite initially feeling left behind, she now pursues appropriateness and excellence in her appearance and will never be among the ignorant persons whose appearance leaves us with a sense of sadness and loss.

Dress Categories

The categories that are most applicable to students' immediate situations are the best place to start. Usually this means beginning with instruction in casual and dressy party categories. The first protocol events should be dressy or semiformal. It is good when students realize that their casual clothes are distinctly different than other dress categories. Following is some information and descriptions from my classes. I discuss the basics, but please know that additional information is available beyond that given here.

Casual

The casual category represents clothes designed for relaxed, unceremonious public outings, events, and sports, as well as common domestic situations. Casual clothes are those ordinary, comfortable garments worn for many informal common activities. These are generally the kinds of comfortable clothes we might wear at home and for certain informal school events, sports, or errands. They are less dressy outfits with several subcategories, including leisure, home wear, active wear, and the closely related area of sportswear. Casual dressing certainly does *not* include soiled clothes, disheveled appearance, poor posture, inconsiderate manners, or sloppy habits.

Casual clothes include daytime apparel such as tee shirts, plaid shirts, polo sports shirts, sweatshirts, jeans, and shorts. Denim skirts, blue jeans, windbreakers, capri and cargo pants are current typical casual styles. Materials typically used for casual garments include cotton, terrycloth, denim, synthetic blends, nylon, polyester, and other washable, durable fabrics. Textures, such as knit and twills, are generally heavier than those used in the finer fabrics in dressier categories.

This broad range of common-sense styles highlights comfort and function, whether at home or outdoors. If we receive an invitation to an afternoon "tailgate" party or picnic, then jeans, capris, or Bermuda type shorts (depending on weather) with casual tops and comfortable shoes are appropriate. Guests would not overdress by wearing a semiformal or suit. Young ladies would not wear high-heeled shoes. If the invitation is for a hike in the mountains, then everyone's sensible choice would be layered casual wear—probably jeans, a tee shirt, a warm top, and sturdy shoes with heavy socks.

However, if the invitation specifies luncheon at a restaurant, ladies and gentlemen avoid ordinary casual attire. Clothes from the daywear category would be the better choice because the restaurant occasion is more "ceremonious" than most outdoor picnics, barbeques, or tailgate parties. If the luncheon were informal and "non-ceremonious," khaki slacks and a collared or polo shirt would generally be appropriate for a gentleman. The more special, "formal," or business-related the event is, the more dignified the attire. Casual clothes are for ordinary, less important events.

Clothes must match the occasion and respect the host's expectations.

Sometimes, an occasion throws us a curve. My husband and I once received an interesting invitation for a dinner party in a vineyard garden that included a five-course catered dinner and featured a presentation of private reserve wines. The stated dress code was "casual elegance." This didn't really mean the "casual" we have been discussing here. It meant that ladies wear comfortable, but elegant, skirts or slacks with low heels. Gentlemen could opt for a summer sports coat and optional tie, but in any case, his clothes need to be very nice. Suitable fabrics for this special soiree would include linens or silks, because they fall into an elegant category yet provide casual summer comfort. The "casual" on this invitation did not refer to daily, ordinary casual clothes, but to comfortable, "elegant" attire suitable for this special occasion and outdoor dining. We had to decipher the proper dress not just from the stated code, but from the type of event.

Normally, the casual category includes a spectrum of clothes suitable for various activities. Active wear, sportswear, and at-home leisure clothing are subcategories of casual wear, and the occasion dictates when to wear each. While most of us don't wear gym clothes at home, adaptable sweatsuits cross over into at-home wear because they are comfortable. Casual leisure wear or at-home clothes cannot be worn everywhere, because they are mainly suitable for chores and relaxing in private.

Sports attire is a generic term for very casual garments, some quite general in function, and others designed for specific sports. Dress codes apply to many sports. An invitation to the tennis club, for example, requires court clothes and tennis shoes with soles that won't mar the court floor. Sportswear appropriateness is as limited as general casual wear. Sweats are not proper for all events, even when casual. Sweats and workout gear are worn where they belong: in a gym or sports-related event—not at church, in an airport, and rarely for a quick errand. True, designers occasionally put forward some "dressier" sweatsuits, court clothes, and jogging suits, but their application remains limited. Sometimes specific sportswear, such as the golf or polo shirt, achieves classic status and makes a transition into a dressier application.

Swimsuits are a subcategory of casual sports clothes. Because they are specifically designed for the beach or pool, not the mall or restaurants, cover-ups are needed when leaving the pool or water area. Like most sportswear, swimsuits are designed for their specific athletic activity. There are, however, variations. I recently saw a pretty swimsuit lightly studded with rhinestones. Here's where discretion and personal style prevail, because on the right person, at the right resort pool, the sparkly swimsuit might be appropriate. The same suit for a high school girl in a swim meet would be overdoing it.

Outdoor activities require common-sense attire fitted to the function. Boats require rubber-soled deck shoes and water-repellent windbreakers. Depending on the boat size and event, a different set of codes can exist. Cruise attire is different than clothes for ordinary boating or fishing activities. It's easy to identify casual clothes as the plainer, tougher, everyday, practical, washable garments. They are comfortable clothes most appropriately worn around home or at a friend's house. They are easily maintained and do not require dry cleaning or much ironing.

Daywear

Daywear is another practical category for young people to understand. Although they often have some familiarity with daywear, I usually focus on this category in the last two years of the protocol program, with older students who already thoroughly understand the casual and semiformal categories. Daywear is a broad category of apparel that includes clothes worn outside the home for a wide range of mostly informal daytime activities between the hours of 8 A.M. and 5 P.M. It generally denotes nicer garments than casual clothes, but less dressy than party or semiformal attire. Daywear is clothing that a person wears to school, work, day events, shopping, meetings, luncheons, appointments, and other outings and activities outside the house. Clothes are always clean and fresh —rumpled, soiled, or tattered is not attractive.

Daywear includes various types of men's pants, slacks, shirts, sport coats, and suits, as well as women's slacks, blouses, suits, and dresses. Versatile daywear is, with its nicer fabrics and styles, generally dressier than casual, at-home leisurewear, sportswear, or work uniforms. Some nicer casual wear may, however, make an acceptable transition into a casual daywear category.

Metropolitan daywear dress codes for women encourage dresses, suits, skirts (from flared to thin pencil styles), tailored blouses, sweaters, pantsuits, and nice slacks as all being acceptable, multipurpose daywear. Some dresses and suits, by fabric, style, color, and accessories, qualify as a dressier daywear appropriate for church and special occasions. Daywear in rural or smaller towns customarily includes nicer casual skirts or slacks, top, and a jacket or sweater, in addition to dresses, as acceptable lady's attire for meetings and get-togethers. Plain silver or gold and trendy jewelry fits comfortably in this category. Bright bangles, sequins, and shiny rhinestones do not belong here; reserve them for dressier categories.

Gentlemen's daywear includes various types of shirts, from polo or golf styles (usually without a club insignia) to button-down long- or short-sleeved shirts, slacks or khakis (not jeans), sweaters, sports jackets, dark shoes, and dark socks. Brown shoes are in the informal daywear category. Summertime grants debonair men the opportunity to wear spectator shoes and leather closed-toe sandals (open-toe sandals are casual). Men usually wear a belt matching their shoe color. Light-colored slacks made of materials such as cotton, synthetic blends, twills, rayon, or microfibers with a short-sleeved cotton shirt generally denote more informal daywear; linens and wools are on the dressier end of men's daywear. (Shorts do not belong in the daywear category; they are casual). The occasion dictates when a tie is required in the daytime category. Basically daytime clothes represent a presentable, dressier "together" look not attained with casual, at-home clothes.

Daywear colors always reflect changing palettes dictated by fashion trends, but generally lighter, brighter colors dominate the daytime category. In cooler seasons, deeper blacks, midnight navy, and winter whites prevail over lighter navy blues and summer whites. Some designers dispute limiting summer white clothes from early spring (on Easter or after May first) to early fall (Labor day), but common sense tells us that bright whites look best in warm weather. Summer color rules vary in temperate regions, with styles and times, but refined, polite society generally observes traditional codes of lighter tones in summer, deeper tones in winter. Darker colors and black move in and out of daytime vogue, but fashion experts generally favor deeper hues for evening affairs and winter months.

Resort clothes can go under casual or daywear categories, and are often brighter and flashier than regular casual sportswear or daywear. Designers sometimes blur boundaries with the addition of sparkling beads, bobbles, or rhinestone details on daywear and even casual clothes. For example, a lady's tee shirt from a resort collection may have lace or beaded accents. Simple Bermuda shorts and a camp-style shirt might be constructed of silk fabric with embroidered details, while a man's basic camp shirt may appear in a colorful silk print.

Shoe colors for men and women are generally as dark as, or darker than, their outfit. White shoes rarely flatter any adult foot, and are mainly worn only in spring and summer months. Hosiery for men matches their slacks. For ladies, light to suntan sheer colors in pantyhose are best with most outfits, except black. Current fashion trends accept tanned, bare legs, with perfectly pedicured feet and no hosiery, for toeless sandals and mules in warmer weather. When pantyhose are worn with sandals, they must be the seamless "sandal toe" style.

Generally all daywear, along with its several subcategories, is nicer than any casual wear. Regular daywear fabrics are mostly practical and comfortable. Some are washable; others must be dry-cleaned. They include cotton, wool, synthetic blends, rayon, microfibers, knit, leather, linens, and tweeds. Tailored slacks, skirts, sweaters and dresses, even in heavier fabrics, are usually considered regular daywear.

Different types of daywear exist for both men and women, ranging from business dress to clothes suitable for an afternoon party or special event. The latter is distinct and dressier, than clothes worn for shopping or a meeting. Clothes worn to church are different, and dressier, than clothes worn to school. Young people benefit from a general understanding about daywear differences. Students can distinguish daywear subcategories by noting fabric and style, which are indicators of suitability. Suitability depends on the importance of the event and the locality.

In protocol classes, further description, comparisons, magazine illustrations or photos, and a "trunk show" with example garments and fabrics will help students recognize subcategory differences. For example, a lady's simple, cotton, knee-length, beige chemise or sheath dress is not the same as a sateen, tea-length, afternoon party dress, or a beige sailcloth skirt, or a crepe suit, or gabardine pleated pants. Yet all are daywear. Each garment is suitably different for various daytime occasions. If that same cotton sheath dress has simple lace trim, or the cotton fabric is eyelet, it could serve for dressier functions, such as a special luncheon or shower, but it still keeps its designation within the daytime boundary. If the color of the cotton sheath is black and the details fancy, the dress could make a suitable transition into the dinner hour but it is not suitable for black-tie affairs.

Fabrics and design indicate importance and suitability in daywear. Cotton is a versatile textile used in both casual and daywear categories. Even finer cottons, such as Egyptian or Sea Island cottons, unless polished, remain in casual and less dressy daywear categories. (One exception, for men, is fine cottons used in evening shirts). Slacks made of sailcloth are heavy and casual, but sailcloth in a skirt moves up into the daywear category suitable for shopping and informal meetings. Crepe is appropriate for special daytime events that require a dressier, elevated tone.

While cotton is a common fabric seen in many casual clothes, a chemise or sheath style dress isn't the casual type of garment most ladies wear around the house. The cotton sheath is dressier than a lady's pleated gabardine slacks because it is a dress. Yet, the slacks are also considered daywear, not casual, because of their style and fabric. Daytime materials are finer than casual denim or twills. The tailored slacks, with the right accessories, are suitable for daytime informal get-togethers or meetings.

A man could wear a black polo shirt with beige slacks in the daytime for an informal meeting or appointment. If he pairs this outfit with a tweed sports coat, it becomes dressier, but the tweed fabric still signifies daywear. If he pairs the same slacks with a dark worsted wool blazer, button down shirt and tie, his outfit moves up a notch into the professional business category. It may even be suitable for dinner.

Nice jeans for men or women may, in some regions, qualify as casual daywear by their color and/or by adding a sweater or blazer and accessories to "dress" up the jeans, but by their nature they remain casual. Jeans remain in the practical and functional casual category. They are not "Sunday best" clothes. (This surprises those who mistakenly consider jeans to be so classic and versatile that they can fit into all categories of dress.) Men's dark sports coats, nice dress slacks and tailored suits are versatile and dressy daywear garments. Ties are worn for the dressiest daytime affairs.

Now let's look at some of the specific, special-purpose subcategories of daywear.

Business Dress. After several years of high school protocol classes, senior students appreciate the additional category of business dress. It can be introduced just as they prepare to enter college life and/or the workplace. This category is not meant for younger students, who need to learn about other categories more useful to their age group.

Overall, "business dress" is a type of daywear. The term is somewhat varied in scope and has several meanings which make this category somewhat hazy, because workplace codes are changing, generally toward broader rules and more relaxed standards. The term needs qualification because different employers have different expectations. Students are challenged to understand some of the variations, but rules still apply in the business world—it is just a matter of *which* rules for *what* business world. The eastern United States business world is more traditional than the western region. There are corporate business looks, casual business looks, and "blue" and "white" collar distinctions; and obviously some jobs, such as with the postal service, military, or police, require uniforms.

Many employers require traditional corporate business dress, while for others, the "casual business" look is acceptable. This is because the working world has changed on many fronts. Technology, for one, changes the workplace today—it may be an office building or home office. The young, high-tech business world is currently overcoming problems with sloppy dress as a new sense of professionalism emerges. Some regions and professions permit more relaxed attire, but even still, what a person wears to work is an important component for success and credibility. Even in the most relaxed work situations, employees have a responsibility to dress credibly and respectfully. A wise employee respects the firm's dress codes, dressing appropriately, conservatively, neatly, and responsibly, as their employer requires for the job.

One recent protocol author says it is important to "know how to dress on business and social occasions, so that the company or firm is proud, not embarrassed, to have you representing them. The executive who shows up for dinner without a jacket and tie in the dining room of a fancy resort like the Greenbrier, in West Virginia, does not cast a good reflection on his company name."[1]

In the senior protocol class, I introduce students to the corporate business look because of its versatile suitability for other occasions as well. Traditional business clothes provide men with budget versatility for many daytime and evening events. No matter what a gentleman's job, business clothes are appropriate for most daytime and evening weddings, lunches, and dinner engagements. A basic dark suit serves a gentleman well for attending funerals, participating in public meetings, being an usher or speaker, and for many church functions. For ladies, a woman's fashionable dark suit can be dressed up or down with the right blouse and accessories. Knowing about this category thus prepares young adults for many future social situations.

Navy, dark gray, and many blacks are good colors for a basic wardrobe. Young men should avoid brown clothes and shoes unless his business will be in the academic world. Browns, tweeds, and classic "sporty" wear are acceptable in the world of learning but not in the professional business world. Men should avoid high polyester content—it is hot and clingy. Use modern, cooler materials that resist "pilling up" as did the original polyesters. In the winter, a gentleman may wear a topcoat, gloves and a hat with his business suit. His hat should have a brim (we aren't speaking about

1. Letitia Baldrige. *Letitia Baldrige's Complete Guide to the New Manners.* New York: Rawson Associates, 1990, 76.

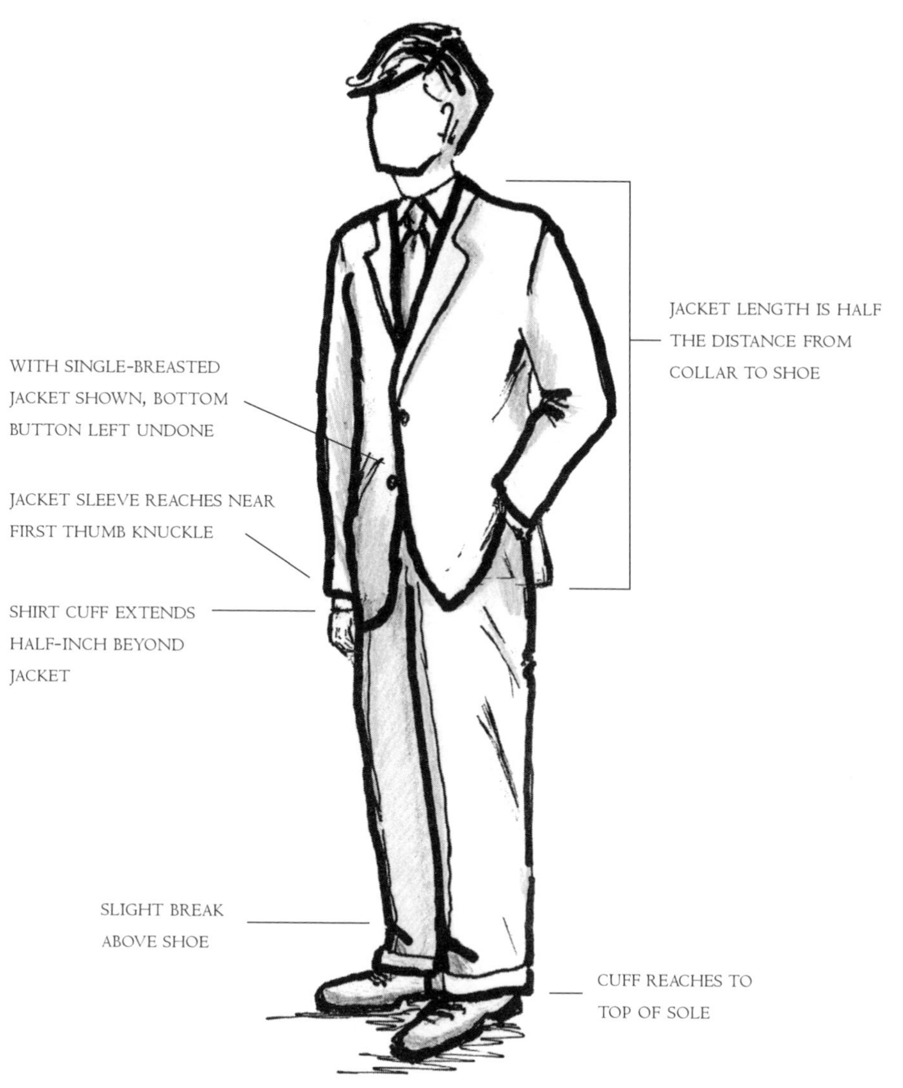

Men's basic suit.

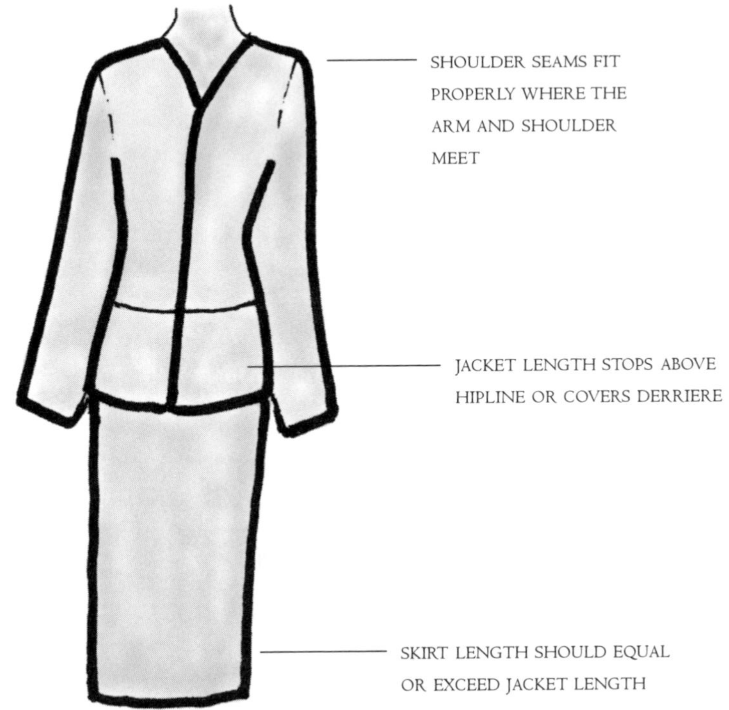

Women's suit with skirt.

Skirt styles.

baseball caps, young men). Both gloves and hat are removed once indoors. The gloves slip into the topcoat pocket before it is hung. A gentleman does not remove his suit jacket.

Women in the professional business world usually wear mid-length dark suits, dresses, pantsuits, or skirts with a lighter blouse, jacket, or nice sweater. Dark pumps, worn with hosiery, are standard; avoid sandals and open-toe shoes. Hats are not worn with women's business clothes. Low cut blouses and very short or tight skirts are out of the question if a woman wants to be taken seriously. Conservative, classic, well-tailored apparel is the appropriate standard. Professional women wear a minimum amount of jewelry, usually not over four pieces at the same time. Gold, silver, or pearls in simple designs are appropriate. Earrings (not too long or dangly) and wedding rings are considered one piece. A necklace, pin, or bracelet is each considered one piece.

Dress for Job Interviews. Our future adults need to realize the importance of a good appearance for job interviews. Business situations require a thoughtful, measured, clean approach. Being well-groomed is a given. This is one time where it is better to be slightly overdressed than not. One of my sons, at college in a large metropolitan area, applied for a delivery job wearing his suit. He was hired on the spot, but not for the delivery job—he was given a sales position. Of course, common sense applies. A guy would not wear a suit when applying for a farm job, but he would show up in neat, clean daywear jeans or slacks and pressed shirt, with combed hair and clean-shaven face (or well-trimmed facial hair). Employers always evaluate demeanor, attitude, qualifications, and attire all together.

Another young man I know of interviewed for a retail clerk position with his shirt's top four buttons unfastened, exposing flashy gold necklaces and a hairy chest. Needless to say, his name was not on the final candidate list, because he ignored the casual business dress code which allows only the shirt's top button to be unfastened. His appearance overrode any ability he possessed. I know another young man who regretted his tattooed arms because it hindered his job advancement—such body and grooming issues go hand in hand with clothes issues.

So what should you wear for an interview? Typically, a dark sports coat or blazer with slacks or a dark suit, dark dress shoes polished to shine (*not* tennis shoes, dark or light), matching socks (*not* light-colored socks), a belt, and a "quiet" tie are a must for most gentlemen's job interviews. Clothes are always clean and pressed. This is a visible sign of a responsible person.

Young ladies have an advantage in job interviews when they wear a modest, tasteful dress or blouse and a skirt that extends past the knee. Pumps are worn instead of sandals.

This brief introduction highlights the most generally accepted requirements. If your students are interested, there are helpful books devoted entirely to business attire and etiquette. The bottom line is dressing neatly and respectfully for the type of job. When applying for a professional job, look professional.

Dressier Daywear. On the dressier end of daywear are nice garments that are not formal in tone, but are worn for special daytime occasions, such as a garden party or eminent guest's reception. A lady may wear a dress or suit, of finer material such as soft crepe de chine, blends, synthetics, sateen, jersey, silk, knit, cashmere, rayon, gabardine, worsted and merino wools, or polished cotton. Dresses, suits, skirts, and nice tops are dressier daywear appropriate for special functions and church. A tea-length afternoon dress in polished cotton, with embroidery, lace, or appliqués, would be the dressiest daywear meant for special afternoon occasions, including parties. It is refreshing to note, as I write this, that current fashion trends are advocating a return to more feminine, "ladylike" attire for women.

An appropriate dressier choice for a gentleman is always a dark navy or black suit. In summer, a gentleman might choose a lightweight sports jacket and linen slacks with spectator shoes for sophisticated daytime social events.

When a daytime event has an elevated tone (e.g., a wedding) you can "dress up" your daywear outfit with a hat and gloves. Hats move in and out of popularity, but are generally a lovely accessory and they serve the useful purpose of shading the face from sun and weather as well as retaining heat in the winter. Brims should not obstruct your neighbors' view. Men always remove hats when indoors, but a lady leaves hers on. Straws and light materials are used in summer hats; heavier materials such as felt, fur, wool, and velvet are used in winter hats. Winter hats are generally not worn after March. In some areas, ladies customarily wear hats to church services. In other regions, hats are worn rarely or only on holidays, especially Easter. For many churchgoers, Resurrection Day marks the time to put away the winter wardrobe and bring forth spring's new lighter look. Traditionally, dress hats are worn with gloves.

Women's gloves in neutral tones (white, bone, beige, brown, or black) are preferred with most daytime outfits. In the spring and summer, washable white, beige, or bone cotton gloves for ladies are appropriate. Leather and suede gloves, in black or brown, are worn in fall and winter. Gloves may be worn without a hat (though hats should be worn with gloves). Shorter wrist-length gloves should leave at least six inches of skin between the sleeve and glove, unless the lady's sleeve extends over the glove end at the wrist. Gloves are removed for activities such as eating, drinking, and communion. Men may wear dress gloves to protect their hands from cold weather. Dark, smooth leather gloves are the most appropriate with daytime attire. Men remove their gloves when indoors and place them in coat pockets.

Church Clothes. A person's attire demonstrates his or her level of regard for an occasion's uniqueness and importance. Thus a day of worship is set apart and designated from ordinary days of the week by a respectful appearance. Clothes indicate our respect for the importance of worship. Garments are part of our visible demonstration of reverence for God and His ways. Flashy, loud, or sloppy clothes that call undue attention to the person wearing them are inappropriate choices in worship services. Etiquette writer Lettita Baldridge agrees with this when she says, "We may be living in a very relaxed, informal time, but that still does not excuse anyone who goes to services in a house of worship dressed inappropriately." She describes clothes that draw attention away from God (in particular, immodest apparel) as inappropriate.

Some churchgoers have become so casual in their appearance that it affects their church demeanor. At some "modern" churches, where the focus appears to be people-centered instead of God-centered, people dress sloppily or provocatively, rejecting the idea of respectful and decent attire as well as reverent behavior. Others sit slouched down while drinking coffee during the service, concurrently "discussing" the sermon with flippant remarks. In contrast, when ladies and gentlemen wear nice clothes, it helps elevate the tone of the gathering, and they are less inclined to these irreverent displays.

Standards matter. Undoubtedly, the following comments will step on a few toes, but students need to remember that casual Birkenstock sandals and unsightly toes best remain in casual settings. To those who insist on their right to dress down, I defer to traditional dress codes as more fitting and proper and ask them to revisit this issue. To those who don't know better, please come up to higher ground and dress up for church. Clothing worn to church is different than that worn on an errand to the supermarket. When parents refuse to dress respectfully for Sunday morning services, they neglect to set the worship day apart, whether or not that is their intention. They need to stop and think about the poor example they set and what their "church" clothes say about their reverence for the Creator of this sacred occasion. Of course, I know of no church that turns anyone away for coming dressed in dirty jeans, tee shirt, and sandals. There are no "clothes police" at the church door. All are welcome, and indeed Scripture forbids showing favor to the well-dressed while ignoring the poorly-dressed. But reverence for God among mature Christians is expressed by reverent decorum and conservative dress set apart from, and above, everyday wear. That's why this type of clothing is affectionately referred to as "Sunday best."

So, what to wear? Traditionally, the best dress codes specify nice daywear, such as a man's dark suit or sports jacket and slacks, as respectful gentlemen's attire for morning church services. Ties are worn with suits but have become optional with sports jackets and sweaters depending on the locality's customs. In some regions, men are comfortably respectful in a nice cardigan sweater and dress shirt with their dress slacks and dress shoes. The point is that they do not dress "down" in their everyday casual clothes for church, but show their reverence by attitude and clean appearance. "Sunday best" is always nicer than the usual daywear.

Church wear for women customarily includes dresses, tailored suits or, in colder climates, nice pantsuits. A low-cut décolleté revealing cleavage, or skirts with high slits, are inappropriate choices for a worship service. Garments made of good materials and dignified in style are suitable church clothes.

For both men and women, traditional Sunday-best daywear has the side benefit of being easily appropriate for many other occasions. Church clothes are often the same type as those worn to funerals, weddings, and for professional business situations. For this reason, I recommend that all young people in my classes place high priority on the purchase of a quality, classic-styled dark suit.

Funerals. As mentioned above, dark suits are proper for funerals. These are solemn occasions and light or brightly-colored clothes are not worn to memorial services out of respect for the bereaved family. Black is the traditional color worn to funerals, though most protocol experts now consider any dark, conservative, and inconspicuous color acceptable, unless you are sitting with the family or asked to be an honorary pall bearer, in which case, black is always worn. Pall bearers always wear suits.

Weddings. Wedding ceremonies vary widely in formality. Dress codes, however, stipulate that women guests avoid wearing all-black business clothes or all-white garments to a wedding (or christening party). All black is considered too sober for the happy occasion, while white is the traditional color for brides (and babies at christenings) on these special days—they are the star attractions, and guests wearing white draw attention to themselves rather than honoring the bride.

First, we look at appropriate wear for female wedding guests.

- Informal daytime weddings: This is the type of wedding in which the bride wears a short afternoon or cocktail dress. Women wear street-length dressy afternoon daywear with raised heels. They may wear hats and gloves, or gloves alone.
- Informal evening weddings: Ladies wear a dressy afternoon or cocktail dress with or without gloves. Dressier fabrics and styles are appropriate in a rainbow of color choices.
- Semiformal daytime weddings: The bride wears a long white dress and short white veil. The women are expected to wear short afternoon or cocktail dresses; hats are optional.
- Semiformal evening weddings: Cocktail dresses; gloves and hats optional.
- Formal daytime weddings: The bride traditionally wears a long white dress with a train, long veil, and optional gloves. Lady guests wear street-length cocktail or afternoon dresses; gloves and head coverings are optional. In some regions, dressy day dresses may be acceptable.
- Formal evening weddings require dressier attire than daytime wear. Dresses may be long or short. Hair ornaments, short cocktail veil, and gloves are optional.
- Generally speaking, a lady should not wear pants to a wedding.

For gentlemen wedding guests, life is much simpler. A dark suit with dress shirt, tie, and black socks and dress shoes is proper standard attire for every male guest at any type of wedding, day or evening, except the formal evening wedding. In this case, if the lady he is escorting wears a longer dress, he may wear a tuxedo. A dark suit, however, is always acceptable unless the invitation specifically requests formal attire. Perhaps this exception in dress codes is the reason that many people categorize business suits as semiformal. Remember, only if the invitation specifies "formal evening wedding" or "black tie" is a gentleman *required* to rent or buy a tuxedo. For all other weddings a gentleman can "dress up" his dark suit and dress shirt with handsome cufflinks and silk tie. He might add a matching breast pocket kerchief and a waistcoat (vest) as other options to customize his black suit for special wedding occasions.

The only occasion when a gentleman wedding guest does not dress traditionally and respectfully in a dark suit is when the invitation specifies a different dress code, for example when the wedding has a customized ceremony that occurs in an unusual place, like at a dude ranch or at sea. Only at these unique ceremonies would a man show up not wearing a tie.

When an invitation states a choice of categories for guest attire, ladies and gentlemen opt for the highest standard given, out of respect for the couple and occasion.

Semiformal and Formal Wear

In the following section, we enter a dressier zone marked by several different terms and interpretations. *Party dress, semiformal, after-five,* and *black tie* are all names of dressier party wear, while the most formal dress category is called *white tie*.

Semiformal. The term *semiformal* has become an increasingly broad dress category, so it is a good place to begin our discussion of dress for special occasions. Everyone realizes that there are some events in life that are more extraordinary and important than regular daily occasions. Various events have distinctive levels of importance that call for celebration: birthdays, anniversaries, births, baptisms, engagements, weddings, and graduations. Today, amid all our modern busyness, we need to appreciate these special occasions more than we do, and one significant way to mark distinctions between ordinary and special events is how we dress for them. When we attend a special event, our attire should testify to the fact. When we dress appropriately for a notable occasion, we show honor, respect and consideration for the guests of honor and the hosts.

As we discuss the range of clothes in the semiformal category, note that regional differences exist in the United States, so accepted "semiformal" dress codes really do vary. In the most proper etiquette circles, *semiformal* has meant and still means "black tie," which implies a tuxedo for men. Increasingly, different areas and some groups broaden this category to include dressy daytime clothes. So, some people now commonly accept semiformal attire to mean dark suits for men and nice dresses with high heels for ladies. Thus, since the meaning of *semiformal* can vary depending on background, the occasion, and the area of the country, hosts who desire strict semiformal wear will often send invitations indicating "black tie." Some

Traditional men's semi-formal or "black tie" tuxedo.

invitations may say "black tie optional." In this case, a considerate guest would dress according to the black tie code if at all possible. Since several interpretations of semiformal exist, it is wise to inquire of a host exactly what type of clothing is expected. It is better not to speculate when you are not certain. No matter which definition of semiformal is preferred, semiformal means "dressy and special," though it is not as grand or elaborate as strictly formal dress.

The broader *party* (or semiformal, using the looser interpretation) category is a good starting point for a school's protocol event, in which young gentlemen escorts will wear a suit but not a tuxedo. The men's dark suit is wonderfully versatile clothing. It covers several categories and many useful purposes, including party dress. Of course, a gentleman's polished leather dress shoes and dark, mid-calf hosiery always match his trousers color. His tie is made from a shiny, colorful silk or similar material. The foundational dress shirt may be white or light-colored. Spread collars are dressier than straight point collars (no button-down collars for party wear). Matching French cuffs are optional with the correct collar style. Jewelry for men, beyond a ring and watch, is debatable. The "less is more" idea is a reliable guide for a refined gentleman.

It is helpful for young ladies especially to realize there are several types of party wear, including *tea-length* afternoon party dresses that reach to mid-calf or slightly lower, as well as dressier *after-five* semiformal clothes. Ladies' less formal party wear, sometimes called "afternoon party dress" is usually made of lightweight materials, such as dotted Swiss or chiffon, with or without appliqués, embroidery, and fancy details. These dresses come in a variety of simpler styles, from a slim-fitting silk sheath to a dress with gathered skirt and princess-cut bodice, but they all express a special afternoon occasion such as a tea, garden party, or special bridal shower. These party dresses are sometimes appropriate for informal (but still dressy) evening affairs when strictly semiformal clothes are not required. Pumps, sandals, or flat-heeled fancy slipper shoes are appropriate with these outfits. The slipper shoes are a smart choice for dressier outdoor lawn parties because their wide, stable heels do not penetrate the turf.

Semiformal garments for women are dressier both in style and fabric than casual or daytime wear. A party dress is different than a regular daytime dress, which is usually more practical and appropriate only for daytime business or activities. A semiformal party dress is also distinct from the usual church dress, although it could perhaps be worn for special church occasions (Easter or Christmas service, an evening wedding, etc.). A semi-formal party dress is never as grand or elaborate as the floor-length gowns in the formal category, but it is always attractive and nice.

Ladies are usually appropriately dressed for dressy or semiformal occasions when they wear a party-type dress in a fine fabric. Depending on the occasion, time of day, and local expectations, velvets, georgette, chiffon, crepe, silks, faille, even shiny chintz or fine wool, in season, can be seen in semiformal clothing for women. (Coarse, textured fabrics don't mix well with party styles, with the exception of finer brocades seen in slim-fitting "cocktail" or "theater" wear). Shiny, metallic-looking materials are common for ladies' tops in this category. Details may include ruffles, touches of lace, velvet, or added sparkles. Glittering jewelry can be worn and short fabric gloves fit in this category.

Semiformal dress lengths are shorter than those in the formal category. A mid-calf to ankle-length after-five dress is a good choice for semiformal occasions. Semiformal dress lengths can range from short to three-quarter-length to ankle-length.

This category's styles usually have a slimmer silhouette than an elaborate, full, floor-length formal gown. The versatile, shorter-length evening dress is acceptable for a variety of events or parties. The mother of the bride and bridesmaids frequently appear in semiformal dresses for daytime weddings.

Black Tie. The tuxedo, according to men's dress expert Alan Fusser, is a type of formalwear originating in the mid-nineteenth century and popularized by Prince Edward because he found it more comfortable for dining than its formal predecessor, the swallowtail coat. "Black tie," a formalwear category to which we have alluded to already, is still a very important one for students to understand. The term is derived from the gentlemen's attire. When the occasion is more than "dressy" or specified as black tie, the strictest etiquette experts classify the tuxedo as men's standard semiformal wear.

Black tie is the type of men's wear often available at a tuxedo shop and seen in many brides' magazines. There are quality dinner tuxedos as well as inexpensive versions. Style experts warn against poorly tailored imitations as a fashion oxymoron, since the purpose of black tie attire is refined elegance in a comfortable fit.

Black tie events are quite special—well beyond ordinary, everyday affairs—and as such require special clothes. Events where black tie attire may be required include some dinners and celebrations, fancy receptions, formal weddings, special gatherings, anniversaries, after-five parties, evening concerts (not rock or popular music), symphonies, and plays, although many men wear dark suits instead of tuxedos at such performances. The opening night of a play, art gallery, or opera, however, are occasions in some cities and social circles for strict semiformal attire—so for these special nights we may see women in semiformal or even formal evening dress, and men in tuxedos. Protocol experts agree that black tie events usually (but not always) occur in the evening after dark.

It is important for young people to understand that black tie wear for men refers to a black or white dinner jacket, worn with a black bow tie, pleated or bibbed-front dress shirt, cummerbund or waistcoat, and dark slacks. According to some protocol writers, and varying with season and region, a white or brightly-colored dinner jacket is recognized as "black tie." Its fabric is lighter weight and particularly suited for summer heat. Increasingly, all clothing except shoes and pants may be selected in many colors and patterns, but black and white remain the traditional choices, black jackets being considered more formal than white. Experts advise men to avoid brocaded or sequined jackets unless they want to be mistaken for a band member.

Let's take a detailed look at the black tie ensemble for men. The tuxedo dinner jacket is more elegant than a suit jacket and has shiny black or midnight-blue, satin or silk grosgrain lapels. It may be double- or single-breasted. The single-breasted model is worn unbuttoned and always paired with a cummerbund or waistcoat. A double-breasted jacket is not worn with a cummerbund and must remain buttoned whenever standing, though it may be unbuttoned when seated. Only peaked or shawl lapels are correct for dinner jackets. Most tuxedo jackets have an inch-long (or slightly more) buttonhole on the breast-pocket side for a boutonniere. Some new designs and colors are currently popular, so a man may wear a dark, jewel-colored jacket in the winter. "Smoking jackets" belong at home, not in public.

The black trousers, never cuffed and with slightly wider legs than suit pants, usually have a shiny single stripe on the outside leg seam in trim fabric that matches the jacket lapel. When the length of the pants is correct (and this applies to any pair of dressy pants), the front crease "breaks" once just above the shoe when the man is standing. At the back of the shoe, the hem stops just above the point where the heel of the sole joins the upper shoe.

Both black and white jackets are worn with a white, pleated or slightly ruffled bibbed-front shirt with double cuffs and turndown or wingtip (more formal) collar. Studs are used instead of buttons. The semiformal turndown collar extends one half-inch above the jacket's collar.

The black bow tie's fabric matches the jacket lapel. The bowtie shape, batwing or butterfly, should not extend beyond the spread collar's outside edge. The pleated folds of the cummerbund face upwards. Solid black patent shoes or black dress oxfords with thin, long, black silk socks (known as hosiery) are standard.

Of course, the gentleman is clean-shaven and well-groomed. Jewelry for men may include a finger ring, a thin dress watch or pocket watch, and cufflinks. Anything more is personal and optional, but my advice is to remain conservative in your liberty: it appears more confidently masculine.

Perhaps it is because every man looks handsome in "black tie" that some people assume this to be the most formal men's attire. But it is not—black tie properly belongs in the dressiest type of *semiformal* category. We will discuss true formal wear later.

Women's Semiformal Wear

Women have a broader range of apparel choices than men for semiformal clothes, though when a man dresses up in a black tie tuxedo, the lady should dress according to the stricter interpretations of semiformal. The couple's attire should not be lopsided. A true semiformal garment is dressier than daywear and even a tailored theatre suit made of fine wool, crepe, silk, or brocade type fabrics. The basic black dress in a fine material is a versatile option that can transcend category standards. It can be adapted for many functions by the simple addition or elimination of accessories, like rhinestone jewelry, scarves, or jackets. It is wise to have such a versatile dress in your closet, because it can be transformed for many events, except the dressiest semiformal and formal affairs.

After-five clothing is a subcategory of semiformal eveningwear. Often called the "cocktail dress," this type of dress is often made of shiny fabric and can be short, either to the knee or mid-calf, but seldom reaches to the ankle as does stricter semiformal eveningwear.

There are multiple choices in the semiformal category besides party dresses and after-five wear. "Hostess" outfits usually include long flowing pants or skirts with pretty tops. Both cocktail attire and hostess clothing are not considered all-occasion semiformal wear because they are designed for specific functions. Hostess outfits are designed for in-home entertaining, while the cocktail dress is a type of after-five party outfit to be worn at the type of function for which it is named.

If the gentleman wears a dark suit when the occasion or invitation does not call for black tie or is in the daytime, then how should the lady dress?

A helpful general rule of thumb is to remember that a lady's attire should match her escort's manner of dress. Therefore she would choose a dressy dress or a more conservative after-five dress appropriate for the event, rather than select fancy semiformal attire. It is usually best to be slightly underdressed rather than overdressed.

The right accessories compliment and complete an outfit. Women's accessories in this category include small evening bags and jewelry such as earrings, necklace, pin, and bracelets with diamonds, rhinestones, and other sparkling gems or bright crystals that add brilliance to the attire in indoor lighting. Accessories possessing classic, timeless qualities can be worn for a lifetime, regardless of changing trends or style.

Short evening jackets, wraps, stoles, and shawls are often needed. A matching or contrasting evening coat, jacket, or shawl wrap has a versatile and long life. Currently we are seeing a return of matching silk coat and dress ensembles. Daytime coats, parkas, or ski jackets are not acceptable in the semiformal/party category.

Open-toe evening sandals or cloth pumps are appropriate. Satin pumps may match the outfit. Daytime leather shoes are not worn, but this does not eliminate a lady's wearing shoes with a lower heel.

White Tie: True Formal Wear

Young people enjoy formal occasions because they require elegant clothes. Today, formal occasions (in the most exacting sense) are increasingly rare, but many state, inaugural, anniversary, charitable, and military balls remain formal events. Formal events might also include a grand, opening-night theater production. All formal occasions demand truly majestic attire, and invitations always specify formal dress when it is expected.

Formal dress is elaborately elegant and festive but different than the black tie. An invitation specifying formal, "white tie," or "tails" means full formal attire from top to bottom for both men and women. Every piece of clothing needs to meet the "formal" standard in its character, style, and exquisite fabric. Unlike the semiformal category, there is no "wiggle" room. Formal events are memorable occasions—an invitation to any formal event is an honor and should be respected as such. When including formal occasions in a school program, remember that formal wear is expensive. Ample advance notice of a school's formal event is helpful for budget planning.

The most regal formal eveningwear for men is the "white tie" black tailcoat. Designers claim that all men's body types look stately in this king of garments. The black, single-breasted, cutaway jacket has long "swallow" tails that should extend slightly below the back of the knees. The sides of the coat gently hug the hips. The narrow, tapered sleeve allows shirt cuffs to extend beyond it about three quarters of an inch. There is also a double-breasted version which does not button in the front. The coats are usually made of wool or a wool/silk blend.

The formal tailcoat requires a white pique bow tie, a starched white pique evening shirt with wingtip collar, and stiff single-cuffed sleeves. The detachable collar extends three quarters of an inch above the jacket's rear collar and sleeves extend beyond the jacket edge the same amount. The shirt has a small tab that attaches to the trousers to keep it in place. Gold, pearl, onyx, or diamond studs and cufflinks are needed in place of buttons. The tie may be a single semi-butterfly or batwing shape and is worn in front of the collar's wing tips. The jacket also necessitates a white pique waistcoat (vest) that covers the waistline with either rounded or pointed bottom front edges, which must not extend or show below the tailcoat edges. Therefore the waistcoat also has a tab by which it fastens to the trousers waistband.

Two narrow, plain "stripes" on the outside leg seam are the most identifiable mark of the formal trouser. The trouser is made of the same material as the tail coat. A longer ride and angled front pleats are subtle tailoring features that assure a proportionately flattering and comfortable fit. The cuffless trouser leg breaks gently above the instep.

Above-the-calf black hosiery, in silk or finely ribbed lightweight cotton, is worn with a black slip-on opera pump or low-cut oxford in patent or shiny leather. The pump may have a grosgrain bow and is the dressiest type of formal shoe for men. This handsome white tie ensemble may also include a black top hat and long, slim silhouetted black overcoat with a fur or velvet collar. Remember, when your invitation specifies "white tie" the courteous response is to dress accordingly, unless your hosts ("whom," as one etiquette expert stated, "you would have to know very well") approve otherwise.

There is a second category of men's true formalwear called "morning dress, for which a long, "cutaway," lighter-colored suit jacket is worn with striped gray trousers. This type of formal wear is sometimes worn by the groom and father at a morning formal wedding ceremony.

For a formal white-tie event, ladies dress in their grandest, most elaborate gowns. Long, floor-length, full-skirted evening gowns made from the finest fabrics are the elegant norm. Beautiful materials, such as taffeta, chiffon, tulle, satin, velvet, brocade, and *peau de soir* are typical formal fabrics.

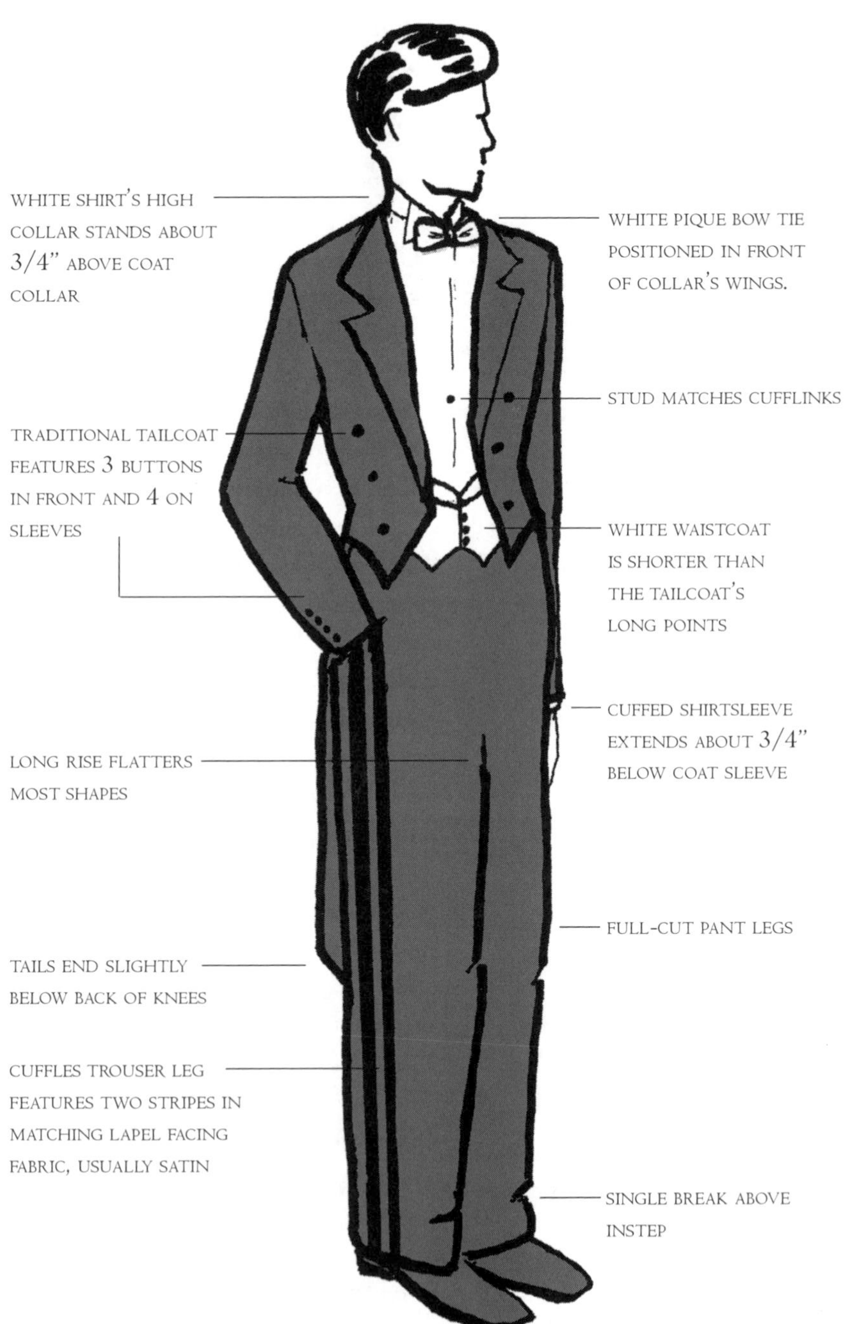

Traditional men's formal: white tie and tails.

Elaborate beadwork and fine laces may be used for design details. Remind young ladies that overlays of tulle and silk illusion are usually reserved for formal occasions rather than semiformal.

Gloves reaching to the elbows are appropriate; longer opera-length gloves are proper with sleeveless gowns. Wrist-length gloves are not formal. Evening coats, jackets, long capes, or elegant fur or wraps are worn. Well designed evening jackets do not go out of style. (Daytime jackets are never worn!) Evening bags are small but beautiful in elegant fabrics and designs. This is the time to wear one's finest sparkling jewelry, but, again, never too many pieces at one time. Hosiery should be sandal toed and sheer. Elegant evening sandals, silk shoes, or satin pumps with heels complete an outfit.

Hairstyles may be worn up off the neck in an elaborate arrangement or kept simple. A woman in a formal evening dress never wears a hat. Bows of satin or velvet and other fancy hair accessories are acceptable.

Conclusion

It takes students several classes to fully understand good dress codes and category differences, but the effort pays off. Building a versatile wardrobe takes time and effort, but wise investments and unrushed deliberation produce an adaptable wardrobe suited for numerous situations. The student who fills his or her closet with the right clothes and knows when to wear them finds life simpler, more elegant, and more enjoyable.

Right Fit and Personal Style

Understanding good grooming and dress categories is a full plate for beginners, but older students nearly always enjoy and find helpful the following additional information about personal style development. If your program has time and students show interest, instruction on flattering individual style, with the goal of helping students appreciate and work with their bodies' uniqueness, is a great addition to the curriculum. Once students understand the basics of dress, the following tips can help young people look their best.

First, both men and women can create a flattering silhouette for their figure type. Lines in clothes create "silhouettes" that affect our overall appearance and sense of proportion. Vertical lines make a person appear taller and slimmer; thus taller people avoid vertical lines and a short person welcomes them. Current styles favor a slim, well-proportioned look, achieved by lengthening lines for a taller overall silhouette appearance. Vertical lines can appear in striped patterns, hanging pendant accessories or ties, details such as button closings, seams, and certain slim-fitting styles. The overall effect or "silhouette" is a long line. Horizontal lines, on the other hand, tend to draw the eye across the body surface, and therefore can make a thin person look wider, shorter, and broader. A very thin or tall person would benefit by wearing styles with horizontal lines while a shorter, heavier person would avoid them.

Broken lines shorten. A combination of contrasting colors or patterns will create a shortened or "chopped" effect. Thus they can reduce a tall person's height, while a solid unbroken color adds length. A short person avoids large plaids and other choppy patterns.

Diagonal lines create dramatic silhouettes and are usually flattering for everyone. Curved lines, from draped fabrics or ruffles, add feminine softness and roundness, which is why most men avoid ruffles.

Colors are another important aspect of personal style. Light colors draw the eye and seem "fuller" while dark colors are usually more slimming. Wearing too many colors at one time creates a sense of confusion. The combination of no more than two to three harmonious colors can be flattering, but more colors appear busy, even clownish. Men's dress styles are more flattering when vivid colors are not used in large amounts. When a gentleman favors strong, bright colors, he does best to indulge his fancy only in small amounts with accessories like his handkerchief and tie. Yellow suits tend to create the image of a canary rather than a respectable gentleman.

Style and Fit for Men

The Suit or Blazer. A well-designed suit with good fit is a very important purchase for a man. Most men look good in the classic style suit jacket that became popular in the 1930s—a style said to have developed first in London. Its popularity is due to its natural, easy cut, slightly padded shoulders, and soft construction. Some men favor side vents for freedom of body movement, while men who like a more tailored fit prefer the center vent. Versions of the wedge-style suit, originally designed for the slight-bodied male, have been a longtime classic. This style has no vents, features tapered sleeves and narrow but padded shoulders, and fits closer at the hips. It is usually tailored in silks and wools and has a stylish, sophisticated look that flatters smaller to average-sized men.

Tailors recommend looking for quality material, construction, and good fit in a man's suit. Many of these points also apply to ladies' clothing purchases.

- Choose good fabrics. Blended natural fibers with small amounts of synthetic fiber content provide durability, comfort, and wrinkle-resistant wearability.
- Choose an experienced tailor or salesperson to assist you with proper fitting.
- Choose small, classic patterns and darker, neutral colors for timeless value.
- Choose well-constructed garments. Look for smooth seams, single row stitching, well-finished button holes and pocket details. Look inside the garment and at the lining to determine how well it is made.
- Choose a suit jacket with well-defined lapel points that will not wrinkle and will return to their original shape when squeezed.

Blazers are a basic component of every gentleman's wardrobe, and for good reason—they can be dressed up or down. Depending on the young man's complexion, a dark navy or black blazer is a suitable first purchase. Younger men generally look better in navy than in black. A blazer provides versatile service with its smart styling. The higher the quality of the jacket, the better it will wear, last, and look. Quality garments are money-saving investments over long periods of time.

The American-style, single-breasted blazer has two to three buttons, natural shoulder styling, breast patch pocket, a buff edge lapel, and lower flap pockets. The English blazer can be either double- or single-breasted with a slightly tapered body. The double-breasted blazer usually has flap pockets and side vents. It is never worn unbuttoned. The English single-breasted blazer usually has two buttons with inset besom pockets. It also has side vents. A finely-woven wool fabric is the best choice of material no matter what the style. Some blazers are available in flannel or camelhair fibers which are also good choices, but quality camelhair may be too pricey for a young gentleman's budget. No matter what your preference, look for materials that will resist wrinkles and lint. Dark colors show lint more easily than light colors, so a good fabric that will resist attracting lint is a must. Suits, blazers, and sport jackets may also be accompanied by a vest, the last bottom button of which is left undone.

A good fit is timeless, though some proportions and details will reflect style trends. Generally the suit lapel should extend slightly short of the half-way mark between the collar and the shoulder line. The jacket should button slightly below or on the natural waistline. The jacket must not be too tight and the sleeves should always reach the wrist (but not so long that the end of the shirt cuff will not show). Trouser legs should gradually taper from the waist to the ankle. Pant leg width will vary with trends, but slimmer-cut pant legs usually look more trim and classic than wide-cut pant legs. The front crease should break once just above the shoe. Cuffs come and go in fashion, but their additional weight does help keep the trouser line straight in a natural, easy line.

People have different body types, and for some it is more challenging to determine what is best for their unique frame. Some are lanky, shorter, rounder, barrel-chested, long- or short-legged, and some are average. An objective look in the mirror will reveal one's body shape and allow informed choices for the wardrobe.

A little training in personal style and fit helps young men and women feel more content and confident by increasing their clothing savvy beyond current casual trends. It helps them to better understand what is best for their individual body type in categories and styles beyond casual.

General body types in men include

- Shorter, thin frame under five feet ten inches tall
- Shorter, rounded or stocky frame, also under five feet ten
- Mr. Average: shoulders wider than hips, medium-sized frame, and average weight
- Tall, lanky, lean body frame over six feet four inches tall
- Heavier set and athletic type having a very muscular, oversized upper body, or barrel chest with shorter legs

Young, growing men may not be sure what body type they have; their bodies are still works in progress. It helps to realize that they probably will develop a similar body shape to one of their parents—when their parents were younger. Most men "thicken up" as they age. For some that is good news and for others it is not, but the right clothes and proper style and fit can create a more flattering look. Garments cover our bodies and express our personalities, but fit and style can actually help our overall appearance. A man's garment must work with his proportions and body shape, "sharpening his keener features and blunting his duller ones." A well-dressed man learns to work with his body type, not against it.

For example, the small and thin guy needs a suit to stretch his length and add bulk to his chest. A single-breasted, three-button suit jacket is best. The jacket should be as short as possible to lengthen his legs yet still cover the derrière. High, broad shoulder pads fill out a thin upper body. Flap pockets pad the hips. For men under five foot ten, cuffs width should be about one and five-eighths inches. Vertical lines, such as pinstripes, and textured fabrics add visual height and bulk.

The average-sized man, about five foot ten to six feet tall, will find that the European wedge-cut suit, with square shoulders and a more fitted waist and hips, is generally flattering, because it creates a triangular silhouette that enhances the male shape. Details must not compete with the overall look—one expert tailor recommends that no detail of the suit stand out with more effect than the total image of the suit. This maintains a sense of balanced proportions, in harmonious relationship to the wearer.

The shorter, stocky man wants to add visual length to his body shape while reducing a heavy or rounded look. A single-breasted, two-button jacket with besom pockets is better than a too-long top jacket with pocket flaps or a double-breasted jacket. A single-vent jacket is the best choice for a slimmer rear view. Keep fabrics dark and use vertical lines in patterns. Trouser pants need to sit on the waist, above any rounded tummy area. A slim cut leg is better than a wide cut.

The tall, lanky fellow wants to reduce height and add visual weight for a better-proportioned appearance. He needs a fuller-cut suit. A double-breasted or single-breasted two-button jacket with flap pockets is flattering. The suit lapel should be a broader cut. His trousers will balance his proportions best when the rise is long, the pleats deep, and wider cuffs are tailored for him. A contrasting but harmonious belt will distract from height. Textured fabrics like flannel or thick camelhair add bulk. So do larger scaled patterns or plaids. He should avoid small patterns or stripes.

The man with the large upper body and proportionately small legs needs to bring visual balance to his frame. He can do this with a single-breasted jacket with natural shoulders, no more than two buttons, possible side vents, and flap pockets. He should also use solid colors or subtle, small stripes in flat woven fabrics. He should avoid heavy, textured, or strongly-patterned jackets. His trousers should fit comfortably, but not snugly. Fabrics with some body such as worsted wool are best to balance the upper bulk. Pleated, straight-flowing pants should have a wider cut leg.

Shirts. When men choose a shirt to wear with a jacket, they face three important considerations: fit, style, and correct proportions. Style involves choosing looks and fabric that are compatible with the suit or sports coat it will be worn with. A casual Harris tweed jacket works well when paired with a rounded collar or relaxed button-down collar. A spread or straight collar works well with dark, dressy suits. Proportions in the shirt collar style are important; a man should consider the collar type and its proportion in relationship to his body. A smaller man wants to avoid high shirt collars that are long and pointed. Men with broad faces or thin necks should not wear the small round or spread collar.

A good fabric in a shirt can compliment the suit, while the wrong choice can hurt the appearance and be uncomfortable to wear. A nylon shirt is a poor choice for a suit because it is too shiny and too hot. Natural fibers like cotton, as well as blends, are superior to synthetic fibers—they are more comfortable, breathe better, and look finer. A quality cotton shirt is versatile and, when blended with a small amount of synthetic fiber such as polyester, it resists wrinkles. It is better than a rayon shirt, which will change shape and wrinkle if it becomes moist.

Men's Accessories

Handkerchiefs. There are several ways to fold the handkerchief properly: (1) A square-folded insert, not to extend more than one and one half inch above the pocket. This method works best with cotton hanks for a formal look. (2) Square-ended fold, loosely stuffed, with three or four points extending upward out of pocket works well for hand-rolled cotton hanks. (3) Patterned designs and silks are best loosely stuffed in the jacket pocket, and look good with blazers and tweeds. A young man needs to know the square fold, but he can learn other folds in the advanced session when there isn't a flood of new information to learn.

A thoughtful gentleman can be prepared to assist others by carrying two handkerchiefs. The extra one, should someone in his party have need for it, is thinly folded and placed neatly inside his jacket, out of sight. His personal handkerchief can be placed in an outside breast pocket as a finishing touch on a dark suit, or in another pocket as he prefers.

Ties. The tie makes a man's final, most important dress statement. Handsome ties exist in a variety of patterns from crested, regimental, and stripe patterns to customized designs with matching blazer buttons. Here again, proportion and fabric is important. Any pattern woven into the material or finely printed should not look busy, or compete with or overwhelm the suit. Therefore a plaid tie is only worn with a solid suit, and the plaid must remain proportionately small. The smaller the pattern or design, the dressier and more appropriate the tie.

Tie widths vary with fashion trends, but three to three and a half inches at the widest point is considered standard and generally appropriate. The

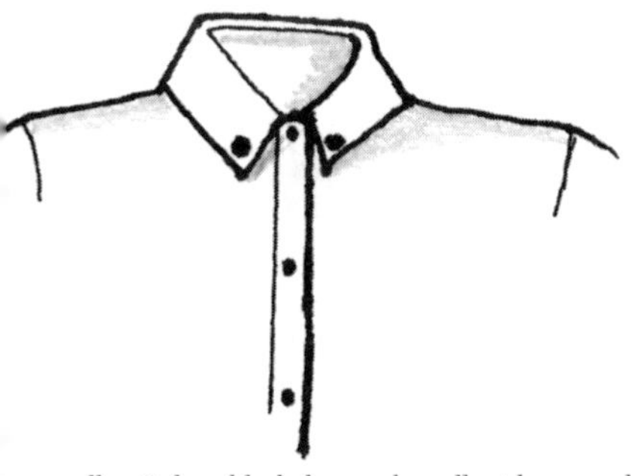

tton collar: Relaxed look that works well with textured kets or sweaters.

Traditional straight-point: flatters rounder and wider faces; good for business dress.

b collar: holds tie and collar higher, which flatters longer ks and rounder faces.

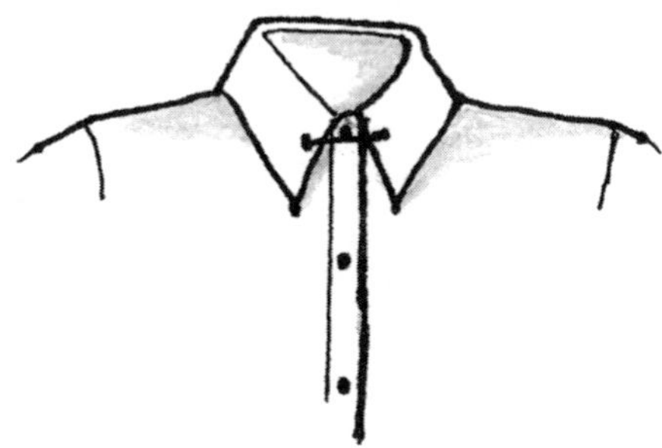

Pinned collar: pin under tie raises the tie higher and keeps the collar in place. Dressy but not formal.

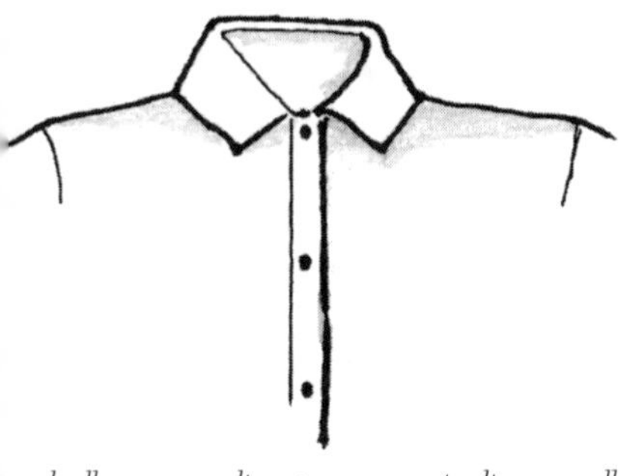

read collar: can compliment a narrower jawline or smaller ad; the dressiest of collars.

Half-Windsor and Four-in-hand: narrow, asymmetrical knots are more casual.

ll Windsor: larger, symmetrical knot is dressiest.

Tie length: point reaches middle of belt buckle.

en's collars, tie knots, and proper tie length. Open and stiff collars, white fabric, and French cuffs are dressier.

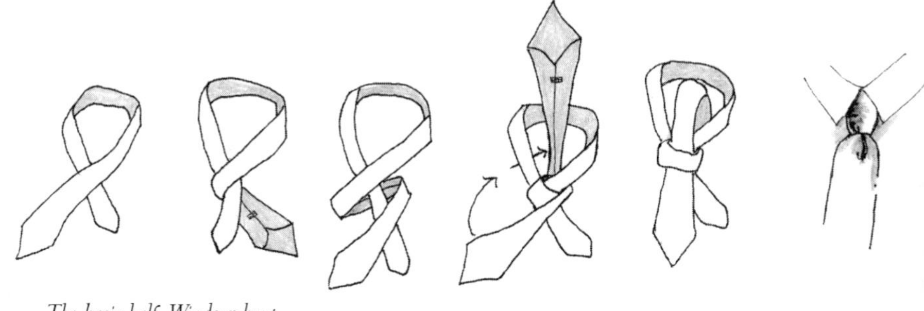

The basic half-Windsor knot.

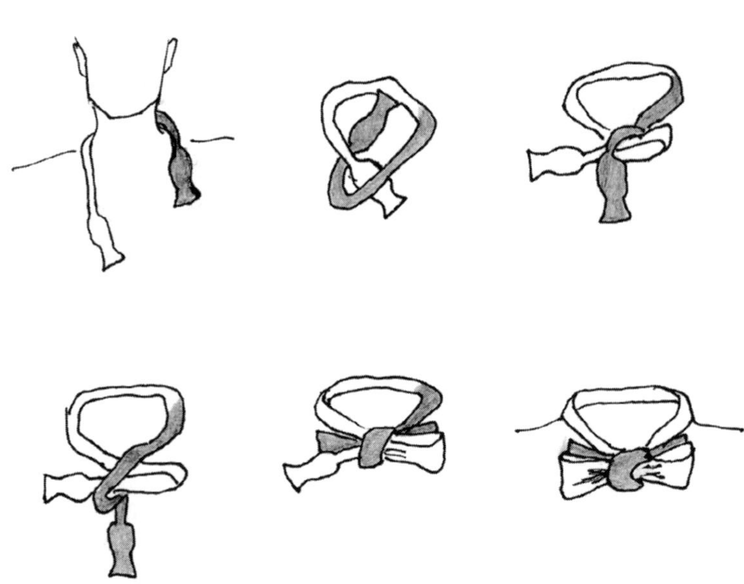

Tying a bowtie.

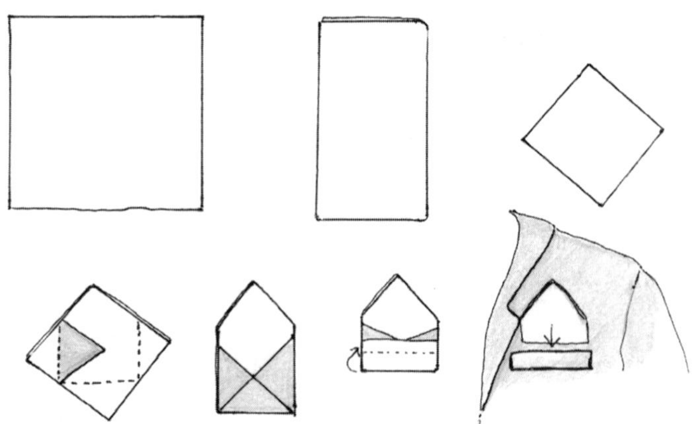

Folding a handkerchief.

knot area should range between one to one and a quarter inch. A knowledgeable fine clothier is a great help in proper tie selection. A good tie can be expensive because it is usually made of fine two-ply cloth such as silk, linen, or wool with slip-stitched, single-needle tailoring. It is often handmade.

Bow ties should be worn with a wing-tip collar shirt; they are not worn with button-down collar shirts. Clip-on ties are never worn by males over age twelve. In a program's dress classes, a mature gentleman should instruct young men on how to properly tie both types of ties, and explain the advantages of the various types of knots.

Men's Jewelry. Functionality and simplicity set the prevailing standards for good taste in men's jewelry. Cufflinks, collar bars, and tie pins or bars look best together when they are made of the same metal. Tiepins and bars move in and out of fashion but provide a finished, dressed-up look. Cufflinks, worn with French-cuff shirts, are dressy and stylish in a variety of metals. Onyx, dark agates, and gold and silver (in a shiny or satin finish) are frequently used in dressy cufflinks. Novelty cufflinks are more informal, but still dressy. Coin cufflinks may be worn with business dress but not with formal attire. Cufflinks and studs should match or at least be harmonious and complementary.

A man may always wear a watch or carry a timepiece in a pocket. Dress watches are thinner than sports watches. Rings for men are optional, but no more than one ring on each hand. Chains or necklaces are usually considered informal. In some circles, men enjoy chain necklaces, while other men think them excessive and feminine. Most dress codes ignore them, but some experts point out that a heavier chain is suitably masculine. An earring's suitability for men is questionable and depends heavily on his social crowd. Earrings are usually only worn by showmen.

Tattoos, though not technically jewelry, are a related topic. Needless to say, these irreversible decorations are not favored for a dressed-up look in our society. They are doomed to be perpetually casual. I know young men who regret having permanent tattoos stenciled on their bodies. These are passing fads that have not withstood the passage of time.

Belts. Keep belts simple and up on the waist. A suit belt should be made of leather in a dark color with a simple metal clasp and hook. Belts should fit flat and comfortably. Make sure the belt is thinner than the suit pant loops before purchasing it. Belts are not worn with suspenders.

Hosiery. Men's dress socks are called "hosiery," but that in no way implies "girlie" hose. Socks should rise above the calf to eliminate exposed skin when the leg is crossed. Natural fibers blended with a small amount of synthetic fiber, such as cotton with nylon, help retain the sock's fit yet remain cool on the foot. Too much synthetic fiber is uncomfortable and hot. Only matching, dark-colored hosiery is worn with dark suits. Avoid navy with black and avoid large prints for dressier occasions. Argyles are worn with tweeds and casual looks.

Underwear. Obvious as it might seem, some students need a reminder that a well-dressed man always wears underwear. It is a necessary part of a gentleman's attire. Briefs versus boxers is a personal preference, but trim silk boxers are comfortable with wool trousers. Undershirts are always worn with dress shirts. Undershirts are available in silk or cotton as well as several style options, including sleeveless and V-neck.

Shoes. A gentleman's shoes should match his attire. To make this point, longtime gentleman and author John Bridges says, "Unless he is a Texas Ranger or a cattle rancher, a gentleman never wears cowboy boots with a suit." Shiny black dress shoes are the correct choice with suits. Every man should own a pair of black leather lace-up shoes. Dark leather oxfords or wingtips are appropriate choices for dress or business attire. Athletic shoes belong in the casual, sportswear category. Leather shoes are the practical choice for comfort, longevity, and appearance. They must be polished and neat in appearance. A good water-repellent spray is invisible and adds protection to a good leather shoe. Men should avoid shoes made or lined with vinyl—they will hold moisture and can create skin problems because the foot cannot "breathe."

Remember, brown shoes are not worn for funerals, business, or weddings—those occasions call for black shoes. Dear Mr. Bridges further comments, "If a gentleman is fortunate enough to have a long life, he will live through many weekends and his brown loafers will get plenty of wear."

Clothes Care. A true gentleman properly cares for his clothes. Suits are hung on wooden or plastic contour hangers when not in use after pockets are emptied. A good suit or blazer should be brushed after wearing. The jacket is left unbuttoned to help retain its shape. It is hung with some air space around the garment to avoid wrinkles. Wool garments are not worn two days in row; this allows them a "rest" time to regain shape and air out. Shirts and undershirts are washed after each time worn. Clean, well-polished shoes are a must for every occasion.

Style and Fit for Women

The female body also comes in different shapes and types. Young ladies appreciate knowing how to make wise purchases—how to find clothes that not only are affordable but also fit well and look good. Otherwise the clothes tend to stay in the closet.

Shopping Tips for Women. When building or adding to their wardrobes, a woman should look for

- Garments and colors that flatter her and her figure type.
- Suitable styles inspired by currently favored designers.
- Quality clothes rather than cheaply made ones.
- Collars and lapels that stand up or lay correctly because the shape is built into their construction.
- Good, comfortable fit at the waist, neck, and arm sleeve seams—not too tight, not too loose.
- Sturdy zippers; buttons with finished buttonholes.
- Clothes with generous seam allowances and hems (important for young ladies who are still growing).
- Patterns, stripes, or plaids that match at the seams.
- Lining of quality, dependable fabric.
- The best quality clothes possible for her budget.
- Clothes to buy out of season for best values.

Avoid:

- Garments with raw edges on the seam borders.
- Hard-to-clean, temperamental, or very delicate fabrics.
- Extremes in fashion trends.
- Clothing with problematic, "fussy" accents, like loose beads or sequins.

The Basic Wardrobe

Fashion consultants generally recommend (in addition to everyday casual clothes) that a lady's minimum wardrobe include the basic garments listed below. Timeless, classic styles in good quality fabrics only vary in hem, jacket, and sleeve lengths from season to season. Begin with basic colors of black, navy, grays, and beiges for mix-and-match versatility. Choose colors that look good with your skin color.

- One basic suit; the best classic colors are dark navy, dark charcoal, or black.
- One pair of slacks that matches the suit jacket.

- One light-colored skirt that coordinates with the suit jacket.
- One light-colored pair of pants that coordinates with suit jacket and other items.
- Three nice blouses: one colored, one white, one print.
- Three pullover sweaters: black, cream or white, and a favorite color.
- One daytime dress suitable for informal occasions.
- Two nice church dresses, one in a flattering color and one black.
- One dressy afternoon dress and coordinating shoes.
- One short after-five dress or ensemble.
- One party dress or semiformal outfit and accessories.
- One long formal dress and accessories.
- One dress coat.
- One sports jacket.
- One evening wrap or jacket.
- Dress shoes.

Finding a Flattering Style and Fit

Regardless of a lady's body type, good fit is important. The jacket should lay flat across her shoulders without gaps or folds in the material. It is important that clothes lead a viewer's eye to the face. Collars should lie nicely at the nape of the neck. Long-sleeved coats and jackets should reach the bottom of the wrist. Classic skirt styles usually feature rear zippers, and may be pleated, straight with a kick pleat, slightly A-line, or in a slimming dirndl style. For average figures, a one- to one-and-a-half-inch skirt waistband is the most flattering.

In addition to the suggestions regarding lines or silhouettes, here are some tips for flattering various body types. Proportion and line are key elements. Because the total look is important, one piece of clothing should not overwhelm the others. For women, a dress or suit's balanced silhouette is defined by the garment shape and the length of sleeves, jacket, and hemlines. For example, a shorter, above-the-hip jacket looks proportionately best with a skirt hem that is just below the knee. Longer jackets look best with longer skirts. Below are some specific tips for different body types.

Slender. Choose textured fabrics and knits such as tweed, corduroy, and velvet in lighter colors and prints. Avoid clingy or snugly fitting clothes, dark or intense colors. Thin women look better in a layered look with shirtwaist dresses and slacks, pleated and full skirts. They avoid vertical lines and silhouettes, scoop necks and V-neck styles, pencil skirts, clothes

Curved lines add softness.

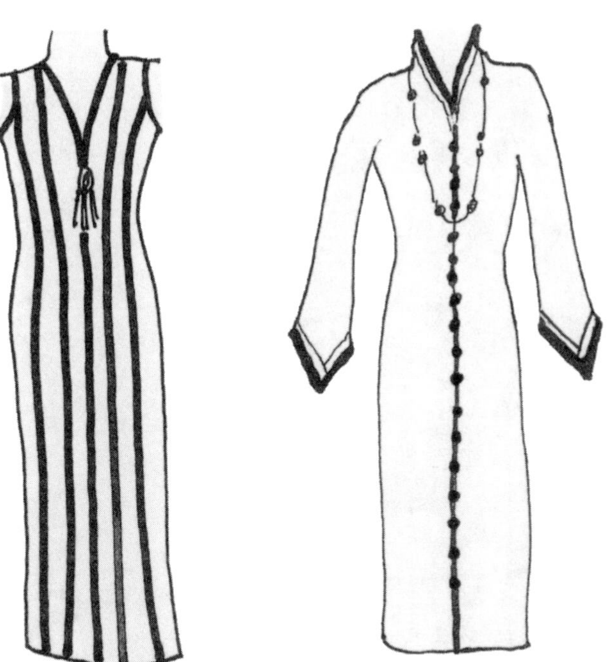

Vertical lines lengthen and slim.

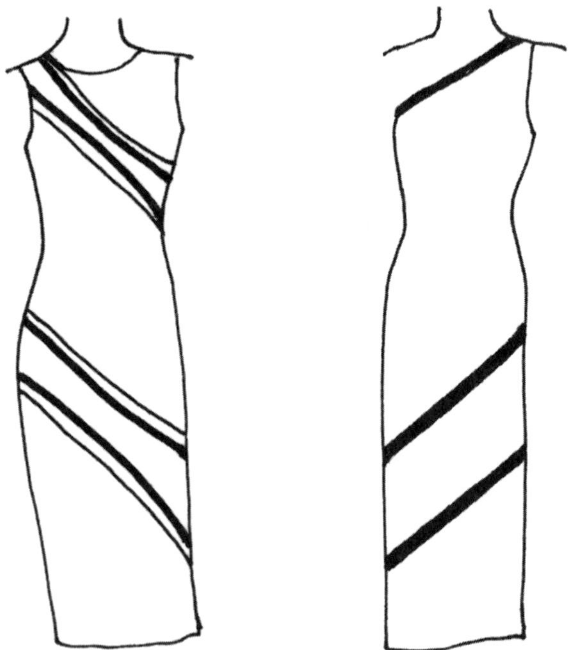

Diagonals flatter most shapes, and add interest and excitement.

Horizontal and broken lines shorten and add width.

without waistlines, and off-shoulder styles. Add fullness with ruffles, scarves, and boots.

Shorter or taller than average. Smaller female body types are easily overwhelmed. Opt for solid colors, simpler styles, and vertical lines. A narrow A-line is more flattering than a full A-line style. Taller body types choose horizontal lines and rounded styles. Tunic tops and contrasting colors are flattering. Rounded lines, such as in saddle pants or boat necklines, reduce height. Bright colors magnify, duller colors slenderize and tone down.

Heavy figure. Choose clothes that emphasize a vertical silhouette such as solid-color outfits and princess-line dresses in neutral and dark colors. Select small patterns and vertical details, and buttons and trims in contrasting colors. Avoid tight clothes, wide belts, bold colors, big patterns, and shiny, heavy, and clingy fabrics. It is important to select fabrics with a dull finish and clothes that fit just right. If the arms are heavy, choose three-quarter length, loose (but not full) sleeves with wide armholes. Avoid sleeveless, strapless, and off-the-shoulder styles.

Triangular shape: large bust, broad shoulders. Choose slightly flared skirts and dresses to add balanced lower proportions. Wear loosely fitted and shirt-style blouses. Favor the vertical lines, moderate V-necklines, and dark-colored bodices. Avoid clingy, tight tops, light-colored bodices, wide belts, rounded necklines, capped sleeves, and shiny or bulky fabrics around the bodice.

Pear shape. Wear darker-colored skirts and pants of medium to light weight in non-shiny fabrics. Choose dresses with slightly flared skirts, not pencil style, paying attention to perfect sizing. Simple princess lines are flattering. Select garments with a broad shoulder line that emphasize the waist for balance. Pair dark pants or skirts with a lighter colored top and box jackets that cover hips. Avoid pleated skirts, gathers, and fullness on the bottom.

Short legs, long waist. Focus attention on the upper face and neck with accessories. Choose styles with collars and draped necklines. Wear solid-color outfits, wide belts, and interesting details on upper bodice. When wearing slacks, keep the leg line unbroken and choose higher-waisted styles in solid colors for pants and skirts. Wear long or short skirts with same-color hosiery.

Long legs, short waist. Lengthen the torso and body line by choosing long, fitted tops that come down to the hips, well-fitting skirts with a drape to one side. Capri pants flatter this body type.

Conclusion

We all want to look our best, and students especially enjoy and benefit from all instruction that helps them understand dress codes and categories. In addition, practical and individualized tips help our young people develop a versatile, flattering wardrobe and present a good public appearance no matter what fashions are in style. Respectfully outfitting the body that God gave us is one more way we can teach our children to obediently honor Him.

Epilogue

Do you agree that how we look and act matter? Must children be respectful and polite, whether they happen to feel like it or not? Can the right manners, communicated through protocol training, make a difference in a child's behavior and character? Can they change culture? Does kindness in seemingly simple actions matter in the greater scheme of things? In God's sight? I hope you answered "yes" to all these questions, and that you found encouraging applications for your home or school from the ideas shared in this book.

Adults who have long benefited from godly training are blessed by the biblical principles that accurately command our every step as long as we live. Our children, however, do not know how to walk in right principles until specifically taught to do so. The next generation needs pragmatic guidelines so they can live honorably and well before God. We have the huge responsibility of tending to their souls as He commands. It won't always be easy, and our efforts will never be perfect. We must, however, stand firm, hold fast, and plant what is good, right, and true using the tools given us. Indeed, when we honor and cultivate Christ's principles in our children, He promises that they will love Him and be strengthened in their walk with Him.

It does not matter whether we are young or old in life—following Christ's principles brings wisdom, joy, and healing. The sooner young people identify themselves with His ways and obediently practice them, the better. Thankfully, applying godly principles in the area of protocol (with God's blessing) teaches children how to stay on the right course. Such application also helps parents properly plant and tend their little ones, drawing water from His well of salvation. This means, in turn, that folly's seeds are removed and wrong ways wither without root. How wonderfully simple, yet profound!

In these last pages, you will discover four essays on protocol. The authors have my sincere gratitude for sharing their articles with us. They expose modern deceptions about protocol, and speak wise words and warnings we need to hear. They challenge us to come and bring our children to higher ground where the way is more honorable, the light shines brighter, and the fruit eternally satisfying.

Part IV

Four Contemporary Essays on Protocol

Manners

Ronald W. Kirk

As a social norm, "manners" carry a bad reputation. When someone mentions the word *manners,* we may instantly think of self-absorbed snobs who use their pretentious and formal manners as a weapon designed to vanquish supposed inferiors. Such social guerilla warfare has long been the ideal for many to measure all common social conduct.

In the great Christian novel *Ben Hur,* the character of the adult Roman Messala returns to his home in Judea after a period of education in the Eternal City. In a reunion with his childhood best friend, Messala sarcastically insults leading character Judah Ben Hur, according to the rigor of noble Roman etiquette.[1] Similarly, in Walter Scott's Christian romantic/historic novel *Ivanhoe,* the noble Norman hosts made the manners of their Saxon guests "the subject of sarcastic observation," while "the untaught Saxons unwittingly transgressed several of the arbitrary rules established for the regulation of society." Moreover, "it was well known that a man may with more impunity be guilty of an actual breach either of real good breeding or of good morals, than appear ignorant of the most minute point of fashionable etiquette."[2] Such hypocritical pomposity was a favorite

1. Lew Wallace, *Ben Hur, A Tale of the Christ* (New York: Grosset & Dunlap, 1922), Book Second, Chapter II.
2. Sir Walter Scott, *Ivanhoe* (New York: A.L. Burt, no date), 174.

"Manners" by Ronald W. Kirk appeared in the June/July 2002 issue of *The Chalcedon Report.*

target of Charles Dickens in virtually all of his stories, and rightly so. Even in these negative literary examples, a better, clearly superior morality and etiquette are implied to exist.

A Balanced View

In reaction, however, anti-manners have now replaced high manners, as dictated by the Hollywood, social-trend-setting elite. With these poor examples, it is now easy to discard manners as superficial or worse, as against the weightier requirements of Scripture. Yet, we ought to be careful of drawing rash conclusions, tantamount to throwing the soup out with the chicken bones. God did not intend His plumb line for a pendulum. Indeed, manners rightfully seen clearly reflect the weightier commands of the Scriptures, including the commandment of Christ to love our neighbors as ourselves.

More pointedly, we observe several examples of good manners in history and literature. Note how young George Washington produced his *Rules of Civility,* which bore on character, and moral and polite conduct. Washington's character, conduct, and accomplishments were renowned in his age, such that Americans have long revered him. The connection between Washington's upbringing in moral manners and his lasting reputation ought to be obvious. Comments from the *Rules,* such as "Associate yourself with persons of good character. It is better to be alone than in bad company," illustrate their Biblical base (I Cor. 15:33).

In her *Little House* book series, Laura Ingalls Wilder presents an elevated example of Christian manners in the home of a late nineteenth-century family. For example, five-year-old Laura in *Little House in the Big Woods* knows it is wicked to cry selfishly or to be envious of her sister. Interestingly, the fine manners of the Ingalls' home are commonly set against the increasing incivility and roughness of the age in which Laura grew up. These books form a textbook of manners and morals remarkably approximating Biblical ideals, though signs of secularization in the home were also beginning to appear.

As late as the 1940s, manners were not yet entirely divorced from their Biblical roots. Emily Post opens her opus volume *Etiquette* with a discussion of the term's true meaning. Attempting to distance herself from mere formality and rigid rules in manners, she asks, "What is the purpose of this rule? Does it help to make life pleasanter? Does it make the social machinery run more smoothly? Does it add to beauty? Is it essential to the code of good taste or to ethics? If it serves any of these purposes, it is a rule to be cherished."[3] Regarding good taste she says, "Good taste is necessarily helpful! It must be the suitable thing, the comfortable thing, the useful thing for the occasion, the place, the time, or it is not in good taste." (Christians would recognize that the experience of true beauty is a blessing from God corresponding to a peoples' responding to His gift of grace [Phil. 4:8].) With respect to men, Miss Post says, "[T]he code of the gentleman is an immutable law of etiquette. Decency means not merely propriety of speech and conduct, but honesty and trustworthiness in every obligation. Integrity includes not only honesty but a delicacy of motive and of fairness in judging the motives of others." Finally, "Etiquette is most deeply concerned with every phase of ethical impulse or judgment and with every choice or expression of taste, since what one is, is of far greater importance than what one appears to be."

Love in Action

Rev. Rushdoony declared that love is law in action.[4] In this sense, self-government and ordinary relational practices (i.e., manners) truly constitute the first sphere of civil government. Where the individual is constrained to do what is right in his conscience, and aided by the Holy Spirit by faith, little coercive government is required and the people are generally free. It is important not to presume upon one's neighbor in his property or person, particularly in absence of a previous relationship which might grant some degree of imposition.

Clearly, as we seek to establish a more Biblical view of human conduct, we must set priorities. In Christian love, kindness, making another comfortable, and providing a beautiful setting are all part of Christian love toward one's neighbor. However, morality and ethical conduct according to the commands of Christ are fundamentally far more important. With respect to the higher expression of the Faith found in Christian liberty (2 Cor. 3:17), self-restraint in manners is essential. No common liberty is long possible in an essentially selfish society.

Conversely, a society where people generally do good to each other is one of the most important foundational elements for a successful gospel mission. With such salt and light, godly influence may work to prepare the

3. Emily Post, *Etiquette* (New York: Funk & Wagnalls, 1945), 1.

4. Rousas Rushdoony, *Law and Society* (Vallecito, CA: Ross House Books, 1986), x.

soil of the people's hearts to receive the Good Seed of the Word of God.

Modern secular education theory requires peer socialization. This is the blind leading the blind, where all fall into a pit. Much better is a home that teaches and practices careful conduct toward one another in life's ordinary activities. If one can learn to love his neighbor, in practice, when that neighbor happens to be his brother or sister, or husband or wife, where it is so terribly easy to be lax in our social conduct, how much more skillful will be the practice of love toward one's neighbor outside the home. Indeed, I have often observed this to be so.

Training our children and ourselves to have good manners, then, is a worthwhile and even imperative Christian endeavor. In an age where examples of good Christian manners may be difficult to find, the traditional manners we practice tend to be the institutionalized result of our sinful disposition. The combined benefit of scriptural and Christian historical and literary insight offer a theoretical and practical set of instructions for a manner of life able to revive Christian civility, gospel influence, and a foundation for the free institutions needed to propagate the kingdom of God.

Boy Meets Girl

Tom Garfield

They were obviously a bit impatient, shuffling and yet tense, eager to depart the classroom in one explosive rush. But the teacher insisted they wait, even if it was a bit longer than usual. The last few girls were still gathering their personal items and heading out the door. Then, as the last young lady passed into the hallway, the teacher reminded the boys to "walk, not run" on their way to the lunchroom. They obeyed, but their steps were jerky, like a Ferrari having to drive twenty-five miles per hour on an open stretch of highway—a good and necessary practice of self-control, with some outside encouragement, of course.

As most of our Logos parents know by now, for several years we have been highlighting the need for upgrading the cultural aspects of our school. One significant form this has taken is in the area of etiquette. Put in biblical language, this is practicing love in the details. "Details" in this case means the small opportunities we have every day to show consideration for others. Even more specifically, we are encouraging the children to make distinctions in how they show consideration for the opposite gender. The Bible is clear about these distinctions, so we believe we should be also, regardless of our culture's never-say-die crusade to eliminate them.

So, for instance, in every grade, the boys are required to allow the girls to leave the classroom first. In the lunchroom, as they file in, the boys are to stand until the girls are seated. Young men are to hold doors for young

"Boy Meets Girl" originally appeared in *Scholasterix*, the newsletter of Logos School, vol. 13, no. 3 (January–March 2003).

women and ladies. (This has the side-effect of young men frequently holding doors even for older male teachers.) During secondary assemblies, the young men are to watch for ladies standing in the back and assist in getting a chair for them. What are the girls and young ladies supposed to do for their part? How do they show consideration for their male peers? The answer: by treating the boys' deference to them with respect, not scorn or mockery. A thankful attitude is pretty much all that's required.

Are we just tying to hark back to the lost age of chivalry in some pathetic, anachronistic manner? After all, our mascot is a knight. Aren't we kicking against the current social goads, or even worse, not preparing the kids for the "real world" out there, where the sexes are really the same?

No, to all of the above. For one thing, the age of chivalry was hardly one we'd like to emulate—it was largely adulterous and generally without a biblical foundation. As for the "real world," by whose definition? God made us male and female, and until He rewires us, that's what we are.

Our goal in this, as with every other aspect of the education we provide, is to prepare the students to think biblically about all they will face before and after graduation. That includes the critical, life-changing event of getting married. To be clear, we are not going into the realm of marital counseling, childrearing, or even providing home management courses, per se. But a young man doesn't turn into a gentleman or know how to show consideration for a young lady by merely turning eighteen—or twenty-one, for that matter. He becomes what he has been practicing to be since he was old enough to observe the model of older men. If he has never seen a gentleman in action or been required to act like one at five, twelve, and fifteen, he simply won't burst into one later, at the point when it matters most to him—that is, when he meets a young lady to whom he does want to show special consideration. The ugly caterpillar won't become the impressive butterfly just by wishing.

To up the ante, God designed most people for the state of marriage, though as Paul tells us, He grants a few folks a special gift of singleness. This means that the vast majority of those sweet little faces coming to kindergarten each morning are heading either for a God-honoring marriage or possibly a series of heart-rending, self-centered relationships. It sounds a little harsh, put that way, but the facts and figures of the "real world" bear this out.

The only question that we face as a Christian school, then, is this: Regarding those facts of life, what kind of behavior will we model and enforce for our students? Will we tacitly adopt the world's view and pretend that how boys and girls treat each other at school is of no consequence to marriage later on? Or will we, under the limited, delegated authority of our parents, seek to model and require the kind of countless small considerations that husbands should demonstrate to their wives, and that wives should demonstrate to their husbands? Which approach is really denying the future reality in the lives of these students? Which approach encourages the biblical mandate that young men are to treat young women "as sisters, in all purity and respect"?

There is a lot to the subject of how boys and girls should interact, wherever they are or however old they are. Suffice it to say here, in all matters of the mind and heart of a student, the Scripture and its principles are neither inappropriate or outdated. Pray for our wisdom in how we promote those principles at Logos.

Manners for Boys

Douglas Wilson

Boys have a need to be respected, but sometimes this need can be communicated in some strange ways. And because boys can gravitate toward such strange forms of communicating their boyhood, they may come to think that "manners are for sissies."

A very easy mistake for boys to make is thinking that masculinity consists of being rudely tough, or gross, or both. A ten-year-old boy can readily think that masculinity is displayed whenever he can make all the girls in his class say *"Eeewwwww!"* This is of course not the case, but we still have to qualify what we are saying.

There is a fine line here because there is a type of boy who is effeminate, and displays that effeminacy through being a "well-mannered" and mousy little boy. This arouses the disgust of the surrounding boys who, in a frenzy of metaphor-mixing, proceed to throw out the well-mannered baby with the mousy bathwater.

In addition, those adults who care the most about "manners" often do not understand masculinity either, and so they cannot help boys make the distinction which they themselves blur. This means that a boy will view all attempts to "teach him manners" as simply an effort by the adult world to make him craven, which he does not want to do. He knows intuitively that a well-mannered boy is not a boy who acts like his sister.

Put another way, manners for boys should be a means of discipling and directing strength, and not a means of denying it. This means that boys

"Manners for Boys" originally appeared in *Credenda/Agenda* 12, no. 3. Reprinted by permission.

need to be taught that manners are a means of showing and receiving honor. Honor is a concept which boys instinctively understand and love, but they still have to be taught to direct it with wisdom. Honor, in its turn, cannot be understood apart from authority and obedience.

As with so many of these things, there is an "intangible" element here. There is an authority which badgers a boy into resentment, and there is an authority which liberates him. A boy might seethe over a mildly cutting remark from his older sister about his dishwasher-loading habits, and then the next moment be daydreaming about a drill instructor screaming in his face from a range of about two inches. When men get to telling stories to one another, boot camp stories are frequently in the mix. They never tell stories about the time their older sister bossed them around the kitchen.

Boys thrive under authority and are not threatened by it. At the same time, the authority must be of the kind which understands masculinity and nurtures it by hammering it. One of the "hammers" should be a short and thorough course in manners.

The heart of masculinity involves the willing assumption of an appropriately assigned responsibility. Manners for boys should be in line with this, and not contradict it. Manners for men should therefore point to or illustrate their distinctive responsibilities, and boys should be in training for this. One of the things we do in our household is that we have the men stand around the dinner table until the ladies are all seated. When my two-year-old grandson is over, this includes him. When he is grown, he needs to have learned, years before his earliest memory, that men have constant responsibilities and duties with regard to women.

Boys should not be allowed to think that manners are something which women impose on men. If they do come to think this, then they will start to react like Huck Finn, chafing under the constraints of civilization. Rather, they should see manners as something which men teach boys to do, for the sake of honoring and protecting women, and for the sake of living graciously with them.

With this as a backdrop, let me offer a few particulars. A priority should be placed on those manners and customs which place a distinction between men and women. In this class we should put men seating women at the dinner table, opening and holding doors, standing when a women enters the room, walking on the sidewalk between a woman and the traffic, and so forth.

In a second class would be manners which discipline a young man to think of the comfort and possessions of others—not tipping back in chairs, not putting feet on the coffee table, and not bouncing the basketball next to the china hutch.

A third category would be in the realm of personal presentation: not dressing like a slob, not bolting food, not wearing a baseball cap indoors, etc. In this last category, a boy is being taught, among other things, to present himself as trustworthy in all the categories.

Fundamentally, all these manners are a way of showing honor to others in areas which are not of cosmic importance. At the same time, because they are acts of love, even if they are love in trifles, God considers them important.

Such manners are places where boys are taught to mute their natural energy. Another set of manners are necessary where boys are taught to release that energy. These channels in which aggressiveness can flow should be well-defined and established. We see here the benefits of organized sports and military training. But even on the playing field, "manners" are still important.

When aggressiveness overflows the banks, or when there are no banks, then we have a major problem. When there is no need for a restraining bank (as is the case for the effeminate boy), then things are a lot quieter—but we still have a major problem. Boys need to be masculine, and true masculinity needs manners.

Modesty Revisited

Wendy Shalit

This afternoon I was reading a magazine for brides in which a woman had submitted the following question: "My fiancé wants us to move in together, but I want to wait until we're married. Am I doing our marriage an injustice?" The editor responded: "Your fiancé should understand why you want to wait to share a home. Maybe you're concerned about losing your identity as an individual. Or maybe you're concerned about space issues."

Space issues? Losing her identity? If this woman cared about those things she wouldn't want to get married in the first place. Her question was a moral one. She wanted to know what would be best for her marriage. And on this—however unbeknownst to the magazine's new-agey editor—the evidence is in: Couples who live together before marriage are much less likely to get married; and if they do marry, they're more likely to get divorced. Yet the vocabulary of modesty has largely dropped from our cultural consciousness; when a woman asks a question that necessarily implicates it, we can only mumble about "space issues."

I first became interested in the subject of modesty for a rather mundane reason—because I didn't like the bathrooms at Williams College. Like many enlightened colleges and universities these days, Williams houses boys next to girls in its dormitories and then has the students vote by floor on whether

---

Wendy Shalit is the author of *A Return to Modesty: Recovering the Lost Virtue* (New York: The Free Press, 1999). This is an excerpt of a presentation she gave at Hillsdale College on November 15, 2000, at a seminar sponsored by the college's Center for Constructive Alternatives, and was printed in *Imprimis* (March 2001). Reprinted by permission from *Imprimis*, the national speech digest of Hillsdale College (www.hillsdale.edu).

their common bathrooms should be coed. It's all very democratic, but the votes always seem to go in the coed direction because no one wants to be thought a prude. When I objected, I was told by my fellow students that I "must not be comfortable with [my] body." Frankly, I didn't get that, because I was fine with my body; it was their bodies in such close proximity to mine that I wasn't thrilled about.

I ended up writing about this experience in *Commentary* as a kind of therapeutic exercise. But when my article was reprinted in *Reader's Digest,* a weird thing happened: I got piles of letters from kids who said, "I thought I was the only one who couldn't stand these bathrooms." How could so many people feel they were the "only ones" who believed in privacy and modesty? It was troubling that they were afraid to speak up. When and why, I wondered, did modesty become such a taboo?

At Yale in 1997, a few years after my own coed bathroom protest, five Orthodox Jewish students petitioned the administration for permission to live off-campus instead of in coed dorms. In denying them, a dean with the Dickensian name of Brodhead explained that "Yale has its own rules and requirements, which we insist on because they embody our values and beliefs." Yale has no core curriculum, of course, but these coed bathrooms, according to Dean Brodhead, embody its beliefs. I would submit that as a result of this kind of "liberationist" ideology, we today have less, not more freedom, than in the pre-1960s era when modesty was upheld as a virtue. In this regard it's important to recall that when colleges had separate dorms for men and women, and all the visitation rules that went with them, it was also possible for kids to circumvent those rules. It was possible, for instance—now, I'm not advocating this—for students to sneak into each others' dorms and act immodestly. But in the new culture of "liberation," a student can't sneak into the dorms and be modest, or, more accurately, she can't sneak out. There is no "right of exit" in today's immodest society. If you don't participate, you're a weirdo. Hence students are not really free to develop their best selves, to act in accordance with their hopes.

Modesty's Loss, Social Pathology's Gain

Many of the problems we hear about today—sexual harassment, date rape, young women who suffer from eating disorders and report feeling a lack of control over their bodies—are all connected, I believe, to our culture's attack on modesty. Listen, first, to the words we use to describe intimacy: what once was called "making love," and then "having sex," is now "hooking up"—like airplanes refueling in flight. In this context I was interested to learn, while researching for my book, that the early feminists actually praised modesty as ennobling to society. Here I'm not just talking about the temperance-movement feminists, who said, "Lips that touch liquor shall never touch mine." I'm talking about more recent feminists like Simone de Beauvoir, who warned in her book, *The Second Sex*, that if society trivializes modesty, violence against women would result. And she was right. Since the 1960s, when our cultural arbiters deemed this age-old virtue a "hang-up," men have grown to expect women to be casual about sex, and women for their part don't feel they have the right to say "no." This has brought us all more misery than joy. On MTV I have seen a 27-year-old woman say she was "sort of glad" that she had herpes, because now she has "an excuse to say 'no' to sex." For her, disease had replaced modesty as the justification for exercising free choice.

In 1948 there was a song called "Baby It's Cold Outside" by Frank Loesser, in which a boyfriend wants his girlfriend to sleep over. His argument is simple but compelling: Baby it's cold outside, and if she doesn't sleep over, she could catch pneumonia and die, and that would cause him "lifelong sorrow." In response, the girl offers several counter-arguments: "My father will be waiting at the door, there's bound to be talk tomorrow," etc. It's a very cute song. And while post-modern intellectuals at progressive institutions like Yale would no doubt say this song proves how oppressed women were in 1948, I would argue that today's culture—in which fathers can't be counted on to be waiting at the door—is far creepier.

The counterpoint to "Baby It's Cold Outside" is a story I read in a women's magazine, written by an ex-boyfriend of an 18-year-old girl whose father had decided that she was too old to be a virgin. After commiserating with the boyfriend, this father drove the pair to a hotel (he didn't trust the boyfriend with his car), where the girl became hysterical and the scheme fell apart. This article was called "My Ex-Girlfriend's Father: What a Man!" And although the story isn't typical, it is quite common these days for parents to rent hotel rooms for their kids on prom nights, which is essentially the same principle. So the father in "Baby It's Cold Outside" waiting at the door, and the older culture that supported modesty, actually made women stronger. It gave them the right to say "no" until they met someone they wanted to marry. Today's culture of "liberation" gives women no ground on which to stand. And an immodest culture weakens men, too—we are all at the mercy of other people's judgment of us as sexual objects (witness the revolution in plastic surgery for men), which is not only tiring but also dishonest because we can't be ourselves.

When I talk to college students, invariably one will say, "Well, if you want to be modest, be modest. If you want to be promiscuous, be promiscuous. We all have a choice, and that's the wonderful thing about this society." But the culture, I tell them, can't be neutral. Nor is it subtle in its influence on behavior. In fact, culture works more like a Sherman tank. In the end, if it's not going to value modesty, it will value promiscuity and adultery, and all our lives and marriages will suffer as a result.

Four Myths Exposed

A first step toward reviving respect for modesty in our culture is to strike at the myths that undermine it. Let me touch on four of these.

The first myth is that modesty is Victorian. But what about the story of Rebecca and Isaac? When Rebecca sees Isaac and covers herself, it is not because she is trying to be Victorian. Her modesty was the key to what would bring them together and develop a profound intimacy. When we cover up what is external or superficial—what we all share in common—we send a message that what is most important are our singular hearts and minds. This separates us from the animals, and always did, long before the Victorian era.

The second myth about modesty is that it's synonymous with prudery. This was the point of the dreadful movie *Pleasantville*, the premise of which was that nobody in the 1950s had fun or experienced love. It begins in black and white and turns to color only when the kids enlighten their parents about sex. This of course makes no sense on its face: if the parents didn't know how to do it, then how did all these kids get there in the first place? But it reflects a common conceit of baby boomers that passion, love and happiness were non-existent until modesty was overcome in the 1960s. In truth, modesty is nearly the opposite of prudery. Paradoxically, prudish people have more in common with the promiscuous. The prudish and the promiscuous share a disposition against allowing themselves to be moved by others, or to fall in love. Modesty, on the other hand, invites and protects the evocation of real love. It is erotic, not neurotic.

To illustrate this point, I like to compare photographs taken at Coney Island almost a century ago with photographs from nude beaches in the 1970s. At Coney Island, the beach-goers are completely covered up, but the men and women are stealing glances at one another and seem to be having a great time. On the nude beaches, in contrast, men and women hardly look at each other—rather, they look at the sky. They appear completely bored. That's what those who came after the '60s discovered about this string of dreary hookups: without anything left to the imagination, sex becomes boring.

The third myth is that modesty isn't natural. This myth has a long intellectual history, going back at least to David Hume, who argued that society invented modesty so that men could be sure that children were their own. As Rousseau pointed out, this argument that modesty is a social construct suggests that it is possible to get rid of modesty altogether. Today we try to do just that, and it is widely assumed that we are succeeding. But are we?

In arguing that Hume was wrong and that modesty is rooted in nature, a recently discovered hormone called oxytocin comes to mind. This hormone creates a bonding response when a mother is nursing her child, but is also released during intimacy. Here is physical evidence that women become emotionally bonded to their sexual partners even if they only intend a more casual encounter. Modesty protected this natural emotional vulnerability; it made women strong. But we don't really need to resort to physiology to see the naturalness of modesty. We can observe it on any windy day when women wearing slit skirts hobble about comically to avoid showing their legs—the very legs those fashionable skirts are designed to reveal. Despite trying to keep up with the fashions, these women have a natural instinct for modesty.

The fourth and final myth I want to touch on is that modesty is solely a concern for women. We are where we are today only in part because the feminine ideal has changed. The masculine ideal has followed suit. It was once looked on as manly to be faithful to one woman for life, and to be protective toward all women. Sadly, this is no longer the case, even among many men to whom modest women might otherwise look as kindred spirits. Modern feminists are wrong to expect men to be gentlemen when they themselves are not ladies, but men who value "scoring" and then lament that there are no modest women around anymore—well, they are just as bad. And of course, a woman can be modestly dressed and still be harassed on the street. So the reality is that a lot depends on male respect for modesty. It is characteristic of modern society that everyone wants the other guy to be nice to him without having to change his own behavior, whether it's the feminists blaming the men, the men blaming the feminists, or young people blaming their role models. But that is an infantile posture.

Jews read a portion of the Torah each week, and in this week's portion there is a story that shows us beautifully, I think, how what we value in women and men are inextricably linked. Abraham is visited by three men, really three angels, and he is providing them with his usual hospitality, when they ask him suddenly, "Where is Sarah your wife?" And he replies, famously, "Behold! In the tent!" Commentators ask, why in the world are the angels asking where Sarah is? They know she is in the tent. They are, after all, angels. And one answer is, to remind Abraham of where she is, in order to increase his love for her. This is very interesting, because in Judaism the most important work takes place, so to speak, "in the tent"—keeping kosher, keeping the Sabbath, keeping the laws of marital purity. Torah is only passed on to the next generation because of what the woman is doing in the home. Yet it is not enough for there to be a Sarah who is in the tent; it is also necessary that there be an Abraham who appreciates her. So I think the lesson is clear if we want to reconstruct a more modest, humane society, we have to start with ourselves.

I don't think it's an accident that the most meaningful explication of modesty comes from the Bible. I was fascinated in my research to discover how many secular women are returning to modesty because they found, simply as a practical matter, that immodesty wasn't working for them. In short, they weren't successful finding the right men. For me this prompts an essentially religious question: Why were we created in this way? Why can't we become happy by imitating the animals? In the sixth chapter of Isaiah we read that the fiery angels surrounding the throne of God have six wings. One set is for covering the face, another for covering the legs, and only the third is for flying. Four of the six wings, then, are for modesty's sake. This beautiful image suggests that the more precious something is, the more it must conceal and protect itself. The message of our dominant culture today, I'm afraid, is that we're not precious, that we weren't created in the divine image. I'm saying to the contrary that we were, and that as such we deserve modesty.

Appendix: 16 House Rules

The following rules are adapted and condensed from a list by Greg Harris called "The 21 Rules of This House."[†] They provide wonderful, clear guidelines for the behavior that Christian parents should expect from their children. Pastor Gene Helsel of Trinity Church in Wenatchee, Washington has kindly added Scripture references to ground and explain each one.

1. We love and obey our Lord Jesus Christ.

If you love Me, keep My commandments. (Jn. 14:15)
Go therefore and make disciples of all the nations, baptizing them in the name of the Father and of the Son and of the Holy Spirit, teaching them to observe all things that I have commanded you; and lo, I am with you always, even to the end of the age. Amen. (Mt. 28:19–20)

2. We love, honor, and pray for one another.

This is My commandment, that you love one another as I have loved you. (Jn. 15:12)
And above all things have fervent love for one another, for "love will cover a multitude of sins." (1 Pet. 4:8)
Let nothing be done through selfish ambition or conceit, but in lowliness of mind let each esteem others better than himself. (Phil. 2:3)
Therefore I exhort first of all that supplications, prayers, intercessions, and giving of thanks be made for all men. (1 Tim. 2:1)

3. We tell the truth.

Lying lips are an abomination to the Lord, but those who deal truthfully are His delight. (Prov. 12:22)
A lying tongue hates those who are crushed by it, and a flattering mouth works ruin. (Prov. 26:28)
Therefore, putting away lying, "Let each one of you speak truth with his neighbor," for we are members of one another. (Eph. 4:25)

[†] A poster of the original 21 rules and an accompanying children's coloring book are published by Noble Publishing Associates (http://noblebookstore.com/).

4. We consider one another's interests ahead of our own.

Be kindly affectionate to one another with brotherly love, in honor giving preference to one another. (Rom. 12:10)

5. We speak quietly and respectfully with one another.

A soft answer turns away wrath, but a harsh word stirs up anger. (Prov. 15:1)

Let no corrupt word proceed out of your mouth, but what is good for necessary edification, that it may impart grace to the hearers. (Eph. 4:29)

6. We do not hurt one another with unkind words or deeds.

And be kind to one another, tenderhearted, forgiving one another, even as God in Christ forgave you. (Eph. 4:32)

7. When someone needs correction, we correct him in love.

Brethren, if a man is overtaken in any trespass, you who are spiritual restore such a one in a spirit of gentleness, considering yourself lest you also be tempted. (Gal. 6:1)

8. When someone is sorry, we forgive him.

Bearing with one another, and forgiving one another, if anyone has a complaint against another; even as Christ forgave you, so you also must do. (Col. 3:13)

Take heed to yourselves. If your brother sins against you, rebuke him; and if he repents, forgive him. And if he sins against you seven times in a day, and seven times in a day returns to you, saying, "I repent, you shall forgive him. (Lk. 17:3–4)

For if you forgive men their trespasses, your heavenly Father will also forgive you. But if you do not forgive men their trespasses, neither will your Father forgive your trespasses. (Mt. 6:14–15)

9. When someone is sad, we comfort him; when someone is happy, we rejoice with him.

Rejoice with those who rejoice, and weep with those who weep. (Rom. 12:15)

That there should be no schism in the body, but that the members should have the same care for one another. And if one member suffers, all the members suffer with it; or if one member is honored, all the members rejoice with it. (I Cor. 12:25–26)

10. When we have something nice to share, we share it.

He answered and said to them, "He who has two tunics, let him give to him who has none; and he who has food, let him do likewise." (Lk. 3:11)

If someone says, "I love God," and hates his brother, he is a liar; for he who does not love his brother whom he has seen, how can he love God whom he has not seen? (I Jn. 4:20)

11. When we have work to do, we do it without complaining.

Now when the people complained, it displeased the Lord; for the Lord heard it, and His anger was aroused. So the fire of the Lord burned among them, and consumed some in the outskirts of the camp. (Num. 11:1)

Rejoice in the Lord always. Again I will say, rejoice! (Phil. 4:4)

12. We take good care of everything God has given us.

He who is faithful in what is least is faithful also in much; and he who is unjust in what is least is unjust also in much. Therefore if you have not been faithful in the unrighteous mammon, who will commit to your trust the true riches? (Lk. 16:10–11)

13. We do not create unnecessary work for others. When we open something, we close it; when we turn something on, we turn it off; when we take something out, we put it away; when we make a mess, we clean it up.

For you, brethren, have been called to liberty; only do not use liberty as an opportunity for the flesh, but through love serve one another. (Gal. 5:13)

If I then, your Lord and Teacher, have washed your feet, you also ought to wash one another's feet. For I have given you an example, that you should do as I have done to you. (Jn. 13:14–15)

14. When we don't know what to do, we ask.

Get wisdom! Get understanding! Do not forget, nor turn away from the words of my mouth. Do not forsake her, and she will preserve you; love her, and she will keep you. Wisdom is the principal thing; therefore get wisdom. And in all your getting, get understanding. (Prov. 4:5–7)

15. When we go out, we act just as if we were in this house.

Let your light so shine before men, that they may see your good works and glorify your Father in heaven. (Mt. 5:16)

16. When we disobey or forget any of the rules of this house, we accept the discipline and instruction of the Lord.

Whoever loves instruction loves knowledge, but he who hates correction is stupid.
A wise son heeds his father's instruction, but a scoffer does not listen to rebuke.
A fool despises his father's instruction, but he who receives correction is prudent.
Harsh discipline is for him who forsakes the way, and he who hates correction will die.
The ear that hears the rebukes of life will abide among the wise. He who disdains instruction despises his own soul, but he who heeds rebuke gets understanding.
(Prov. 12:1; 13:1; 15:5; 15:10, 31–32)

Selected Bibliography

Christianity, History, and Culture

Dawson, Christopher. *Religion and the Rise of Western Culture: The Classic Study of Medieval Civilization.* New York: Doubleday, 1991. This is an excellent discussion of the impact of Christianity throughout history.

Caldwell, Mark. *A Short History of Rudeness: Manners, Morals, and Misbehavior in Modern America.* New York: Picador, 1999. I found this book in the library. The author, a university professor, traces how certain manners have been regarded in history and how manners change, currently "not for the better." His conclusion is that manners are related to morals but ironically that idea makes him nervous.

Calvin, John. *Golden Booklet of the True Christian Life.* Trans. Henry J. Van Andel. Grand Rapids: Baker, 2000.

Henisch, Bridget Ann. *Fast and Feast: Food in the Medieval Society.* University Park, PA: Pennsylvania State University, 1997. A fascinating study, using primary sources and illustrations from thirteenth through fifteenth centuries about foods, dining and social attitudes.

Pernoud, Regine. *Women in the Days of the Cathedrals.* Trans. and adapted by Anne Cote-Harriss. San Francisco: Ignatius, 1989. This book's discussion includes etiquette, manners, and behavior from centuries past that have influenced us.

Rushdooney, Dr. Rousas. *By What Standard?* Tyler, TX: Thoburn Press, 1983.

Schaffer, Francis. *A Christian Manifesto.* Westchester, IL.: Crossway Books, 1982.

Spurgeon, Charles. *Evening by Evening.* Nashville, TN: Thomas Nelson, 2000.

Taylor, James S. *Poetic Knowledge: The Recovery of Education.* New York: State University of New York Press, 1998. The author, a teacher of English and American literature, humanities, western civilization, and philosophy of education in private schools and colleges, comments on writers and philosophers from Socrates until the current time. He calls the reader to consider the effectiveness of poetic knowledge in life and education, which includes aesthetics and an appeal to the senses as well as the mind. Beauty is imperative in all learning.

Visser, Margaret. *The Rituals of Dinner: The Origins, Evolution, Eccentricities and Meaning of Table Manners.* New York: Grove Weidenfeld, 1991. This is not an etiquette book, but is a well-researched and fascinating study about dining habits, methods, and customs.

General Etiquette and Protocol Books

Baldrige, Letitia. *Letitia Baldrige's Complete Guide to the New Manners.* New York: Rawson Associates, 1990. This seasoned protocol author has a heart for kind manners.

Bates, Karen Gribsby and Hudson, Karen Elyse. *Basic Black: Home Training for Modern Times.* New York: Doubleday, 1996. A practical book full of courteous etiquette for various occasions. The authors promote kindness, consideration and politeness as a duty in daily living.

Bridges, John. *How to be a Gentleman: A Contemporary Guide to Common Courtesy.* Nashville: Rutledge Hill Press, 1998. A small, smart and easy-to-read book for men with a multitude of practical dos and don'ts between its little covers.

Brosseau, Jim, ed. *Town and Country Social Graces: Words of Wisdom on Civility in a Changing Society.* New York: Hearst, 2002. An interesting collection of commentaries on the necessity of polite behavior.

Ford, Charlotte. *Etiquette: Charlotte Ford's Guide to Modern Manners.* New York: Crown, 1988. Don't let the date fool you. She offers traditional protocol with helpful hints ignored in many newer books.

Lichter, Linda S. *Simple Social Graces: Recapturing the Joys of Gracious Victorian Living.* New York: Regan Books/Harper Collins, 1998. The author researched past norms and mores regarding Victorian manners and culture in America: "The Victorians would say that a culture of self-indulgence in which parents don't take responsibility for teaching their children character and civility takes its toll on children's development of self-restraint and social conscience. And so the cycle is repeated, as adults expect little of themselves and even less of their children." While the author applauds "the ideals, grace, and beauty that sprang from a shared code of values," she also discusses some controversial issues. One may not agree with some of her subjects or conclusions, but this book is informative and helpful for its historic prospective. The bibliography in itself is noteworthy for readers who like to study historic traditions.

Martin, Judith. *Miss Manners' Guide for the Turn of the Millennium.* New York: Pharos, 1989. Put this one on your reading list when you go to the library. Parents will enjoy Miss Manners' expertise and literary style.

Martin, Judith. *Miss Manners' Guide to Excruciatingly Correct Behavior.* New York: Atheneum, 1982. This book is detailed and always makes for a fun read, but material is arranged in a way that makes it difficult to find immediate answers to general protocol.

Platz, Ann and Susan Wales. *Social Graces.* Eugene, OR: Harvest House, 1999. The authors term themselves "daughters of the South." Their warm influence for gracious living is evidenced in this small, "folksy," and beautifully illustrated book. Some of their suggested etiquette reflects regional differences. Their selection of small quotes is interesting. This diminutive size of this little book reflects the fact that it is only an introduction to general good manners.

Post, Peggy. *Emily Post's Etiquette.* New York: HarperCollins, 1997. If you can only buy one book, this would be a good one. It is full of standard socially acceptable protocol for most situations.

Segaloff, Nat. *The Everything Etiquette Book.* Holbrook, MA: Adams Media, 1998.

Children and Teens

Baldrige, Letitia. *Letitia Baldrige's More than Manners! Raising Today's Kids to Have Kind Manners and Good Hearts.* New York: Rawson Associates, 1997. A general etiquette book for parents who want to teach their children proper behavior. This book is usually available in public libraries.

Burgess, Gelett. *Goops and How to Be Them: A Manual of Manners for Polite Infants Inculcating Many Juvenile Virtues Both by Precept and Example.* New York: Dover Publications, 1968. Originally published in 1900 by Fred Stokes Company. An entertaining instructional booklet with rhymes and drawings for young children.

Eberly, Sheryl. *365 Manners Kids Should Know: Games, Activities, and Other Fun Ways to Help Children Learn Etiquette.* New York: Three Rivers Press, 2001. The format of "a manner a day" along with activities makes this a practical book for parents who want to teach their children general protocol and manners.

Garretson, John. *The School of Manners; or, Rules for Children.* London, 1701. Reprinted London: Farady House, 1983. This book underscores the fact that good manners are timeless.

Hartley, Fred, et al. *The Teenage Book of Manners—Please!* Westwood, NJ: 1991. Quick, easy reading with cartoons about basic good manners and polite behavior for preteens and younger teenagers.

James, John Angell. *Addresses to Young Men: A Young Man's Friend and Guide through Life to Immortality.* Morgan, PA: Sola Deo Gloria, 1995. Reprint of Hamilton Adams & Co. (London), 1860. This is a book for the young man who desires to seek God and live nobly. With books like this, it is no wonder that past generations raised strong men who, like mighty oaks, led responsible lives of obedient reverence and godly usefulness in Christ. We are still blessed by their influence.

Martin, Judith. *Miss Manners' Guide to Rearing Perfect Children: A Primer for Everyone Worried about the Future of Civilization.* New York: Galahad, 1993. Enjoy Martin's sage advice and humor in this book geared toward protocol and parenting.

Nehlsen, Nancy. *Table Manners for Kids: Tots to Teens.* Featuring Marjabelle Young Stewart. Public Media and Attica Recording Studio, 1993. A 34-minute video covering formal dining basics.

Odor, Ruth Shannon. *A Child's Book Manners.* Cincinnati: Happy Day Books, 1990. A small, inexpensive Christian book for toddlers and very young children. Nice for bedtime reading, this book opens the door for discussion on good behavior.

Specific Topics

Caselton, Margaret. *Beautiful Napkins: Stylish Ideas for Your Table.* Philadelphia: Running Press, 1999.

Martin, Judith. *Miss Manners' Basic Training: Eating.* New York: Crown, 1997. All about dining etiquette and, like all Martin's books, witty and fun to read. She is never caught with egg on her face.

Post, Elizabeth L. *Emily Post's Complete Book of Wedding Etiquette.* Revised Edition. New York, HarperCollins, 1991.

Dress

Bridges, John and Bryan Curtis. *A Gentleman Gets Dressed Up: Knowing What to Wear, How to Wear It, and When to Wear It.* Nashville: Rutledge Hill Press,

2003. Like all of Bridge's and Curtis's books, this one demonstrates a lively flair for succinct, practical, and amusing advice that makes protocol for men come alive. Their books are some of my family's favorites, even though we disagree with a few of their opinions.

Feldon, Leah. *Dressing Rich: A Guide to Classic Chic for Women with More Taste than Money.* New York: G. P. Putnam's Sons, 1982. This book still contains good information on various regional standards and elegance dress with discussion about investment purchases, principles of good dressing with design, line, proportion, color and fabrics.

Flusser, Alan. *Dressing the Man: Mastering the Art of Permanent Fashion.* New York: HarperCollins, 2002. Like Mr. Flusser's earlier book, *Style and the Man: How and Where to Buy Fine Men's Clothes,* this is an affordable and excellent reference for every gentleman's library.

Gersham, Suzy Kalter. *Best Dressed: The Born to Shop Lady's Secrets for Building a Wardrobe.* New York: Three Rivers Press,1999. This is an entertaining, lighthearted book with budget stretching ideas in wardrobe planning and shopping. Her helpful advice on how to be well dressed is comprehensive.

Greenleaf, Clinton T., III. *A Gentleman's Guide to Appearance.* Holbrook, MA.: Adams Media, 2000. A small but thorough and quick reference in achieving a masculine, classic professional appearance.

Hix, Charles. *Man Alive!* New York: Simon Shuster, 1984. In spite of the dated photos and chapter headings there is much good information on classic styles, fabrics and types of men's clothes. I found it in the library.

Klensch, Elsa. *Style.* New York: Perigee, 1995. Klensch's fashion savvy book is as interesting as her television programs.

Rubenstein, Hal and Jim Mullen. *Paisley Goes with Nothing: A Man's Guide to Style.* New York: Doubleday, 1995. A little book about style for men, full of ideas and spiced with humor.

Weber, Mark and the Van Heusen Creative Design Group. *Dress Casually for Success . . . for Men.* New York: McGraw Hill, 1997. This book's format makes it easy and quick to retrieve information on various wardrobe topics. The knowledgeable writers provide solid helpful information on a good appearance.

This book was typeset in Adobe Pagemaker 7
using Centaur MT, Birch, and Corvinus Skyline

Designed and typeset by Jared Miller